*Integrating Aerospace Science
into the Curriculum: K-12*

Gifted Treasury Series
Jerry D. Flack, Series Editor

Integrating Aerospace Science into the Curriculum: K-12

Robert D. Ray
and
Joan Klingel Ray

1992
TEACHER IDEAS PRESS
A Division of
Libraries Unlimited, Inc.
Englewood, Colorado

TEACHER IDEAS PRESS
A Division of Libraries Unlimited, Inc.
P.O. Box 6633
Englewood, CO 80155-6633
1-800-237-6124

Library of Congress Cataloging-in-Publication Data

Ray, Robert D.
    Integrating aerospace science into the curriculum, K-12 / Robert
D. Ray and Joan Klingel Ray.
        xxi, 191 p. 22x28 cm. -- (Gifted treasury series)
        Includes bibliographical references.
        ISBN 0-87287-924-0
        1. Aeronautics--Study and teaching.   2. Gifted children-
-Education.   3. Talented students--Education.   I. Ray, Joan
Klingel.   II. Title.   III. Series.
    TL560.R38   1992
    375'.6291--dc20   91-47024
                                                            CIP
                                                            Rev.

*This book is dedicated to
the children who inspired and motivated us
to seek new and innovative activities
for teaching aerospace.*

Contents

Preface from the Series Editor

It is a pleasure to introduce the fourth volume in the Teacher Ideas Press Gifted Treasury Series—*Integrating Aerospace Science into the Curriculum: K-12*. The Gifted Treasury Series is committed to bringing significant curricula, resources, and teaching strategies to teachers, administrators, media specialists, parents, and others concerned with the education of our most able youth. Doctors Robert Ray and Joan Ray admirably exemplify the meaning of this commitment in the pages that follow. Here are no silly or frivolous topics, silly activities, or fun-and-games kits to waste the precious school time of gifted youths. *Integrating Aerospace Science into the Curriculum: K-12* outlines and explores curricula based on one of humanity's greatest arenas of fascination and accomplishment: human flight.

The breadth and depth of the curriculum strategies, resources, and student explorations span a timeframe of thousands of years. From Daedalus and Icarus to the Wright Brothers, from Dr. Robert Goddard to the visions of present-day aerospace scientists have for the future, the authors lead educators to ways and means of opening up the visionary and exciting world of science to students of all ages. But, it would be wrong to think of this superb text as exclusively science-bound. As with other texts in the Gifted Treasury Series, this book accentuates interdisciplinary, integrated, and holistic learning for students. Meaningful content, from mythology to the inventions of Leonardo da Vinci to the plans for future space stations is explored. Academic rigor is ever strived for. Simultaneously, the process skills of creative and critical thinking and independent and small-group investigative research are facilitated through the many wonderfully challenging activities provided. Moreover, exemplary student products will come forth as students respond to the exciting explorations the authors recommend.

This Gifted Treasury volume is definitely user-friendly. Classroom teachers, media specialists, and resource teachers for the gifted who do not have a strong background in science will delight in the ease with which this book will empower them to teach, explore, and demonstrate a critical body of science knowledge to students. In one instance, students need only manipulate and experiment with two sheets of notebook paper to begin to understand how and why parachutes work. Present-day, science-shy teachers who employ this book will soon be teaching physics to their students with comfort, ease, *and* confidence!

A hallmark of the Gifted Treasury Series is the proven worth of the activities and resources that are advocated. No idea or strategy is suggested that has not been tried and been proven worthy of replication. As series editor, I can personally attest to the workability of the exciting lessons outlined in the pages of this book. Two years ago, on a cold February morning, I sat transfixed in Robert Ray's first-grade classroom in Colorado Springs, Colorado, as I observed six- and seven-year-old children recite Sir Isaac Newton's third law of motion and discuss the history of the Apollo phase of the NASA Space Program. None of Dr. Ray's students were identified as gifted students, but he taught them as if they were, and they responded in kind. In the University of Colorado Super Saturday Program, Dr. Ray has challenged and inspired identified gifted students to achieve remarkable levels of accomplishments in both the building of their scientific knowledge base and in the creation of remarkable aerospace projects.

Integrating Aerospace Science into the Curriculum: K-12 is a book with a vision. It begins with an exploration of the myths of past civilizations, but it finds its heart and soul in the future. Ultimately, it will help the concerned and creative teachers or mentors to inspire their students to reach for the sky and to touch the stars.

Jerry D. Flack

Acknowledgments

The authors thank the following persons for the many kindnesses extended to them during the preparation of this book: Dr. Jerry Brown, Director of Education, United States Space Foundation; Captain Dale Gardner, U.S. Navy, NASA Astronaut; Richard P. MacCleod, President, United States Space Foundation; Rudi Banuelos, Jackie and Eric Peterson, Dewey Reinhard, and Wilbur Wassaw, all of Colorado Springs; the library staff at the Penrose Public Library (Colorado Springs), the United States Air Force Academy, and the University of Colorado at Colorado Springs (especially Laurie Williams, Inter-Library Loan Office); personnel at the Teacher Resource Centers at the Johnson Space Center, Houston, Texas, and at the United States Space Foundation, Colorado Springs, Colorado; and staff of the NASA-NEWEST Workshop for Teachers, summer 1989, Johnson Space Center, and of the "Getting Comfortable Teaching with Space" Teachers' Workshop (July 30-August 3, 1990), co-sponsored by the U.S. Space Foundation and the U.S. Air Force Academy, Colorado Springs.

We also thank the student artists from schools in Colorado Springs and Cherry Creek (Denver), Colorado, and Rockville, Maryland, for their illustrations. With the exceptions of the eleven figures drawn by the authors and figure 5.4 drawn by the art teacher at Turman Elementary School, Harrison District 2, Colorado Springs, the artwork in this book was contributed by students ranging in grade level from third through senior high school. Following is a list of illustrations and names of the respective artists/photographer:

Figure		Artist/Photographer
1.1	Da Vinci's parachute	Lisa Sciotto
1.2	Da Vinci's ornithopter	Brandon Miera
2.1	Montgolfier balloon	Sarah Cicotello
2.2	Dirigible	Candice Wright
3.1	Forces on a kite	authors
3.2	Making a kite	authors
3.3	Cayley's glider	Lisa Sciotto
3.4	An airfoil	authors
3.5	Bernoulli's Principle	authors
3.6	Otto Lilienthal gliding	Kelly Reid
3.7	Otto Lilienthal's gliders	Lisa Sciotto
3.8	Making a paper glider	authors
3.9	Hargrave's box kite	Lisa Sciotto
3.10	Parts of a modern airplane	authors
3.11	Four forces of flight	authors
3.12	Blériot's airplane	Lisa Sciotto
3.13	*Sopwith Camel*	Lisa Sciotto
3.14	Sample weather chart	class project
4.1	B-29 bomber	Scott Hornick
4.2	Modern helicopter	authors
4.3	Making a "heli-pencil"	authors
4.4	Boeing 707	Kelly Reid

Introduction

Why Use Aerospace Science in the Classroom?

"If you want to grab kids' attention and interest," advises Richard P. MacCleod, president of the United States Space Foundation, "you should recognize that they are mainly interested in three things: ghosts, dinosaurs, and space. But among these three, the one that is going to be the greatest force in their futures is space."[1] Indeed, not just space science but every man-made object that flies through the air or into space seems to arouse the curiosity of persons young and old. The study of such objects is called *aerospace science* with *aerospace* compounded from *air* and *space*. With today's gifted and talented students as the major pool for tomorrow's scientists, engineers, researchers, teachers, physicians, professors, astronauts, test pilots, and other professionals whose knowledge and talent will be crucial to the continued successes of the American aerospace programs, it is only logical to include aerospace science in the gifted and talented curricula of elementary, middle, and secondary schools. Aerospace science offers the "right stuff" for all students but especially gifted and talented education.

The Association for the Gifted, a division of the Council for Exceptional Children, advocates the following criteria for gifted and talented education in the United States and Canada:

> Curriculum for the gifted and talented should include content which is more than information and facts. It should include skills, experiences, and processes. The content needs more academic rigor, real-world orientation and decision-making, and should be interdisciplinary. Content for the gifted and talented should remain abreast of changes in society, such as the area of technology, so that a gap does not occur between reality and curricular content.[2]

A healthy dose of such standards into *all* curricula and classrooms — whatever the grade and whatever the giftedness of the students — would surely enrich and enhance education generally. What this book will show is that few curricula are more academically rigorous, more problem-solving directed, more imaginative, more hands-on oriented, more real-world related, and more interdisciplinary than aerospace science.

Furthermore, even though this book, part of the Gifted Treasury Series, is targeted at teachers and library media specialists who work with gifted and talented students, it also is a resource for everyone involved with the education of America's youth. These persons need not have been science majors in college to include various aspects of aerospace science in their classroom and library programs. One of the authors — a primary school teacher with an academic background in history, reading, and bibliotherapy — began using aerospace science merely as a context within which to teach various skills (reading, writing, problem solving, communication) and content areas (social studies, art, health and drug awareness, and basic science) only to discover that it was a powerful magnet for students. The editor of this series visited this author's classroom and observed the responses of so-called average students to the aerospace science-based curriculum and later wrote that the teacher taught "all ... students as if they were gifted students and, quite amazingly, they respond[ed] in kind."[3] Even more remarkable results occurred when the same teacher taught aerospace science to primary-level children in the Super Saturday Program for the Gifted and Talented at the University of Colorado at Colorado Springs. Those who regularly work with the gifted and talented can expect to give much more to their students and can expect much more from them by including aerospace science in curricula and program offerings.

Franklin C. Owens, deputy director of the National Aeronautics and Space Administration's (NASA) Educational Affairs Division, cites research indicating "that if we don't turn children on to science and technology by the third grade, the chance of their studying those fields later in life dramatically diminishes." Likewise, Harold R. Bacon, deputy chief of staff for aerospace education with the Civil Air Patrol-United States Air Force and an experienced teacher in junior high through university levels, champions "putting aerospace into all aspects of the curriculum, starting with kindergarten."[4] This book will help you do just that.

How This Book Can Launch Your Aerospace Curriculum

As this book will attest in its chapter-by-chapter bibliographies, many resources are available to teachers who desire to include an aviation or space unit in their classrooms: resources that comprehensively cover the history of flight in general, that address space, that provide aerospace activities for elementary, middle, and secondary students, that offer activities focusing on spacecraft, or that focus on airplanes. There are books about the flying brothers, Montgolfier and Wright, about the flying Charleses, Lindbergh and Yeager, about helicopters, X-planes, and supersonic aircraft (see bibliography for recommended titles).

However, our teaching and research experience shows that while one book discusses the story of flight or of a particular aspect of flight, we need to seek yet another book to uncover activities appropriate for the classroom. Although some of the activity books give brief snippets about aerospace history, such as names and dates of major flights, they really do not explain the significance of those names and flights—how one flight relates to another subsequent flight, or what scientific and technological principles were involved in the flight. Finally, many activity books are simply weak in giving procedures for activities and experiments. This book fills some of those gaps, keeping in mind the teacher-as-reader.

From Toys to Technology:
The Science and Story of Aerospace Advances

Our book not only tells the story and explains the science of aerospace, but also suggests ways of integrating such information with other curricular areas through hands-on activities. It tells the story of how humanity first took to the skies and ultimately traveled through space. Chapter 1 provides a brief overview of the history of flight. Chapters 2 and 3 explore balloons and kites to demonstrate the principles learned from experimenting with objects often thought to be simple toys. Chapter 4 explores the development of aircraft during periods of war. Chapters 5 and 6 explore the development of the space programs. Interviews with a balloonist and an astronaut provide an opportunity to meet experts in two chronologically distant forms of flight.

"IMAGINATION IS MORE IMPORTANT THAN KNOWLEDGE" (ALBERT EINSTEIN)

As figure I-1 shows, the foundation of the "Steps to Outer Space," as well as the unfolding of the unknown top step of the future, is *imagination*—the underlying quality of the gifted and talented individual. The intervening steps cite the imaginative accomplishments of flight pioneers from the Montgolfier brothers' early experiments with hot-air balloons to the astronauts' spacewalking outside the space shuttle.

Basic scientific principles relative to flight are interwoven with the historical stories behind the "Steps to Outer Space." For the elementary teacher who is a generalist, we present the science so that teachers whose backgrounds do not include formal science education can understand it. The elementary-level science material includes some sample activities that teachers can use to introduce the basic principles of science necessary for students' understanding of flight and space travel, as well as activities directly related to these areas. All of the activities are designed to get *you*, our teacher-colleague, launched, and we encourage you to supplement them with your own materials and ideas. Resources for additional activities and background materials are listed in the bibliographies.

Fig. I.1. The Steps to Outer Space.

For the junior and senior high school levels, the book suggests areas in aerospace studies where teachers of different subjects can collaborate. For example, a team of English, history, geography, and physics or biology teachers can collaborate on curriculum planning around an aerospace theme. Students can begin to see the interrelatedness of knowledge when presented through a multidisciplinary approach.

THE AEROSPACE MAGNET

To facilitate such interdisciplinary teaching, this book discusses the interdisciplinary potential in using aerospace science as a curricular development tool. The discussion covers the theoretical and practical ways that aerospace science can enhance the teaching of various skills and content areas, ranging from art to social studies. You might know this as a *curriculum web*[5]; for its application in this book, we call it the *Aerospace Magnet* because aerospace science attracts other fields or skills that, in turn, are made more exciting and challenging for students by their presentation within the aerospace context. Rather than isolated as a separate unit or chapter, the Aerospace Magnets will appear where appropriate throughout the book, suggesting the interdisciplinary nature of aerospace science.

Whenever this Aerospace Magnet symbol appears, there is a hands-on activity that teachers can use in their classrooms. These activities range from simple science experiments (complete with step-by-step procedures and an explanation of materials and the scientific principle involved) that primary school students can perform to projects in literature appropriate to a high school honors English class. For advanced science and mathematics students, teachers can use ideas for integrating basic science and math concepts and procedures with aerospace science. (For example, when the physics teacher discusses gravity, the gravitational forces of the planets, or the effects of zero or microgravity and high gravity on astronauts during space flights can be included.) Grade-level applicability of each Aerospace Magnet is suggested by the labels "Beginning," "Intermediate," "Advanced," or "General." In addition to activities, the Aerospace Magnets include cross-references to additional books and teaching materials, as applicable.

One example of the way aerospace science relates to other fields and students' real-life choices is career planning. Interwoven with the story and science of aerospace are intermittent suggestions about potential careers in the field and ways to integrate this material into the school curriculum. Aerospace is a continuously evolving field, requiring high degrees of expertise in all areas: art, history, medicine, pilotage, and technology, to name a few. By the time today's gifted first-graders reach junior high, they need to start thinking seriously about career possibilities so they can take the appropriate coursework to be admitted to a college or university that will prepare them eventually for their chosen careers. Some of these careers will be in fields that today do not even exist.

Finally, in addition to chapter-by-chapter bibliographies that include some commentaries, the book provides a bibliography of bibliographies of resources (publications, audiovisual materials, software, names and addresses of clubs and organizations) relevant to aerospace science education and available to the teacher and library media specialist. The concluding "Appendix of Useful Addresses" is a handy reference for contacting key agencies and resource suppliers. This book consolidates information, thus saving the user's time.

The Teacher-Library Media Specialist Team

That the classroom teacher and the library media specialist will work as a team in this endeavor is a given. Just as a space launch requires the collaboration of various experts, the tripartite task of exciting, challenging, and motivating all students—especially gifted and talented students—requires collaboration. Jerry D. Flack, in an article for *School Library Media Quarterly*, and David V. Loertscher, in *Taxonomies of the School Library Media Program*, argue for such teamwork and provide models for joint ventures in curriculum development.[6] However, there is also a more down-to-earth reason to encourage teacher-library media specialist cooperation in teaching space science or anything else: in these days of tight school budgets, pooling fiscal resources will advance the school's accumulation of physical resources and vice versa. With these criteria in mind, the book includes Aerospace Magnets labeled "Library Research" to suggest areas where the teacher and library media specialist can work as a team. As they guide the students in library research, the team members should emphasize the importance of *diligence and accuracy* in the research process—whether that research occurs in the library or the laboratory. As the story of aerospace progress makes clear, flight pioneers from the Montgolfiers to the moonwalkers needed to apply themselves as devoted researchers. Emphasizing this, the teaching team can help students reach for the stars.

Notes

[1]Richard P. MacCleod, president, United States Space Foundation, interview with author, 12 January 1991. Likewise, teacher Iris Harris, whose aviation-centered classroom is featured in the December 1990-January 1991 *Air and Space Smithsonian*, remarks, "Two kinds of books never stay in the library.... Dinosaur books and aviation and space books." (p. 78). See Michael Parfit, "Flight School," *Air and Space Smithsonian*, 5 (December 1990-January 1991): 78-83.

[2]Beverly N. Parkes, "First Steps toward Program Standards in Educating the Gifted and Talented" (Report prepared as a result of the Association for Gifted Symposium I, Fort Worth, Texas, 13-14 March 1987), 15-18.

[3]Jerry D. Flack, letter to author, 7 February 1989.

[4]Owens and Bacon made these remarks at the Fifth National Symposium of the United States Space Foundation's session on "Aerospace Education: Preparing for Life in a New Era," Colorado Springs, Colorado, 7 April 1989.

[5]Jerry D. Flack, *Inventing, Inventions, and Inventors: A Teaching Resource Book* (Englewood, Colo.: Libraries Unlimited, 1989), 4-8.

[6]Jerry D. Flack, "A New Look at a Valued Partnership: The Library Media Specialist and Gifted Students," *School Library Media Quarterly* 14 (1986): 174-79. David V. Loertscher, *Taxonomies of the School Library Media Program* (Englewood, Colo.: Libraries Unlimited, 1988).

Bibliography

Andrews, Sheila Briskin, and Audrey Kirschenbaum. *Living in Space*. Book 1 for grades 1, 2, 3; Book II, for grades 4, 5, 6. Washington, D.C.: U.S. Government Printing Office, 1987.
     Full of hands-on activities; but be thoroughly sure you work out the procedures for them before using this series in the classroom.

Bacon, Harold R. Civil Air Patrol-United States Air Force. Remarks made at the Education Forum at the Fifth National Symposium of the United States Space Foundation, Colorado Springs, Colo., 7 April 1989.

Boyne, Walter J. *The Smithsonian Book of Flight for Young People*. New York: Atheneum, 1988.

Bryan, C. D. B. *The National Air and Space Museum*. 2d ed. New York: Harry N. Abrams, 1988.

Dewaard, E. John, and Nancy Dewaard. *History of NASA: America's Voyage to the Stars*. New York: Exeter Books, 1984.

Dye, Aimee. *Aviation Curriculum Guide for Middle School Level, Secondary School Level*. Washington, D.C.: Department of Transportation, Federal Aviation Administration, n.d.
     To secure a free copy of this, contact the FAA's regional office at the address given for your state in "Appendix of Useful Addresses."

Flack, Jerry D. *Inventing, Inventions, and Inventors: A Teaching Resource Book*. Englewood, Colo.: Libraries Unlimited, 1989.

Flack, Jerry D. "A New Look at a Valued Partnership: The Library Media Specialist and Gifted Students." *School Library Media Quarterly* 14 (Summer 1986): 174-79.

Gelman, Rita Golden, and Susan Kovacs Buxbaum. *What Are Scientists? What Do They Do? Let's Find Out*. New York: Scholastic, 1991.
     Introduces beginning students to the various types of scientists in the context of space creatures visiting Earth.

Harris, Iris, and the Alabama State Department of Education. *Aviation and Space Curriculum Guide, K-3*. Washington, D.C.: Department of Transportation, Federal Aviation Administration, 1990.
For a copy of this manual, contact the FAA's regional office at the address given in the appendix. Lots of activities; work out the procedures carefully before using the activities in class.

Housel, David C., and Doreen K. M. Housel. *Come Fly with Me: Exploring K-6 through Aviation/Aerospace Concepts*. Lansing, Mich.: Michigan Aeronautics Commission, 1983.
Lots of activities.

Johnston, William B., et al. *Workforce 2000: Work and Workers for the Twenty-first Century*. Indianapolis, Ind.: Hudson Institute, 1987. (Prepared for the Department of Labor).

Kopp, O. W., Mary Head Williams, Audean Allman, and Jean Rademacher. *Elementary School Aerospace Activities: A Resource for Teachers*. Washington, D.C.: National Aeronautics and Space Administration, 1977.
May be in your public library; was for sale through the Superintendent of Documents, U.S. Government Printing Office, Washington, D.C. 20402 (stock number 033-000-00693-4).

Loertscher, David V. *Taxonomies of the School Library Media Program*. Englewood, Colo.: Libraries Unlimited, 1989.

MacCleod, Richard P., interview with author, 12 January 1991.

Martin Marietta Astronautics Group Careers. Denver, Colo.: Martin Marietta Astronautics Group, 1989.

McAleer, Neil. *The OMNI Space Almanac*. New York: OMNI World Almanac, 1987.
Great photos; teachers and advanced students will find this a good read.

National Air and Space Museum and National Aeronautics and Space Administration. *Discovery* (n.p., n.d.).
For a copy of this looseleaf-bound manual, contact the Smithsonian Institution whose address is in the appendix. Includes a sketchy historical survey. Good on activities.

Ontario Science Centre. *Scienceworks: 65 Experiments That Introduce the Fun and Wonder of Science*. Reading, Mass.: Addison-Wesley Publishing, 1988.
Dozens of simple activities for teachers to do with beginning students to introduce basic scientific principles.

Owens, Franklin C. Division of Educational Affairs, NASA. Remarks made at the Education Forum at the Fifth National Symposium of the United States Space Foundation, Colorado Springs, Colo., 7 April 1989.

Parkes, Beverly N. "First Steps toward Program Standards in Educating the Gifted and Talented." Report prepared as a result of the Association for Gifted Symposium 1, Fort Worth, Texas, 13-14 March 1987, 15-18.

Stine, Megan, et al. For the Smithsonian Institution. *More Science Activities*. New York: GMG Publishing, 1988.

Strickler, Mervin K., Jr. *A Model Aerospace Aviation Curriculum Based on August Martin High School* [in Queens, New York]. Washington, D.C.: Department of Transportation, Federal Aviation Administration, n.d.
Contact the regional FAA office, whose address is in the appendix.

Strongin, Herb. *Science on a Shoestring*. Menlo Park, Calif.: Addison-Wesley, 1976.
Great activities for primary-level teachers.

Taylor, John W. R., and Kenneth Munson. *History of Aviation*. London: Octopus Books, 1975.
Extremely thorough; by the people who do the definitive *Jane's All the World's Aircraft*.

Tolman, Marvin N., and James O. Morton. *Physical Science Activities for Grades 2-8*. Science Curriculum Activities Library. West Nyack, N.Y.: Parker Publishing, 1986.
Contains over 170 easy activities, including units on gravity and centrifugal force useful for aerospace curricula.

U.S. Department of Transportation, Federal Aviation Administration. *Aviation Science Activities for Elementary Grades*. Washington, D.C.: U.S. Government Printing Office, 1983.
Contact the regional FAA office; address in appendix.

_____. *Demonstration Aids for Aviation Education*. Washington, D.C.: U.S. Government Printing Office, 1987.
Contact the regional FAA office; address in appendix.

Walpole, Brenda. *175 Science Experiments to Amuse and Amaze Your Friends*. New York: Random House, 1988.
Recommended for beginning students; includes a unit on flight.

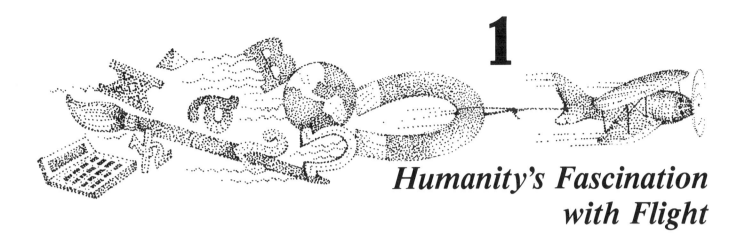

Humanity's Fascination with Flight

In the National Endowment for the Humanities report *American Memory*, Dr. Lynne Cheney rhetorically asks, "If literature connects us to permanent concerns, then shouldn't every young person read it?"[1] Although space science might suggest to some persons an exclusive focus on science and technology, the study of humanity's perennial fascination with flight and the unknown represented by the heavens is an exciting literary and historical area for students — one that reminds them that tomorrow's aerospace plane and space stations owe much to yesterday's genius and spirit. This permanent human concern with flight is seen in mythology and literature.

Flight, Mythology, and Literature

Mythology, as Joseph Campbell tells us, provides stories that help us come to terms with being human. These stories deal with human longings, fears, worries, and joys that have been part of human life since it began. In a way, they also play a role in space science. Speaking in Colorado Springs, Colorado, on January 4, 1990, Army Brigadier General Robert Stewart, a mission specialist on two space shuttle launches (STS-41-B, STS-51-J), who made the first untethered flight with NASA's manned maneuvering unit (discussed in chapter 6), stressed that although science and technology are responsible for physically putting persons in space, there is a spiritual propulsion that spurs humanity's desire to explore the heavens. He observes that this spiritual propulsion, which sends humans skyward, is sometimes neglected here on earth when we deal with the mundane details of everyday life:

> One of the root causes of the social problems is that people don't think in terms of magnificence any more. They think in terms of the next meal. Well, the next meal is important ... but you've got to feed his soul too. That's what I think we've lost sight of — feeding the human spirit.[2]

Space travel, Stewart concludes, is a way of nourishing the human spirit.

MYTHOLOGY

- Library research, language arts, critical thinking, oral communication, working in groups

- Intermediate and advanced

For a class unit on mythology organized by the teacher and library media specialist, divide the class into research teams and ask each team to investigate mythology for stories and legends about humanity's fascination with flight. Notice that many of the gods worshiped by early human beings lived in the heavens or had the ability to fly or both. Ask students to consider why people gave their deities this attribute; in other words, what does this attribute given to deities tell us about the human perception of the ability to fly?

Using such resources as Bulfinch's *Mythology* and other related works suggested by the library media specialist, students should be able to identify such figures as Pegasus, Mercury or Hermes, Jove and his son Phaethon, Daedalus and his son Icarus and their respective connections with flight. After reading about these figures, the team members should speculate what the myths are telling us in terms of warnings, lessons, and themes. What might flight have symbolized to early humanity? (Teachers might wish to provide guidelines for their students to facilitate their speculations.) Each team should be responsible for reporting its findings and speculations to the class; depending upon the grade level, students should be able to cite sources correctly, to summarize and interpret information, and to write up their findings. Also, in your unit on mythology, students can write and illustrate a modern myth dealing with flight.

FLIGHTS OF FANCY IN EARLY FICTION

- Library research, language arts, oral communication

- Intermediate and advanced

Students may want to explore early conceptions of flight in literature. Here are some readable suggestions: Jonathan Swift, *Gulliver's Travels* (1726); Dr. Samuel Johnson, *Rasselas* (1759); Edgar Allan Poe, "The Unparalleled Adventures of One Hans Pfaall" (1835), and "The Balloon Hoax" (1844-45); Jules Verne, *From the Earth to the Moon* (1865) and its sequel *Round the Moon* (1870), "A Balloon Journey," *Five Weeks in a Balloon* (1863), and *Around the World in Eighty Days* (1873); and H. G. Wells, *The War of the Worlds* (1898) and *The First Men in the Moon* (1901). The reading might even include old Buck Rogers and Flash Gordon comics, two characters who made space travel a part of popular culture decades before Sputnik. For additional literary resources, see Freedman's *2000 Years of Space Travel*; the library media specialist can also create a bibliography and/or display of books on the subject that would interest your students.

Writing assignments and discussions about the readings within their historical context might focus on how literature can prepare people for facing future reality, as well as motivate and inspire them to "create" their futures. For example, the Father of Rocketry, American physicist Dr. Robert Goddard, attributed his inspiration to study rockets to his reading of Verne's *From the Earth to the Moon* and *Round the Moon*.[3]

Leonardo da Vinci: From Palette to Pilot

Leonardo da Vinci (1452-1519), the archetypal Renaissance man, may well be familiar to many students as one of the greatest artists of all time. Younger students may identify the name Leonardo—as well as the names of three other great Renaissance artists, Raphael, Donatello, and Michelangelo—with the Teenage Mutant Ninja Turtles® of cinema and cartoon fame.[4] However, few students probably know of Leonardo da Vinci's ideas about flight.

About the time that Christopher Columbus was sailing across the Atlantic in search of new worlds, da Vinci was working in Florence and Milan, Italy, on descriptions and drawings of flying machines. Although model helicopters dating back to the Middle Ages have been uncovered, da Vinci worked independently on designing a helicopter that theoretically operated by a screw type of rotating mechanism to raise the vehicle straight up. (See chapter 4 for a discussion of helicopters.)

Although the idea for a helicopter may have predated da Vinci, as far as evidence shows, he was the inventor of the *parachute* (figure 1.1).[5] As can be seen in our artist's rendition of da Vinci's sketch, his parachute looked like a pyramid-shaped tent with a pole extending from its apex to the point where the shroud lines meet. Although evidence varies on whether da Vinci's ideas for the helicopter and parachute ever went beyond sketches, some historians say he made working versions of both items and perhaps even flew his own helicopter—although the chances of his doing the latter are slim.[6]

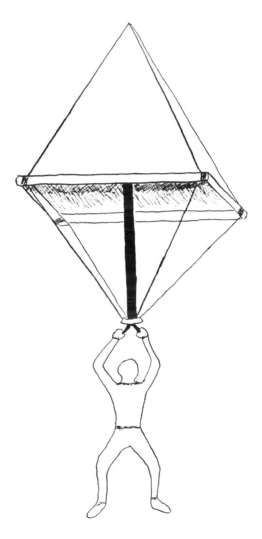

Fig. 1.1. Da Vinci's parachute.

From observing birds, da Vinci believed that an object needed flapping wings in order to fly. This is a different idea about flying than that exhibited by his helicopter. Based on his bird watching, da Vinci left writings about and made drawings of an *ornithopter*, or flapping-wing aircraft (figure 1.2), that he apparently envisaged could fly when empowered by the pilot's arm and leg movements. However, a bird is proportionately much stronger than a person; thus, a person never could have moved da Vinci's heavy ornithopter through the air.

Yet, the ornithopter was a precursor of the *glider*, which is discussed in chapter 3. Using modern, lightweight but strong materials, human beings would be able to supply human power to flight by 1977.

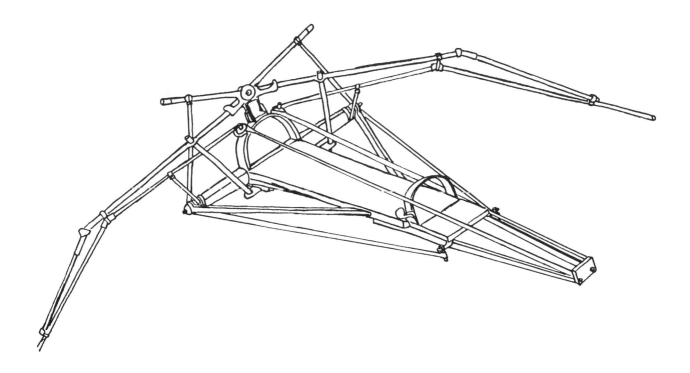

Fig. 1.2. Da Vinci's ornithopter.

Da Vinci's observations and ideas about human flight might have accelerated the development of aviation, but his scientific manuscripts and drawings remained unknown until 300 years after he died.

UNDERSTANDING THE FORCE OF GRAVITY AND MAKING SIMPLE PARACHUTES

- Science, mathematics, problem solving

- Beginning, intermediate

Making and launching a small, simple parachute helps students understand the pull of gravity and how it can be resisted. *Gravity* is a force that pulls objects to the ground or earth. It is one of the four forces of flight, the other three being *lift, drag*, and *thrust*, which will be discussed as we proceed. Although da Vinci implicitly understood the principle of gravity, the person who articulated the law of universal gravitation was the great English scientist Sir Isaac Newton (1642-1727). The law of gravity appeared in his most famous work, *The Mathematical Principles of Natural Philosophy* (originally titled *Philosophiae Naturalis Principia Mathematica*), published in 1687. This publication also presented the laws of motion, which will be discussed under jet engines in chapter 4.

Before actually constructing the parachutes, teachers can illustrate the concept of gravity by first giving each student two sheets of paper of equal size and weight. Ask students to observe their papers closely. Crumple up one sheet in a tight wad and leave the other as it is, asking students to do the same with their two sheets. Then, with all students holding their wadded paper and their sheet of paper in their hands, ask the students which they think will hit the floor first if both are dropped at the same time and from the same height. Allow time for predictions and then, on cue, students drop their papers simultaneously. Ask the students to explain why the crumpled paper took less time to fall, or fight the force of gravity, even though both papers were the same weight. (Answer: The crumpled paper had less surface area to resist the push of air. The open, flat sheet of paper had more surface area and had to push more air aside as it fell; thus, it fell more slowly. This is the principle behind a parachute.)

From the paper-dropping activity, you and your students can proceed to making parachutes according to the following instructions:

Materials: Sheet, string, magic markers, washers, scissors, yardsticks/rulers, hole puncher.

Procedure: Tear an old sheet into enough 12"x12" squares so that each student has one. Depending on the age level, students (or if the students are too young, the teacher) will do the following: First, cut a small hole (a hole puncher works well here) ½" from each corner of the square, where the string is to be inserted. Second, using felt-tip markers, students may draw their own designs on the parachute. Third, cut the string into four 16" segments, which the students should measure with yardsticks. Fourth, tie one string segment to each corner of the sheet through the punched holes. Fifth, gather the loose ends of the string segments together and tie them through a washer.

Students may then go outside to test and enjoy their parachutes by wrapping the strings and washer very loosely around the sheet and throwing the parachutes in the air. (Note: For safety, make sure each of the students has an individual testing area.)

An excellent description of da Vinci's work on parachutes, as well as a brief history of parachutes, is provided in Engle's *Parachutes: How They Work*. Additional basic science activities in this area can be found in Strongin's *Science On a Shoestring*, pp. 135-37. As a variation on the parachute activity described, the class may want to build a papier-mâché paratrooper to go with the parachute. For help on this, see the Smithsonian's *More Science Activities*, pp. 76-78.

BE AN INVENTOR!

- Science and problem solving

- Beginning and intermediate

Be a multidisciplinary Renaissance person like da Vinci: design a parachute protecting a raw egg from breaking when it is dropped from a specific height. What materials would you use? Why? What dimensions would you use? Why? Construct a model of this parachute and demonstrate it. For further information on this activity of "braking an egg," see Housel and Housel's *Come Fly with Me!*, p. 173; and Caballero's *Aerospace Projects*, p. 46.

UNDERSTANDING GRAVITY'S EFFECTS

- Science (physics, biology), mathematics, problem solving

- Intermediate and advanced

Intermediate students can calculate how much they would weigh if they landed on particular planets by multiplying their earth weights by that planet's surface gravity. Earth's surface gravity is 1.0. We know the approximate surface gravities for seven planets: Mercury = .26; Venus = .86; Mars = .39; Jupiter = 2.64; Saturn = 1.07; Uranus = .91; Neptune = 1.12. Earth's satellite, the Moon, has a surface gravity that is one-sixth (about .17) of the earth's; this explains why the Apollo astronauts who walked and worked on the Moon (chapter 5) could each wear, without any discomfort, a portable life support system (chapter 5) that weighed 104 pounds on earth. How much did it weigh on the Moon? If you went to the Moon, how much would you weigh? Our nearest star, the Sun, has a surface gravity of about 28; figure out how much the portable life support system would weigh there. Would it be feasible—notwithstanding the Sun's intense heat—even to ask astronauts to carry such a life support system there?

Advanced students can work with their physics and/or mathematics teacher on Newton's law of gravitation and its application in everyday life. They can learn about acceleration gravity and discuss why NASA officials were so tense when America's first astronaut, Commander Alan B. Shepard, reentered the earth's gravitation in his Mercury capsule, *Freedom 7*, and experienced high gravity (high g's) to the extent of 11 g's. Nowadays, astronauts rarely experience high gravity beyond 3 g's during their missions.

The advanced students' physics teachers can relate the study of gravity and centrifugal and centripetal force to space. (The nonscience teacher wanting to learn something about centripetal and centrifugal force can look ahead to chapter 5's Aerospace Magnet, "Understanding Newton's First Law".) If astronaut John Glenn, whose earth weight was 170 pounds, experienced 6.7 g's of gravitational force at the liftoff of his Mercury capsule *Friendship 7*, how much did he weigh under the force of the high g's? For a discussion of astronauts preparing in a centrifuge for high gravity at launch and landing, see the section on "Conditions of a Space Flight: From High Gravity to Zero Gravity" in chapter 5.

AEROSPACE ARITHMETIC

- Mathematics, problem solving

- Beginning

At the primary level, use simple math problems with an aerospace theme. As Jack Barker, public affairs officer for the Federal Aviation Administration (FAA)'s Southern Region says, "Two hours plus two hours to fly here is better than two apples plus two apples."[7] Simply use flight-oriented illustrations to explain the basic arithmetical principles—from adding rockets to subtracting helicopters.

MEET SIR ISAAC NEWTON

- Library research, language arts, history of science, art

- General

Have students find materials about Sir Isaac Newton in the library; advanced students might want to look at the *Encyclopedia of Philosophy*, which has a good bibliography on him. Ask students to find the popular story about Newton's realizing the existence of gravity (while gardening in 1666, he observes an apple fall from a tree); what is the philosophical point of this little story? (Because great discoveries can come from simple, everyday occurrences, it is important to be observant of the world around us. Just as the Wrights discerned the principles of airplane flight from working with a simple kite, so Newton discovered gravity by merely watching an apple fall.) What else did Newton discover? Have beginning-level students draw pictures of Newton working in his garden and making the discovery about gravity. Take a discovery walk. Take students to a place where they can sit and observe others at work or play. Have them take paper and pencil and record their observations. Encourage them to make connections and think like a scientist.

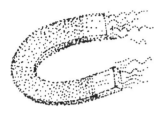

DRAW LIKE DA VINCI AND WHAT ELSE DID DA VINCI DO?

- Art, problem solving

- Beginning and intermediate

Students are usually intrigued by da Vinci's sketches of a parachute and an ornithopter (figures 1.1 and 1.2). Have them draw their own versions of these items. Ask them to design their own flying machines. Additional illustrations of da Vinci's aircraft appear in two books by Gibbs-Smith: *Leonardo da Vinci's Aeronautics*, pp. 7-18, and *Aviation: An Historical Survey from Its Origins to the End of World War II*, p. 17.

With the help of your school art teacher and library media specialist, arrange for an exhibit in the library of your students' work.

Show students examples of da Vinci's art using photographic reproductions in slides, art books, and posters. Have them look at his most famous painting, *Mona Lisa*. What do they think her face is conveying? Why? Which of da Vinci's paintings do they like the best? Why? Using the same approach, show the class the paintings and sculptures of other great artists of the Renaissance such as Michelangelo and Raphael. Ask the school art teacher to come to your classroom and discuss with the class the question, "What is great art?" Do your students have favorite artists? Who? Why?

Based on the sophistication of da Vinci's descriptions and sketches regarding flight, we can infer that he had an understanding of basic *aerodynamics*, the study of the movement and forces exerted by air and other gases. Teachers interested in presenting science lessons about aerodynamics have many resources, including the U.S. Department of Transportation, FAA's *Aviation Science Activities for Elementary Grades* and *Demonstration Aids for Aviation Education*, as well as Housel and Housel's *Come Fly with Me!*

Subsequent to Leonardo da Vinci, people continued to wonder, dream, and imagine about flight and the possibilities of *human* flight. However, it was not until the last two decades of the eighteenth century—over 250 years after da Vinci's death—that people actually figured out a way to ascend above the earth. This occurred in a small French town, when Monsieur Montgolfier was looking at his kitchen fireplace and wondering why the smoke and ashes rose into the air. To see how Monsieur Montgolfier's sitting in his chair watching the kitchen fire ultimately led to astronauts' sitting 381 miles above the earth in the space shuttle *Discovery* to launch the Hubble telescope, we turn to a study of lighter-than-air aircraft in chapter 2.

MAKE AN AEROSPACE DICTIONARY

- Language arts, science

- General

Have students start their own aerospace dictionaries in which they write out key words and corresponding definitions. From this chapter, for example, they could include *gravity, parachute*, and *aerodynamics*. Depending on the students' level, for aerodynamics the teacher might even want to define *gas* so students don't confuse it with what goes into cars: a gas is one of the three forms of *matter*, or what everything is made of. (The other two forms of matter are liquid and solid.) A gas is invisible and can take any shape and volume, expanding to fill a very big space or contracting to fill a little space. Beginning students might want to add the words *expand* and *contract* to their dictionaries. The air that we breathe is a gas. (The fourth Aerospace Magnet of chapter 2 is a simple experiment dealing with a gas, showing that hot air expands and cooled air contracts.)

Notes

[1]Lynne V. Cheney, *American Memory: A Report on the Humanities in the Nation's Public Schools* (Washington, D.C.: National Endowment for the Humanities, 1987), 10.

[2]Sue McMillin, "Space travel feeds the 'spirit,' general says," *Colorado Springs Gazette Telegraph*, 5 Jan. 1990, B2, col. 3.

[3]Charles Harvard Gibbs-Smith, *Aviation: An Historical Survey from Its Origins to the End of World War II*, 2d ed. (London: Her Majesty's Stationery Office, 1985), 41.

[4]The Renaissance, a period in European history from the fourteenth to sixteenth centuries, was characterized by brilliant achievements, particularly in art, literature, and science. The hub of activity was Florence, Italy, where universal genius was highly valued. A person who demonstrated such genius was known as a *Renaissance man*, a term we still use today to describe an individual of extraordinarily versatile and brilliant achievements. The concept is personified by Leonardo da Vinci: artist, poet, scientist, engineer, and inventor. For more on the idea of "Renaissance" individuals, see the material on Sir George Cayley, including the relevant Aerospace Magnet, in chapter 3.

[5]Gibbs-Smith, *Aviation: An Historical Survey*, 9.

[6]Air Force ROTC, *Aerospace Science: History of Air Power* (Maxwell Air Force Base, Ala.: Air University Press, 1986), 1-6.

[7]Michael Parfit, "Flight School," *Air and Space Smithsonian* 5 (December 1990-January 1991): 83.

Bibliography

Air Force ROTC. *Aerospace Science: History of Air Power*. Maxwell Air Force Base, Ala.: Air University Press, 1986.

Bulfinch, Thomas. *Mythology*. New York: Crowell, 1970.

Caballero, Jane A. *Aerospace Projects for Young Children*. Atlanta, Ga.: Humanics, 1983; rev. ed. 1987.

Campbell, Joseph, with Bill Moyers. *The Power of Myth*. New York: Doubleday, 1988.

Cheney, Lynne V. *American Memory: A Report on the Humanities in the Nation's Public Schools*. Washington, D.C.: National Endowment for the Humanities, 1987.

Engle, Eloise. *Parachutes: How They Work*. New York: G. P. Putnam's Sons, 1972.

Freedman, Russell. *2000 Years of Space Travel*. N.p.: Holiday House, 1963.

Gibbs-Smith, Charles Harvard. *Aviation: An Historical Survey from Its Origins to the End of World War II*. 2d ed. London: Her Majesty's Stationery Office, 1985.

_____. *Leonardo da Vinci's Aeronautics*. London: Her Majesty's Stationery Office, 1967.

Housel, David C., and Doreen K. M. Housel. *Come Fly with Me: Exploring K-6 through Aviation/Aerospace Concepts*. Lansing, Mich.: Michigan Aeronautics Commission, 1983.

McMillin, Sue. "Space Travel Feeds the 'Spirit,' General Says," *Colorado Springs Gazette Telegraph*, 5 Jan. 1990, p. B2, col. 3.

Parfit, Michael. "Flight School," *Air and Space Smithsonian* 5 (December 1990-January 1991): 78-83.

Stine, Megan, et al. *More Science Activities*. New York: GMG Publishing, 1988.

Strongin, Herb. *Science on a Shoestring*. Menlo Park, Calif.: Addison-Wesley, 1976.
    Great activities for primary-level teachers.

Lighter-Than-Air Aircraft
Balloons, Dirigibles, and Blimps

As we saw in chapter 1, humanity has been fascinated with flight for ages. However, it was not until the end of the eighteenth century that human beings finally took to the skies. They used lighter-than-air aircraft, the balloon being the most basic type. The fear that accompanied people's fascination with flight was in some ways overcome by the hoopla that surrounded early hot-air and hydrogen balloon flights. In a sense, the balloon enabled humanity literally to rise above its fears and take the first steps to the sky.

Lift and Gravity:
Two of the Four Forces of Flight

The balloon is the simplest aircraft. Made of a spherical or sausage-shaped lightweight bag or envelope of paper, silk, or rubberized material, the balloon is filled with heated air, a hot-air balloon, or hydrogen or helium, a gas balloon. Hydrogen and helium are lighter-than-air gases. These gases or heated air give the balloon its *lift*. Remind your students that because an uninflated balloon is heavier than air, it remains on the ground, just as an uninflated toy balloon remains on the table or floor; however, when balloons are filled with hot air, hydrogen, or helium, they float into the air. Lift is one of the *four forces of flight*. Lift is the force that enables an object to overcome the pull of *gravity*—another of the four forces of flight—which, as we saw in the discussion about parachutes in chapter 1, is the force that pulls things back down to the earth.

JUMP INTO SCIENCE!

- Science, problem solving, oral communication

- Beginning

Review the force of gravity by having students jump; ask them why they come back down to the ground. Ask them if they have seen pictures in books or on television of astronauts in the space shuttle experiencing a condition known as zero gravity or weightlessness. Ask them to describe what they saw. Ask them what would happen to those astronauts if they jumped, even once.

How a Hot-Air or Gas Balloon Works

A hot-air balloon rises because the heated air inside the bag is hotter and thus less dense and lighter than the air outside the bag. A gas balloon rises because the gas (originally hydrogen, but nowadays helium) inside the balloon is lighter and less dense than the air outside. As the gas balloon ascends, the air pressure surrounding the balloon decreases, causing the gas inside the bag to expand. As either type of balloon starts to lift from the ground, the pilot of the balloon can gain *altitude* (height) by discarding what is known as *ballast*, anything heavy such as bags of sand or bags of gravel that weigh the inflated balloon down. When the balloonist wants to descend, lifting gas is released from the balloon. The balloon will be pulled to the ground by the force of gravity, just as a helium-filled toy balloon would start to lose altitude if the gas were slowly released. All of this may seem conceptually simple, but it was not until the end of the eighteenth century that a balloon capable of lifting objects and people into the sky was invented.

TERMS

- Language arts
- General

Add the following words and definitions to students' dictionary of aerospace terms: *lift, altitude, helium, hydrogen*, and *ballast*. Have intermediate and advanced students look up the derivation of the word *ballast*: waste plus load.

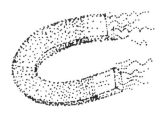

AIR TAKES UP SPACE

- Science
- Beginning

To show that air takes up space, simply have a student blow up a paper bag or a balloon. Explain to the class that although we cannot see air, it occupies space.

PRINCIPLES OF AIR

- Science and language arts
- Beginning, intermediate

Hot air expands and rises; cooled air contracts and descends. The teacher can demonstrate this basic scientific principle by performing with the class any of several simple experiments related to the properties of air. Here is one:

Materials: An uninflated balloon, empty pop bottle, one pan filled with water and one pan filled with snow or ice, a hot mitt (like that used in cooking) or strong tongs, and an electric hot plate.

Procedure:
1. Place the uninflated balloon over the pop bottle.
2. Place the bottle with the balloon on top in the pan of water and heat the pan of water on the hot plate. The heated air molecules will expand, thus causing the balloon to expand. (Keep in mind that there is not *more* air; the air molecules are simply spreading further and further apart or becoming less dense.)
3. Using the hot mitt or tongs, carefully remove the bottle with the balloon on top from the pan of hot water and place it in the pan filled with ice or snow. The coldness causes the air molecules to contract, so the balloon gets smaller.

Result: Hot air expands and rises; cooled air contracts and descends.

To enhance the link between language and science among beginning students, have students dictate to you what took place during the science lesson. This dictation can be jotted on a language experience chart for study and future review by the students. When you record the students' dictation, you may choose to divide the lesson into the component steps of a science experiment:

1. Hypothesis—a good guess the students make before the experiment expressing what they think will happen.

2. Materials—what are used in the experiment.

3. Procedure—what is done during the course of the experiment (directions).

4. Result—what happens as an outcome of the experiment.

Depending on the age level of the students, you might choose to incorporate such skills as the teaching of spelling, punctuation, and sequencing as you write down what the students dictate to you. This technique can be used for other science lessons given in this book.

Additional simple science experiments similar to the one provided on the properties of air may be found in Elementary Science Study, *Teacher's Guide for Gases and "Airs"*; the U.S. Department of Transportation, FAA's *Aviation Science Activities for Elementary Grades* and *Demonstration Aids for Aviation Education*; Walpole's *175 Science Experiments*; and Iris Harris's curriculum manual cited in the bibliography to the introduction.

If the balloon is to carry passengers, a basket is fastened to it by strong tapes (hot-air balloons) or cords or nets (gas balloons). Remember, the balloon will rise in the air provided the balloon and its attachments weigh less than the volume of air displaced. For example, a balloon filled with helium rises because it weighs less than the air it displaces. Conversely the balloon will drop towards the earth if it loses some of its lifting gas, thus decreasing its volume.[1]

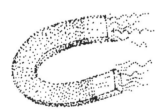

ARCHIMEDES' PRINCIPLE AND BUOYANCY

- Science (physics), social studies, language arts, careers

- Intermediate, advanced

Archimedes (ca.287 B.C.-212 B.C.) was a Greek mathematician, physicist (one who studies matter, energy, and their relationship), and inventor. Among his many discoveries is what has become known as *Archimedes' Principle*. The story is told that a ruler asked Archimedes to find a way of telling whether his crown was pure gold or an alloy of gold and silver. Upon stepping into his bathtub, Archimedes realized that a given weight of gold would displace less water than that same weight of silver because silver is less dense than gold and occupies greater volume. Ecstatic at this discovery, he supposedly ran through the streets naked, screaming "Eureka! Eureka!—I have found it! I have found it!" Archimedes' Principle states: a body immersed in fluid is buoyed up by a force equal to the weight of the displaced fluid. This rule applies to floating and submerged objects and to all fluids. It explains why ships are *buoyant* in the water and why helium balloons float in the air.

The science (physics) teacher can illustrate Archimedes' Principle. Weigh an object (of known volume) two times: first, weigh it in the air; second, weigh it in a tub of water. What is the difference in the weights taken under different conditions? How does this difference compare with the weight of the water displaced during the second weighing process? Relate this to how helium balloons float up and into the air.

A good film about Archimedes' Principle is *The Blimps: Clearly Identified Flying Objects*, Public Relations Film Library, 114 East Market Street, Akron, OH 44316.

Have intermediate students add *physicist* to their dictionaries. Invite a physicist from industry or education to your class to tell students about the job. Does this physicist's job relate to the airplane or space indistry? If so, how? (Remind your students that the first American female astronaut, Sally Ride, has a Ph.D. in astrophysics; several other astronauts are physicists too.) Ask the physicist ahead of time to bring a few simple, exciting experiments or demonstrations to the school to do for your students. After the physicist's visit, have the class write and send thank-you notes.

Advanced students also might be interested in having a physicist from higher education or industry visit and talk about career options in this science.

Balloons were the first historically recorded successful aircraft. They continue to be used today to help advance the exploration of the skies. As the National Research Council report, "The Uses of Balloons for Physics and Astronomy," explains, the short lead times, low costs, and wide range of flight opportunities of balloons make them superior even to satellites for investigating the space environment nearer the earth. The balloon has also been integral to work on developing spacecraft and space flight instrumentation.[2] For example, scientists use balloons to collect small meteorites, and to study planets and stars, thus advancing space programs.[3] Given the importance of the balloon as not only the first step towards the sky, but also as a continuing tool for space exploration, it is worthwhile to learn something about balloons and ballooning as a starting point in the study of space science.

The First Balloonists:
The Montgolfiers and Hot Air

In 1782 a French paper maker, Joseph Montgolfier, sat in front of his fireplace, wondering why smoke, sparks, and other solid matter were steadily rising up the kitchen chimney. Believing that the smoke and bits of matter were borne up the chimney by some type of gas, Joseph and his brother Etienne conducted a number of experiments related to the flying ability of increasingly large balloons fueled by fires of straw and wood placed in the base of the balloons. On June 5, 1783, in their native village of Annonay, the Montgolfiers inflated a large bag (35 feet in diameter) made of sackcloth lined with paper; the air was heated by a straw fire underneath the bag, which ascended 6,000 feet skyward. When the air cooled down, the balloon floated back to the ground, only to catch fire and burn. The local villagers who witnessed the flight were amazed and frightened—too frightened to help put out the flames.[4]

The Montgolfier brothers did not understand that their balloons ascended because they contained heated air that was lighter than the surrounding air. Instead, they mistakenly thought that the balloons rose because the burning fuel created a gas that was lighter than air—like the gas Joseph Montgolfier had concluded was sending the smoke and sparks up his fireplace chimney—which they called *Montgolfier gas.*[5]

NOT SO MYSTERIOUS FLOATING POWDER

- Science

- Beginning, intermediate

Even without a fireplace, you and your students can reproduce a situation similar to that experienced by Joseph Montgolfier.

Materials: An electric lamp with the shade removed, and a small amount of talcum powder or cornstarch.

Procedure: Light the lamp and let the bulb get hot. Holding the powder or cornstarch in your hand over the light bulb, ask students what they think will happen when you start to sprinkle the contents of your hand over the hot bulb and why. Then sprinkle a little talcum powder or cornstarch in the air a few inches above the light bulb.

Result: The powder or cornstarch will rise and float around because the air heated by the hot light bulb is lighter than the surrounding air. The students can watch the currents caused by the rising heated air as the powder/cornstarch floats.

Animal Aeronauts

Word of the Montgolfiers' first flight rapidly spread and excited all of France. In a demonstration for King Louis XVI and Queen Marie Antoinette on September 19, 1783, Joseph and Etienne sent the first living passengers aloft in a balloon: a duck, sheep, and rooster were in a cage attached to the balloon. These animal passengers landed safely, and their flight led the way for human beings to fly. (As we will see in chapter 5, America and the Soviet Union sent dogs and chimpanzees into space before sending human beings.) Pilâtre de Rozier became the first human aeronaut when on October 15, 1783, he ascended 84 feet over Paris in a tethered balloon designed by the Montgolfiers.

On November 21, 1783, in Paris, de Rozier and the Marquess d'Arlandes made the first free or untethered manned flight. Ascending 3,000 feet, they stayed aloft for twenty-five minutes and flew over Paris, landing 5 miles from their point of origin. An excellent source for a print of this Montgolfier balloon, as well as prints of other aviation and aerospace vehicles, is the publication *Discovery*, available from the Smithsonian Institution or the United States Space Foundation, whose addresses are given in the "Appendix of Useful Addresses." For a student's illustration of a Montgolfier balloon, see figure 2.1.

Fig. 2.1. Montgolfier balloon.

Balloons

Thousands watched the de Rozier and d'Arlandes flight, including the King and Queen of France and the American envoy to France, Benjamin Franklin, who was in Paris negotiating the Treaty of Paris by which Great Britain formally ceded independence to the thirteen colonies. Like Leonardo da Vinci, who is mentioned in chapter 1, Franklin was a Renaissance man: writer, statesman, educator, printer, and inventor. (We will encounter Franklin and his famous kite experiment in chapter 3.) A few months later, he prophetically wrote to the great British scientist Sir Joseph Banks, president of England's Royal Society, calling the French balloonists "ingenious men" whose work will prove useful to "science and society."[6]

Subsequent hot-air balloons became known as *Montgolfières*, and after centuries of dreaming about flight, human beings finally flew at their own will.[7]

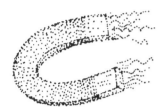

MODEL HOT-AIR BALLOON

- Science, art, language arts

- Beginning and intermediate

The class can make a papier-mâché model of a hot-air balloon.

1. Blow up and securely tie a round balloon.

2. Cover the balloon with several layers of tissue paper soaked in liquid starch.

3. Allow the paper to dry overnight.

4. The next day the paper will be hard, and the balloon can be popped by carefully inserting a needle or pin through the papier-mâché covering.

5. Cut an opening in the bottom of the paper and remove the balloon.

6. Using four strings about 1 foot long each, attach a construction paper basket to the balloon.

The basket and paper balloon may be decorated as desired. This can be extended into a creative writing activity. Ask students to write about a trip in their balloon, telling such things as where they would go, whom they would take along, and the exciting adventures that would take place.

Jacques A. C. Charles and the Robert Brothers

Even in 1783, the first year of flight, the Montgolfier brothers were not alone in their pioneering efforts. A contemporaneous fellow Frenchman, Professor Jacques A. C. Charles, a distinguished physicist, was independently experimenting with balloons. Supported by the French Academy of Sciences, which was intrigued by the potentials of balloon flight, Charles knew the work of English chemist Henry Cavendish, who in 1766 had discovered the gas hydrogen, which he called "inflammable air." Charles concluded that "Montgolfier gas" or heated air would not be as light and thus neither as efficient nor as safe as hydrogen—which we now know is fifteen times lighter than air—for raising a balloon. However, a problem arose: how to contain the hydrogen within the balloon?

Working with two brothers, A. J. and M. N. Robert, who had discovered a method for coating silk with rubber that resulted in a relatively gastight product, Professor Charles was able to launch an unmanned balloon 2,000 feet into the sky on August 26, 1783. Within two minutes, it disappeared from sight, reappearing just momentarily across the Seine.

SEPARATING WATER INTO HYDROGEN AND OXYGEN

• Science

• Intermediate and advanced

Ask your school science (chemistry) teacher to demonstrate to the class how hydrogen can be made by separating water into hydrogen and oxygen through electrolysis.

LEARN ABOUT HYDROGEN

• Library research, science, oral communication

• Intermediate and advanced

Have some of your students look up the properties and uses of hydrogen and report on them to the class.

Less than a month after Pilâtre de Rozier's November 21 flight over Paris, Professor Charles, accompanied by his technician, M. N. Robert, made the second manned balloon flight on December 1, 1783. One of the witnesses of this flight was the ever-curious Benjamin Franklin, who had ridden in his carriage to the launch site, just about where the Eiffel Tower now stands. Training his small telescope into the sky, he watched the balloonists waving white pennants to the crowd below. When someone wondered aloud, "Of what use is a balloon?" Franklin made the foresighted reply: "Sir, of what use is a newborn baby?"[8] This was the first manned hydrogen-filled balloon flight. Witnessed by half of the Paris population, the Charles-Robert flight lasted more than two-and-a-half hours, climbed to an altitude of 820 feet, and covered over 27 miles, a notable improvement on the Montgolfier flight. Flying solo in a second flight for the day, Charles rose to some 9,000 feet. Succeeding hydrogen balloons became known as *Charlières*. Although hydrogen is, itself, highly explosive, Charlières rapidly became more popular than the Montgolfiers, which were perceived as even more hazardous than gas balloons because they were fueled by fires of wood and straw. Consequently, by the end of the 1700s hot-air balloons had all but disappeared, not returning until the advent of modern-day sport balloons from the 1960s to the present.

Helium Replaces Hydrogen

After helium was discovered in 1868, this nonexplosive gas replaced hydrogen—the flammability of which destroyed many lives and aircrafts—as the preferred gas for filling a gas balloon. Safer than hydrogen, helium has 92 percent of hydrogen's lifting capacity. The world's supply of helium comes mostly from America, where there are several major natural gas fields in Texas, New Mexico, Kansas, Oklahoma, Arizona, and Utah.

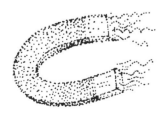

DESIGN A POSTCARD

• History of science, language arts, art

• Beginning

Design a postcard for an important event in ballooning history. On the back of the card, write a short message to a friend pretending that you had really witnessed the event.

YOU ARE THERE!

• Library research, social studies, language arts

• Intermediate and advanced

Have the students use the library to find more about specific key events in ballooning. Then tell your students: "Pretend you are at the scene of an important ballooning event. Record the actual facts of the event, as well as your own feelings and impressions, as the event takes place. When writing the facts, remember the five W's: who, what, when, where, and why. Keep in mind that if another person were to read your account of the event, your goal would be to have such a vivid rendition that the reader would be able to say: 'I am there!' "

Balloons in Battle

Within eleven years of the Montgolfier brothers' pioneering flight, balloons flew into action in the Napoleonic Wars. The French used tethered balloons to observe the movement of enemy troops. During the American Civil War (1861-1865), the Union army had a balloon corps that reported troop movements and helped direct the artillery. When Paris was surrounded by enemy German troops during the Franco-Prussian War (1870-1871), the Parisians were able to send vital communications literally over the heads of the enemy troops by launching balloons that carried people and mail: airmail had begun. Tethered balloons were used as observation posts in World War I (1914-1918), during which England used *balloon barrages*: enemy planes had to fly over tethered balloons from which steel cables, capable of mangling airplanes, were suspended. Such barrages were used again during World War II (1939-1945). The Japanese sent more than 9,000 balloon bombers, which inflicted relatively minor destruction, to America's west coast. Today, in addition to their popularity for sport, balloons are used by scientists to carry instruments to study atmospheric conditions such as wind, moisture, temperature, pressure, man-made contaminants, and cosmic rays from distant galaxies. Unmanned balloons used for these investigations transmit their findings by radio signal. In addition, balloons are used to test the upper atmosphere, which is important to the space program.

The Modern Hot-Air Balloon

Paul "Ed" Yost, who had originally been hired by the General Mills Company to work on high-altitude hydrogen balloons, was the first person to apply modern-day technology to the eighteenth-century invention, the hot-air balloon. Yost conducted a series of experiments on hydrogen-filled balloons made of polyethylene, a soft, moldable plastic made by General Mills. In 1953 he piloted an 8,000-cubic foot polyethylene balloon to which he had fastened a blowtorch to heat the gas. With the help of grants from the Office of Naval Research (ONR), Yost and his colleagues at Raven Industries, Inc., investigated topics related to human-carrying balloons, including coatings for envelopes and burner performance for naval balloons that would be used to carry supplies. Refining the work done by the Montgolfiers, Charles, and others, Raven produced a "modern" hot-air balloon, which they dubbed "the Vulcoon" (a portmanteau word composed of "Vulcan," the Roman god of fire, and "balloon"): a 30,000-cubic foot polyurethane coated nylon envelope, 40 feet in diameter, with a burner fueled by bottled propane. The first "modern" free balloon flight carrying people occurred at Bruning, Nebraska, on October 10, 1960. The flight ended quickly, however, because of burner problems. Learning from the experiment, Raven built a prototype of the modern burner. In November Yost ascended 9,300 feet above Strato Bowl, South Dakota, in a balloon with the improved burner. Although this was just 300 feet higher than Jacques A. C. Charles had gone on his second flight in 1783, Yost's feat helped to revive popular interest in hot-air ballooning as not only a method of supply transportation, but also an enjoyable sport.[9]

Balloons in Space

The expandability of the balloon has inspired ideas for expandable space structures. As Edwin J. Kirschner points out, such structures have many advantages: "They are lightweight and can be folded into high-density packages requiring relatively little lift to be placed in orbit. When in space they can be rapidly inflated."[10]

With the sophisticated uses of balloons planned for the space program, it is hard to believe that ballooning began with the successful flight of a duck, a sheep, and a rooster — from barnyard to outer space.

LEARN HOW BALLOONS WORK

- Library research, science, oral communication, problem solving, language arts, art

- General

Using resources available in the school and/or public library, students can investigate how a pilot controls a hot-air balloon and a gas balloon. (See Bansemer, Fillingham, and Kirschner in the bibliography to get started.) Students can also find illustrations identifying the parts of hot-air and gas balloons and explain the parts. With the increasing popularity of sport ballooning, students may investigate the requirements for securing a balloonist's license from the FAA. (Note: One can secure this license at age 16.)

If there are sport balloonists in your community, students might invite them to the school for an interview. Students' questions should include not only factual material (such as how the balloon operates), but also such information as why the individual has chosen to be a balloonist. Did reading any of the myths or literature about flight in general, such as those mentioned in chapter 1, or about balloons, in particular, inspire the balloonist to pursue this activity? Encourage your students to ask divergent or open-ended questions rather than convergent or close-ended ("yes" or "no") questions.

The balloonists may even be willing to bring their balloons to the school to demonstate a tethered launch. If this occurs, be sure to work in advance with the principal and other officials to be sure that all necessary permissions are secured. The students can write reports about, as well as illustrate, their findings, and present them to the class. Students might also design, write, illustrate, and produce a class *Balloon Bulletin* fact sheet or newspaper for distribution around the school before the visit.

Meet a Balloonist:
Dewey Reinhard

Following is a personal interview with the famous balloonist, Dewey Reinhard, who lives in Colorado Springs, Colorado, and whose ballooning feats have earned him the International Montgolfier Award.

Author: Mr. Reinhard, how did you first become interested in ballooning?

Reinhard: Although I've always been interested in aviation, I really got involved with ballooning as a result of reading an article in the *National Geographic* back in the 1950s about four people who tried to fly a gas balloon called *The Small World* across the Atlantic Ocean from the Canary Islands to Barbados. It was a very exciting story that always stuck in my mind and eventually led me to make my own transAtlantic attempt in a balloon. This article in the '50s was before I was an airline pilot, but it so impressed me that I knew I wanted to be a balloonist as a result of reading it.

Author: But in this day and age of jet travel, why do you favor flying balloons?

Reinhard: I fly balloons because it is challenging; it's fun; it's beautiful; and you can do things in balloons that you can't safely do in any other aircraft. You can pick pine cones out of the tops of trees when flying in the mountains, and you can pick wild flowers when swooping very low over the prairies east of Colorado Springs while flying within 6 inches of the ground. I guess flying in balloons is therapeutic for me. I don't do it for a living or for money. I do it for enjoyment and — hopefully — to expose my friends and family and other people to the wonders and joys of ballooning.

Author: I've heard that you prefer to fly helium balloons rather than hot-air balloons. Why do you choose helium?

Reinhard: Actually, I don't normally fly helium balloons because it — the helium — is so expensive. Most of my individual flights are much longer in duration. However, I probably accumulate more hours of helium flying in a year than I do hot air in that same time period. The helium balloons are particularly challenging to fly because of their navigation. The challenge in flying a gas balloon is first, planning the flight. A flight can last anywhere from four hours to forty-eight hours. You have to have decent weather when you take off, and then you have to try to forecast the weather conditions at your landing place, which may be 500 or 600 miles away. Also, I find the appearance of a traditional netted helium balloon kind of romantic for me. It's the original design and original appearance of a balloon that dates back to just after the Montgolfier brothers. But the thing that I like best about helium balloons is that they are totally silent. The night flying is absolutely incredible! You just take your place above the earth and drift silently across the countryside.

Author: I know that you try to interest young people about ballooning. How do you do this?

Reinhard: I very much enjoy going to different schools and talking with the students about ballooning. All children — both young and old — are excited when they hear the noise of the inflator fan and burner during the inflation of a hot-air balloon. As the balloon stands up and rises to a vertical flying position, just that act of getting a balloon upright to take form gets even me excited! Small children like the special shapes that balloons come in, like Mickey Mouse, Tony the Tiger, and Bugs Bunny. These especially appeal to children. After all, balloons are happy things, whether they be toy balloons or real flying balloons. Just being around balloons tends to make people of all ages happy.

Author: What's your experience in dealing with high school students about ballooning?

Reinhard: Again, the majesty and gigantic size — some of them 85 feet tall — of the balloon really seem to impress them. I think that the balloon flight represents a serenity that high school kids find difficult to come by. If they have a basic interest in aviation — and after all, hot-air ballooning *is* the *first* way man flew — they will be intrigued by balloons: some people are just born to fly! And the majesty, beautiful colors, and the serenity and freedom of the balloon to go where the wind takes it — these are all things that appeal to and excite the enthusiasm of kids. But I always remind them that the balloon is a happy environment that you *have to* treat with respect.

Author: Please tell me about some of your exciting experiences and adventures as a balloonist.

Reinhard: Probably one of my greatest and most exciting adventures was when I attempted to cross the Atlantic. We took off from Bar Harbor, Maine, on October 10, 1977, in our 86,000-cubic-foot balloon called *The Eagle*. We were hit by a sonic boom from the Concorde [for an explanation of sonic booms, see chapter 5]; saw whales underneath us; and a bird collided with the balloon in the middle of the night and fell into our gondola. We covered 220 miles in forty-six hours, but we were forced down off the Canadian coast by a terrible storm. We were picked up by the Canadian Coast Guard, and perhaps *that* was the most dangerous part of this trip because the Coast Guard lowered a giant hook over the side of their ship that probably weighed half a ton to hook on to our gondola.

On par with that flight would be our 1988 flight in the (James) Gordon Bennett Race from Lech, Austria. We left at night and flew through the Austrian Alps. The wind we needed to get the track we wanted was below the mountain-top level. Sometimes the wind would carry us around the peaks and other times we had to work like crazy to get over them. We had a lot of turbulence. After twenty-two hours of ballooning, we were getting low on ballast, and so we were forced to land through deep cloud cover in Central Yugoslavia. Then we had some very interesting experiences with the Yugoslavian police and farmers. We wound up placing something like fifth or sixth in the race.

In 1987, I also flew out of the Austrian Alps from a place called Seefeld. Our goal was to reach the North Sea or English Channel and make it across (the Channel) so that we'd land in England. We didn't do that! But we had an exciting night of flying by instinct. We had a radio tuned off-station so that when we were getting too close to power lines, we could hear the buzzing on the radio. We didn't do too well in this competition, but we were the only balloon to head North: the others flew to Yugoslavia! We landed in Germany.

HOW FAST CAN A BALLOON TRAVEL?

- Mathematics, social studies, language arts

- Intermediate

In the interview, Reinhard mentions that the *Eagle* "covered 220 miles in forty-six hours." How many miles per hour did the balloon travel? Using a large map, students should plan a balloon voyage, plot the course, and figure out the distance. Then, using the data from the first problem, they can calculate how long (approximately) the trip would take them if they were to travel at the same speed. If any of your students have read Jules Verne's *Around the World in Eighty Days*, have them plot the route, determine the distance, and calculate how many miles per hour that balloon would have had to travel to go around the world in eighty days.

MAPS AND ATLASES; LONGITUDE AND LATITUDE

- Social studies, library research (using an atlas)

- General

In Dewey Reinhard's interview, as well as throughout this chapter (including the "Ballooning Timeline" at the end of the chapter), many geographical locations are mentioned. Some of these locations are Paris and Annonay, France; Venice, Italy; London, England; Seefeld, Austria; the Austrian Alps; Germany; Yugoslavia; South America; the Canary Islands; Barbados; Japan; Bar Harbor, Maine; Philadelphia; Lakehurst, New Jersey; Nebraska; South Dakota; the six states with major helium fields (Texas, New Mexico, Utah, Arizona, Kansas, and Oklahoma); Colorado Springs, Colorado; the Atlantic and Pacific Oceans; the Seine River; the North Sea; and the English Channel. Leonardo da Vinci worked in Florence and in Milan, Italy. Using an atlas, students can locate these places and identify them with colored push pins on a large world map. Depending upon the age of the students, the class's mapwork can include the study of longitude and latitude. (For example, Seefeld, Austria is found at 47° 15' N and 11° 00' E in the Alps.) Here's another library research assignment: Reinhard mentions the Gordon Bennett Race. Who was James Gordon Bennett and why is there a balloon race with his name?

Mastering the Winds:
Dirigibles

Despite the early popularity of soaring skyward in a balloon, people soon realized that the balloon had one major drawback: control. Balloons are at the mercy of the winds. Even today, although balloons have improved control of their vertical movement, they have limited *lateral*, or sideways, control—so limited that they take first priority when meeting any other type of aircraft.

From the earliest days of ballooning, people sought to develop a balloon that could be fully controlled by its own power and steered while in the air. An aircraft with these capacities came to be known as an airship or *dirigible*, which means "directable" or "steerable," from the Latin word *dirigere*, meaning to direct or guide. In 1852 a Frenchman, Henri Giffard, built and flew the first dirigible, actually landing where he had planned. Although Giffard's dirigible was relatively unstable, he had taken another step in advancing humanity's ability to conquer the sky by providing some control for his aircraft. For a student's drawing of a dirigible, see figure 2.2.

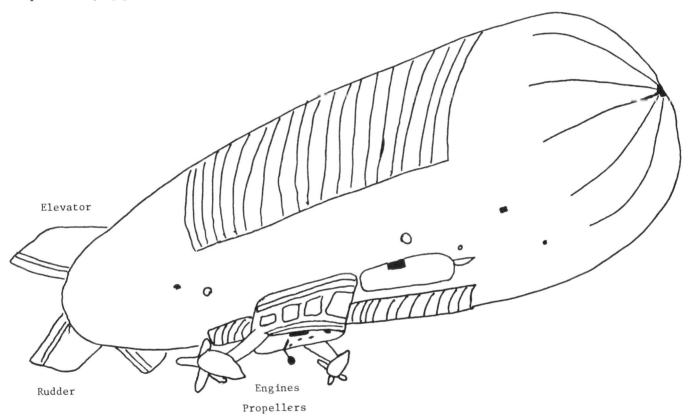

Elevator

Rudder

Engines

Propellers

Fig. 2.2. Dirigible.

The Other Two Forces of Flight:
Thrust and Drag

Like balloons, airships are lighter-than-air aircraft. As shown in figure 2.2, a dirigible has a large oblong or cigar-shaped main body containing hydrogen or helium. In other words, the airship contains a gas that is lighter than air. The gas causes the airship to ascend and keeps it up in the air like a gas balloon. The airship's body is cigar shaped or oblong to help it gain lift or overcome gravity. However, even more important than helping the dirigible to gain lift, its streamlined design minimizes the *drag*, or resistance to forward movement. Thus, the airship's ability to move through the air is enhanced by *streamlining*: designing or contouring the aircraft to reduce its resistance to movement through the air. Drag—the force that slows down an object's movement through the air—is the third of the four forces of flight. Because streamlining helps to overcome drag, it is used in the design of kites and aircraft.

Unlike balloons, airships have steering mechanisms called a *rudder* and *elevators*. These are attached to the rear or *tail* of the airship. As the name suggests, the elevator helps the airship go up or down. The rudder, located at the rear underside of the airship, steers or turns it to the left or right. In addition, the airship has on its underside *engines* or motors to power it through the air by empowering the dirigible's *propellers*, twisted blades that turn when they are powered by the engine and thereby pull an aircraft through the air. The engines and propellers provide *thrust*, the fourth and final force of flight. Thrust is the force that drives the aircraft forward. Thus, the dirigible brings into play all four forces of flight. The parts of the dirigible are visible and labeled in figure 2.2. These same parts, serving the same functions, are on airplanes, discussed in chapter 3.

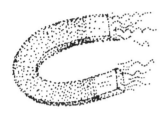

THE FOUR FORCES OF FLIGHT

- Science, language arts
- General

Periodically review with the class the four forces of flight: lift, gravity, drag, and thrust. Although they are mentioned here, they will be discussed in much greater detail in chapters 3 and 4, where Aerospace Magnets give ideas for presenting the forces in their relation to the airplane. By familiarizing students with the names and definitions of the forces now, however, you will prepare them for dealing with the airplane, Bernoulli's Principle, airfoils, Newton's third law, and other related topics. Have students add each of the four forces of flight, as well as *streamlined* and *propellers*, to their dictionaries of aerospace terms.

The Zeppelins

With the invention of lightweight gasoline engines in the early 1900s, dirigibles became lighter in weight, which facilitated control and lift. Dirigibles were built and flown in many countries. However, probably the most famous contributor to the development of dirigibles was Count Ferdinand von Zeppelin, a retired German army officer, who designed and built over twenty-five dirigibles. The body of his dirigibles consisted of a framework of aluminum covered by linen cloth. Because they are supported by an interior metal framework, Zeppelin's airships are called *rigid airships*. The interior of his dirigibles was divided into compartments filled with balloons of hydrogen. Two cars, one for the engines and the other for the crew, were suspended from the bottom of the framework. His first airship, the LZ-1, was 420 feet long and could travel about 17 miles per hour. Later, some *zeppelins* flew at over 75 miles per hour.

DIRIGIBLE TRAVEL

- Mathematics
- Intermediate

Count Ferdinand von Zeppelin's dirigible flies 65 miles per hour. The distance from city A to city B is 3,875 miles. How long will it take to make the flight? Choose a city within your state and calculate how long a flight will take from home.

The First Mass Air Transport System

The zeppelins, named after their inventor, proved quite popular and marked the beginning of mass transport by air. Students may have seen a zeppelin in the movie *Indiana Jones and the Last Crusade* in the scene where Indiana and his father escape from Germany. This scene portrays the roomy and luxurious mode of travel that zeppelins provided. Passengers on board enjoyed beautiful lounges, dining rooms, and sleeping cabins. Even including today's jumbo jets, the dirigible was the largest passenger-carrying aircraft ever to exist.

With comfortable airships available for commercial travelers, flight was no longer a unique opportunity for daring adventurers as in the days of the Montgolfiers. In 1909 Zeppelin established a German airline (DELAG), which carried more than 35,000 passengers between 1910 and 1914, the beginning of World War I. During the war German zeppelins dropped bombs on English cities. (For more on this use of zeppelins, see the section on aircraft in World War I in chapter 3.)

The Dirigible Boom

After World War I, dirigibles became even more popular internationally. In 1919 the English-built dirigible, *Beadmore R-34*, became the first dirigible to cross the Atlantic in both directions.[11] In 1923 the United States' *Shenandoah* became the first dirigible to use helium, leading experts to proclaim it the safest flying machine ever built.[12] In 1929 the commercial dirigible, *Graf Zeppelin*, flew around the world in a little over twenty-one days. Used later for regular passenger service between Germany and South America, it made over 125 Atlantic crossings.

Despite these success stories, misfortune seemed to plague the dirigibles. One after the other caught fire in midair, crashed to the ground, or fell into the sea. For example, in 1925 the *Shenandoah* was caught in a strong wind and broke into three pieces, crashing and killing many of its crew. The wreck itself was so spectacular that crowds came to see it and even made raincoats, called *Shenandoah slickers*, out of its fabric.[13]

The most famous, and the last, of the airship disasters happened in 1937 and involved the German-built *Hindenburg*. The largest dirigible ever built, it was 812 feet long, which is the length of about thirty city buses placed end-to-end. The *Hindenburg* had been constructed to use helium. However, because the United States refused to allow Germany to use its helium, the *Hindenburg* was forced to use hydrogen, which is highly inflammable. After making thirty-six safe flights over the Atlantic between Germany and America, it crashed while making a routine landing in Lakehurst, New Jersey, on May 6, 1937. Atmospheric electricity apparently ignited a hydrogen leak and the *Hindenburg* was engulfed in flames; more than thirty people were killed.

USING DIRIGIBLES AND AIRCRAFT IN MATH PROBLEMS

- Mathematics

- Intermediate and advanced

Count Zeppelin IV wishes to reestablish his great grandfather's dirigible airline. He needs to raise a total of $63 million to do so. Bank 1 gives him a loan at 6 percent interest; bank 2 supplies the balance at 7.5 percent. The count paid each bank the same total amount of interest in dollars. First, calculate how much money he actually borrowed from each bank; then, calculate how much interest he paid to each bank in dollars.

What Is a Blimp?

The *Hindenburg* disaster abruptly ended the use of dirigibles as a means of mass transport. The United States, England, Italy, and the Soviet Union all had previously built and flown dirigibles, most of which were abandoned after the *Hindenburg* accident. Although airships saw some use by the U.S. Navy in World War II to patrol the coast and escort naval ships, subsequent crashes effectively ended the military use of airships. Today, the few airships in operation are mainly used for advertising (e.g., the Goodyear airship) and for carrying airborne television cameras over parades and football games. Unlike the *Hindenburg*, which had an interior metal frame and was a rigid airship, the Goodyear airship is a smaller, nonrigid airship, with no interior metal framework. Thus, the Goodyear airship is a *blimp*, a name which, according to one source, is derived from "b" for balloon and the word "limp," the state of the nonrigid airship before it is inflated.[14] Yet another source claims that the word *blimp* was coined in 1915 by a British naval air officer, A. D. Cunningham, who, when thumping on an inflated airship envelope, noted that it made a "blimp"-like sound.[15]

MEET THE COUNT

• Library research, language arts, critical thinking

• Intermediate and advanced

Students can investigate the life and accomplishments of Count Ferdinand von Zeppelin, then write a dialogue in which they talk with Zeppelin about why he so steadfastly pursued the development of his dirigibles while others were developing airplanes. Or, have students theorize on paper why Zeppelin didn't forego the development of his dirigibles with the advent of heavier-than-air aircraft (airplanes).

THE BETTER WAY TO FLY: JUMBO JETS OR DIRIGIBLES?

• Library research, oral communication, critical thinking

• General

With the help of the library media specialist, have students compare the interior design of a dirigible that was used for passenger service, such as the *Hindenburg*, with the interior design of a modern-day commercial jumbo jet. (Chapter 4 has information comparing jumbo jets with dirigibles; the latter were the bigger of the two.) In terms of comfort, safety, speed, or any other features the class selects, ask students to decide in which they would rather fly and why.

BALLOONING BOOKS

• Language arts, oral communication

• General

Depending on class level, have the students read, write about, and discuss one or more of the books dealing with balloons listed in chapter 1. Intermediate students also might read a poem called "The Balloon" by A. Tennyson in Padraic Colum's *Roofs of Gold: Poems to Read Aloud*. Intermediate and advanced students will laugh out loud at Edward Lear's "Limericks" in Ogden Nash, comp., *Everybody Ought to Know*. Younger beginning students will enjoy some of the following books about ballooning: Adrienne Adams, *The Great Valentine's Day Balloon Race*; Mary Calhoun, *Hot-Air Henry*; Eleanor Coerr, *The Big Balloon Race*; Ron Wegen, *The Balloon Trip*; and Brian Wildsmith, *Bear's Adventure*. Students in grades 4-6 will enjoy the novel by William Pene du Bois, *The Twenty-One Balloons*. Some poems about balloons and ballooning include e.e. cummings's "Who Knows if the Moon's" in both William Cole, ed., *Poems of Magic and Spells* and Sara Hannum and Gwendolyn Reed, *Lean Out of the Window*. The library media specialist can find poems on almost every possible topic for students K-12 in Dorothy B. Frizzell Smith and Eva L. Andrews, comp., *Subject Index to Poetry for Children and Young People: 1957-1975*.

After reading others' books, stories, and poems about balloons and ballooning, students may wish to try their own hands at creative writing on the same subject.

A Ballooning Timeline

September 19, 1783 Hot-air: The first living passengers—a duck, a sheep, and a rooster—are sent aloft in a balloon built and launched by Joseph and Etienne Montgolfier.

November 21, 1783 Hot-air: In a Montgolfier balloon, de Rozier and d'Arlandes make the first free flight, staying aloft for twenty-five minutes.

December 1, 1783 Hydrogen: Jacques A. C. Charles and M. N. Robert make the first manned hydrogen balloon flight. The hydrogen balloon, built and flown by Charles, stays aloft for more than two-and-a-half hours and covers over 27 miles.

1783 Hydrogen: The French government forms an air arm to the army.

June 14, 1784 Hot-air: Madame Thible, a popular French opera singer, becomes the first woman balloonist as she ascends over Lyons.

September 15, 1784 Hydrogen: Vincent Lunardi launches a balloon from London, England—the first balloon launched outside France.

January 7, 1785 Hydrogen: Frenchman Jean-Pierre Blanchard, joined by the first American to fly, Dr. John Jeffries, makes the first flight from one nation to another. Flying across the English Channel from England to France, they deliver the first airmail letter.

1792-1802: Balloons are used for reconnaissance during the French revolutionary wars.

January 9, 1793 Hydrogen: Blanchard makes first American balloon ascent at Philadelphia, in presence of George Washington.

October 22, 1797 Hydrogen: Frenchman A. J. Garnerin makes first parachute jump from a balloon.

August 22, 1849 Hot-air: The first air bombing raid in history occurs when Austrian pilotless hot-air balloons carrying bombs are sent against Venice.

1852 Hydrogen: French engineer Henri Giffard builds the first dirigible.

1861-1865 Hydrogen: Balloons are used for observation during the American Civil War.

1870-1871 Hydrogen: During the Franco-Prussian War, with Paris under siege, almost regular airmail service is accomplished involving sixty-six balloon flights.

1910-1914 Hydrogen: The German dirigible airline, DELAG, carries more than 35,000 passengers.

1914-1918 Hydrogen: Balloons are used for observation and directing gunfire during World War I.

1919 Hydrogen: The English-built dirigible, *Beadmore R-34*, becomes the first dirigible to cross the Atlantic in both directions.

1923 Helium: The United States' *Shenandoah* becomes the first dirigible to use helium.

1929 Hydrogen: The German commercial dirigible *Graf Zeppelin* flies around the world.

May 6, 1937 Hydrogen: The German dirigible *Hindenburg*, the largest flying machine ever built, explodes and is consumed by fire at Lakehurst, New Jersey. This halts dirigible transportation.

1939-1945 Hydrogen: During World War II some 9,000 *Fu-Gos*, small balloons carrying explosives, are sent from Japan to the United States. The Fu-Gos make 250 recorded landfalls, causing six deaths, but minimal property damage.

October 10, 1960 Hot-air: The official birth date of the modern hot-air balloon is marked by the first man-carrying free flight at Bruning, Nebraska. Ed Yost, an American balloon researcher, is largely responsible for this development.

August 16-17, 1978 Helium: The first transatlantic flight from Maine to France is completed in the balloon, *Double Eagle II*.

INTERVIEWS AND TIMELINES

• Library research, social studies, language arts, art, working in a group, acting

• General

Students may divide into groups, each group choosing one topic from the "Ballooning Timeline" for research and subsequent presentation. The results of each group's research can be presented in a mock journalistic interview, a dramatization, a panel discussion, or a mock television interview. Students can videotape these presentations with the help of the school media center instructor and/or perform their interviews, skits, etc. at a school assembly. Students can also make an illustrated timeline of ballooning events for display; a roll of white shelving paper works well for this activity. On the timeline, they can intersperse ballooning events with important dates in world history. Display the timeline in the classroom or ask the library media specialist for permission to do so in the library so your class can share its ballooning expertise with the rest of the school.

Notes

[1]*Children's Britannica*, 1988 ed., s.v. "balloon."

[2]Edwin J. Kirschner, *Aerospace Balloons: From Montgolfiere to Space* (Blue Ridge Summit, Pa.: AERO [Tab Books], 1985), 67-68.

[3]*World Book Encyclopedia*, 1989 ed., s.v. "balloons." by Don Piccard.

[4]Charles Coulston Gillispie, *The Montgolfier Brothers and the Invention of Aviation 1783-1784* (Princeton: Princeton University Press, 1983), 3.

[5]Air Force ROTC, *Aerospace Science: History of Air Power* (Maxwell Air Force Base, Ala.: Air University Press, 1986), 1-14.

[6]Thomas Fleming, ed., *The Founding Fathers: Benjamin Franklin, A Biography in His Own Words* (New York: Newsweek Book Division, 1972), 362.

[7]John W. R. Taylor and Kenneth Munson, *History of Aviation* (London: Octopus Books, 1975), 20.

[8]Taylor and Munson, *History of Aviation*, 23; Air Force ROTC, *Aerospace Science*, 1-14; David Schoenbrun, *Triumph in Paris: The Exploits of Benjamin Franklin* (New York: Harper and Row, 1976), 391-92.

[9]Alden P. Armagnac, "Gas Flame Lifts New Hot-Air Balloon," *Popular Science* 179 (August 1961), 47-50; Dick Wirth and Jerry Young, *Ballooning: The Complete Guide to Riding the Winds* (New York: Random House, 1980), 48-49.

[10]Kirschner, *Aerospace Balloons*, 79.

[11]David C. Cooke, *Dirigibles That Made History* (New York: G. P. Putnam's Sons, 1962), 42.

[12]Cooke, *Dirigibles*, 46.

[13]Ivan Rendall, *Reaching for the Skies* (New York: Orion Books, 1989), 34.

[14]Air Force ROTC, *Aerospace Science*, 2-15.

[15]*Webster's New World Dictionary*, 2d. college ed., s.v. "blimp."

Bibliography

Adams, Adrienne. *The Great Valentine's Day Balloon Race*. New York: Scribner, 1980.

Air Force ROTC. *Aerospace Science: History of Air Power*. Maxwell Air Force Base, Ala.: Air University Press, 1986.
An easy-to-read history of flight with special emphasis on military uses.

Armagnac, Alden P. "Gas Flame Lifts New Hot-Air Balloon," *Popular Science* 179 (August 1961), 47-50.

Bansemer, Roger. *The Art of Hot-Air Ballooning*. Clearwater, Fla.: Gollum Press, 1987.

Burton, Walter E. "Bringing Back Hot Air Balloons," *Popular Science* 179 (July 1961), 124-27, 190.
Gives step-by-step instructions for making model hot-air balloons and discusses the revival of interest in hot-air balloons.

Caballero, Jane A. *Aerospace Projects for Young Children*. rev. ed. Atlanta, Ga.: Humanics, 1987.

Calhoun, Mary. *Hot-Air Henry*. New York: William Morrow, 1981.

Children's Britannica. 4th ed. 1988. s.v. "balloon."

Coerr, Eleanor. *The Big Balloon Race*. New York: Harper and Row, 1981.

Cole, William, ed. *Poems of Magic and Spells*. New York: Collins-World, 1965, 1971.

Colum, Padraic. *Roofs of Gold: Poems to Read Aloud*. New York: Macmillan, 1964.

Cooke, David C. *Dirigibles That Made History*. New York: G. P. Putnam's Sons, 1962.

du Bois, William Pene. *The Twenty-One Balloons*. New York: Viking, 1947.

Elementary Science Study. *Teacher's Guide for Gases and "Airs."* Nashua, N.H.: Delta Education, 1987.
    Available at many public libraries and curriculum collections or write to Delta Education, Inc., Box M, Nashua, N.H. 03061-6012.

Fillingham, Paul. *The Balloon Book: A Complete Guide to the Exciting Sport*. New York: David McKay, 1977.

Fleming, Thomas, ed. *The Founding Fathers: Benjamin Franklin, A Biography in His Own Words*. New York: Newsweek Book Division, 1972.

Garrison, Paul. *The Encyclopedia of Hot Air Balloons*. New York: Drake Publishers, 1978.

Gillispie, Charles Coulston. *The Montgolfier Brothers and the Invention of Aviation 1783-1784*. Princeton: Princeton University Press, 1983.
    A scholarly, beautifully written and illustrated book by an eminent historian; teachers and advanced students will enjoy this book.

Halperin, Richard P. *Physical Science*. New York: Barnes and Noble, 1983.

Hannum, Sara, and Gwendolyn Reed. *Lean Out of the Window*. New York: Atheneum, 1965.

Jackson, Donald Dale. *The Aeronauts*. Alexandria, Va.: Time-Life Books, 1980.

Kirschner, Edwin J. *Aerospace Balloons: From Montgolfiere to Space*. Blue Ridge Summit, Pa.: AERO (Tab Books), 1985.

Nash, Ogden, comp. *Everybody Ought to Know*. Philadelphia: Lippincott, 1961.

National Air and Space Museum (Smithsonian Institution). *Discovery*, n.d.
    Great pictures of flying machines throughout history. Based on the collection at the Smithsonian's Air and Space Museum, Washington, D.C.

Reinhard, Dewey. Interview with author. Colorado Springs, Colorado, 12 April 1990.

Rendall, Ivan. *Reaching for the Skies*. New York: Orion Books, 1989.
    Written for a British television series; a good read and great photos; for teachers and advanced students.

Schoenbrun, David. *Triumph in Paris: The Exploits of Benjamin Franklin*. New York: Harper and Row, 1976.

Smith, Dorothy B. Frizzell, and Eva L. Andrews, comps. *Subject Index to Poetry for Children and Young People: 1957-1975*. Chicago: American Library Association, 1977.

Taylor, John W., and Kenneth Munson. *History of Aviation*. London: Octopus Books, 1975.
    Detailed and thorough; great pictures.

U.S. Department of Transportation, Federal Aviation Administration. *Aviation Science Activities for Elementary Grades*. Washington, D.C.: FAA, 1983.
    Contact your regional FAA office for a copy; address in appendix.

_____. *Demonstration Aids for Aviation Education*. Washington, D.C.: FAA, 1987.
    Contact regional FAA office.

Walpole, Brenda. *175 Science Experiments to Amuse and Amaze Your Friends*. New York: Random House, 1988.
    Easy for the teacher, too!

Webster's New World Dictionary. 2d college ed. Cleveland, Ohio: William Collins, 1980.

Wegen, Ronald. *The Balloon Trip*. New York: Clarion Books, 1981.

Wildsmith, Brian. *Bear's Adventure*. New York: Pantheon Books, 1981.

Wirth, Dick, and Jerry Young. *Ballooning: The Complete Guide to Riding the Winds*. New York: Random House, 1980.

World Book Encyclopedia, 1989 ed. s.v. "balloons," by Don Piccard.

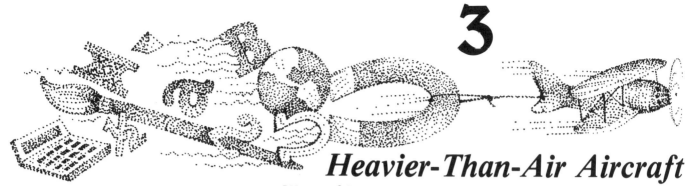

3

Heavier-Than-Air Aircraft
Kites, Gliders, and Propeller Airplanes through the "Golden Age of Flight"

Kites

Complicated ideas frequently have simple origins. What may seem a simple toy can sometimes play an important role in the development of complex equipment. For example, in chapter 2 we saw how balloons powered by air, hydrogen, or helium led to the development of the dirigible, whose controllability marked yet another step in humanity's desire to master flight. Like the balloon, the kite is normally regarded as a child's toy. However, the kite played a major role in aerospace history. In fact, this chapter points out that the Wright brothers owe much of their success in aerospace to what they and others learned from flying kites.

Whereas a balloon is a *lighter-than-air aircraft*, whose flight is supported by its *buoyancy* in the air, a kite is a *heavier-than-air aircraft* grounded by a flexible line. Heavier-than-air aircraft derive their lift from *aerodynamic forces*. The four forces of flight—lift, gravity, drag, and thrust—were examined in the discussion of dirigibles in chapter 2; these forces also affect the flight of kites and airplanes. However, because a dirigible is lighter than air when its envelope is filled with a buoyant gas like helium, lift works differently with heavier-than-air aircraft than it does with lighter-than-air aircraft. Whereas the lift for balloons is provided by a lighter-than-air gas, the lift for a kite or airplanes comes from wind pressure. We can get a preliminary idea of how lift and the other three forces of flight affect airplanes by looking at them in relation to a kite.

Forces of Lift and Drag on Kites

Just as an airplane needs lift greater than its own weight to overcome the pull (force) of gravity and fly, so, too, does a kite. How does a kite achieve such lift? If you recall the ordinary diamond-shaped kite (figure 3.1) you may have flown as a child, you will remember that the kite's strings are so arranged that when you fly the kite it is neither vertical nor flat; rather, a flying kite tilts or leans at an angle. The front edge of the angle, called the *leading edge*, is higher than the rear edge, called the *trailing edge*. The kite's tilting angle is called the *angle of attack*: the angle at which the kite—or an airplane's wing—meets the air stream. This tilt affects how the kite rises into the air.

30

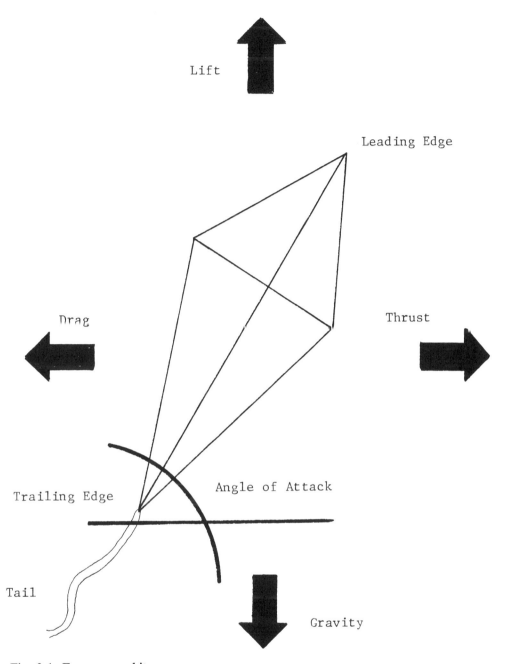

Fig. 3.1. Forces on a kite.

Holding the kite string as you run, you will find that your ground speed gives air speed to the kite that has lifted off the ground. As you release additional string, the kite rises higher and higher. This upward force is lift. It is created by air moving past the kite, supporting it in flight. Specifically, some lift comes from the air's impact against the kite's lower surface at the angle of attack. However, the most lift comes from the air going above the kite, which goes farther and faster than the air passing underneath the kite, thus creating an area of lowered air pressure. Lift is produced when the greater air pressure below the kite pushes it up into the area of lowered pressure above the kite. The greater the difference between the air pressure above and below the kite, the greater the lift, and the larger the surface area of the kite, the greater the total lift. This is why very large kites can produce such strong lift that they break their lines and fly away. More on angle of attack, as well as Bernoulli's Principle and Newton's third law, is discussed in relationship to airplane wings later in this chapter.

If you hold the kite string tightly and pull it towards you, you will feel a pull from the flying kite as the air attempts to hold it back. This is drag: resistance to the direction of flight produced by air moving past the object. The larger and rougher a surface area, the more drag produced because air does not flow quickly around big bulky objects. This is why a simple streamlined kite, whose shape minimizes drag, flies better than a big bulky kite, whose shape produces greater drag. Using the next Aerospace Magnet, you and your students can make and fly simple diamond-shaped kites that will help demonstrate lift and drag, as well as the angle of attack.

GO FLY A KITE!

- Language arts, science (physics), physical education
- General

Have your students add to their dictionaries the term *angle of attack*. Make simple diamond kites according to these directions. Also see figure 3.2 for help.

Materials: For each student or student-team, you will need:

1. A large plastic trash bag (without drawstrings) or a large sheet of tissue paper such as that used for wrapping gifts.

2. Glue.

3. Tape.

4. Kite sticks (for each kite, use one 36" stick for the spine and one 30" stick for the spar or crosspiece; kite sticks are available at hobby shops, or you can use flat sticks of a strong light-weight wood such as spruce [not balsa, which breaks easily] cut to the appropriate lengths).

5. Scissors.

6. Knife.

7. Light but strong string (also available from a hobby shop or from a variety store that sells kites).

8. Strips of old sheets for the tail.

9. Yardstick.

Kite-Building Procedure: (See figure 3.2, which you might want to draw on the blackboard or copy onto a large chart for students to see.) Using one kite stick, cut to 36", for the *spine* (the vertical backbone of the kite) and the other, cut to 30", for the *spar* (horizontal crosspiece that helps to shape and support the kite).

1. Glue the spar about 9"-10" from the top of the spine, directly at the spar's center, so that the glued sticks look like a cross, as shown in figure 3.2, and you have 15" of spar on either side of the spine.

2. Cut a notch or a slice at each end of the spar and spine: make the notch at the centers of the ends of each piece of wood, cutting in a perpendicular ($\perp$) direction from the edge.

3. Attach string from the notch at each end of the spar to the notch at each end of the spine so that the string outlines the kite's diamond shape; the string is the frame for the kite, giving the kite its final shape.

4. Tie the ends of the string, wrapping the string around each end a few times to prevent the string from cutting into the wooden sticks and splitting them farther along the notch line.

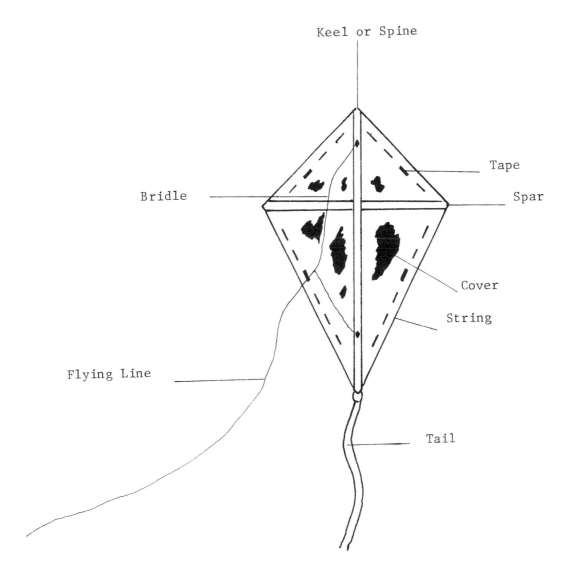

Fig. 3.2. Making a kite.

5. Lay out on a flat surface—the floor works best—either the lightweight plastic trash bag (cut open) or the big piece of tissue paper and place the glued wooden sticks with the string attached on top of the plastic or tissue; the plastic or tissue paper will be the *cover* or *face* of the kite, which provides the *lifting surface*. The plastic or paper should be about 1" larger on each side than the actual string frame.

6. Cut the plastic or tissue as needed to the proper shape and dimensions; be absolutely sure that you have 15" (or an equal amount if your spar is less than 30") of cover or surface on either side of the spine (*keel*)—otherwise the kite will veer off to the right or left. (Think of the surface or cover on either side of the spine as "wings.")

7. Fold the edges of plastic or tissue paper neatly over the string and glue or tape it so it holds.

8. Cut a piece of string 54" long for the *bridle*, which will help guide and hold the kite correctly into the wind.

9. Connect the bridle to two points along the spine, one near the top and one near the bottom.

10. Tie your flying line (one end of a ball of lightweight string) a few inches below midway along the bridle.

11. Tie the *tail*, which will give stability and control, to the very bottom of the spine. The drag provided by the tail will keep the kite's trailing edge pointed away from the wind. This, in turn, keeps the kite pointed correctly to achieve the best lift and thus the best flying. The tail may be as long as 60" or so, but experience will be the best teacher on this. Too much tail will give too much drag; too little tail can cause the kite to spin and whirl out of control.

Kite Flying: Go to a large open area (no trees, buildings, power lines, antennae) at a park or playing field and have a kite-flying contest. Remember: safety first! Review safe kite flying with your students. In addition to going to an open location, remind your students: never use wire or metallic string for kites; do not climb trees, poles, buildings, etc. to rescue the kite; never fly your kite in the rain or near or in a thunderstorm; never fly your kite near street or airport traffic.

After the Flight: When you go back to school, have the students write poems or essays about kite flying.

For more information about kite building and kite flying, see especially the pamphlets for teachers and students published by Estes Industries, a rocket and kite company, in Penrose, Colorado 81240 (see appendix). For the teacher, there is Robert L. Cannon's "Kite Flying Teacher's Guide" (catalog number 84,719), and for students there is the same author's "Let's Go Fly a Kite" (catalog number 84,717C). These pamphlets give lots of instructions and advice about kite building and flying, including important safety directions. For persons interested in building a variety of kite types, see Bruce H. Mitton, *Kites, Kites, Kites: The Ups and Downs of Making and Flying Them*.

Kite History

Kite flying is based on principles of science, particularly aerodynamics. How and where kite flying began, however, are matters of speculation. Some historians believe that the Chinese flew kites at least 2,000 years ago. One popular legend holds that the first kite was a Chinese farmer's reed hat held by a string.

From China, kites spread to Malaya, Polynesia, Japan, and Egypt. As the kite was adopted by these peoples, it gained ceremonial, magical, and religious significance. Stories about the kite were handed down from generation to generation. For example, one ancient story of the kite comes from the Polynesian islands. The islanders worshiped the twin brother gods and kite flyers, Rongo and Tane. Tane was even depicted as a kite who was constantly catching his long tail in a tree. According to the story, to see whose kite would fly higher, Tane challenged Rongo to a kite-flying contest. Rongo secretly attached a long tail to his kite before the contest and consequently won. For this reason, when the Polynesians flew their kites, the first kite to go up was named and dedicated for Rongo.

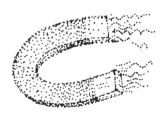

MAPWORK IN KITE HISTORY

• Social studies

• General

Have students locate China, Polynesia, Japan, and Egypt on your wall map and identify these places with colored push pins.

Kites at Work

In the Far East, kites advanced to a high degree of design and performance. They were associated with mysticism and mystery. However, when the kite was introduced to western Europe and the New World, people began to discern practical functions for it. As early as 1749—thirty-four years before the first manned hot-air balloon flight—two University of Glasgow (Scotland) students made the first recorded weather experiments with kites. However, the real advances in using kites for scientific study came in 1883 with the work of British meteorologist E. Douglas Archibald. He attached an *anemometer* or wind gauge to kites to measure the wind's velocity some 1,200 feet above the earth. This highly successful experiment gave him the distinction of introducing the kite as an important meteorological tool. In this field kites replaced balloons, which had been used to measure wind velocity, but which had also tried the patience of eighteenth- and nineteenth-century scientists because the balloons flew in arcs when tethered and flew away when untethered—taking the scientific instruments with them!

Although Archibald made great contributions to the scientific use of kites, the most famous kite flyer in history, scientific or otherwise, is Benjamin Franklin (1706-1790). Franklin was present at the balloon flights of the Montgolfier brothers and Jacques A. C. Charles in France in 1783. Thirty-one years earlier, on a stormy day in June 1752, in Philadelphia, Pennsylvania, Franklin made his now legendary kite experiment, which showed that lightning and electricity were identical. (Contrary to popular misconception, he did not discover electricity by this experiment; electricity had already been identified.) For this experiment, Franklin used a simple diamond kite made of a silk handkerchief and cedar strips connected to a wire, and provided with a tail, loop, and twine. Where the twine and silk ribbon were attached, he secured a key. A printed account, purportedly in Franklin's words, appeared in the *Pennsylvania Gazette*, October 19, 1752, and is reprinted in his *Papers*:

> As soon as any of the Thunder Clouds come over the Kite, the pointed Wire will draw the Electric Fire from them, and the Kite, with all the Twine, will be electrified, and the loose Filaments of the Twine will stand out every Way, and be attracted by an approaching Finger. And when the Rain has wet the Kite and Twine, so that it can conduct the Electric Fire freely, you will find it stream out plentifully from the Key on the Approach of your Knuckle.[1]

From this experiment, Franklin reasoned inductively that lightning and man-made electricity were the same, and that buildings could be protected from lightning by an iron rod connected to the earth by a wire. This principle is familiar to us today as the lightning rod, which is even used at the top of the external liquid fuel tank on the space shuttle (see chapter 6).

Kites have been practical tools in many areas, scientific and otherwise, throughout history—from meteorology to electricity, from aerial photography to building bridges. However, kite flying, since its origin, has also been a recreational pastime that all can enjoy.

READING POEMS ABOUT KITES

- Language arts

- General

Poems about kites that you and your class might enjoy include: R. Williams, "King Arthur and His Knights," in William Cole, ed., *Oh, What Nonsense!* (level: beginning and intermediate); M. Sawyer, "Kite Days," in Sara and John E. Brewton, *Sing a Song of Seasons* (level: intermediate); L. Cohen, "A Kite is a Victim," in Lillian Morrison, comp., *Sprints and Distances: Sports in Poetry and the Poetry in Sport* (level: intermediate); S. Yamaguchi, "The String of a Kite," in Edith Shiffert and Yuki Sawa, trans., *Anthology of Modern Japanese Poetry* (level: intermediate and advanced); J. Farrar, "Threnody," in Leland Blair Jacobs, ed., *Poetry for Autumn* (level:

beginning); and H. Summers, "Kite," in Thomas Lask, ed., *The New York Times Book of Verse* (level: intermediate and advanced).[2] Ask students how their own experiences as kite flyers compare or contrast with the poets' descriptions. Students also could write their own poems.

KITE FLYERS AROUND THE WORLD

- Library research, social studies, language arts, art, working in a group

- Intermediate, advanced

Enhance students' multicultural awareness by studying kites around the world. In Greece, Japan, and China, kite flying is an important part of national culture. With the help of the library media specialist, have students investigate how and when kites are used today in those countries and elsewhere. What types of kites are flown? For what events or holidays? Who flies the kites? Students can prepare oral and/or written reports. They should also locate the country on which they focus on the map with a push pin. Student teams may wish to draw or make a kite similar to the one used in the country chosen. In addition to Mitton's book cited earlier (see bibliography), students can use Clive Hart, *Kites: An Historical Survey* and Jane Yolen, *World on a String: The Story of Kites*, which has good photographs of children from different countries flying kites. Your library media specialist can help you and your class find other resources as well.

Kite + Glider = Primitive Airplane

One of the first persons to relate the principles of a kite to human flight was Sir George Cayley (1773-1857), baronet. Like Leonardo da Vinci and Benjamin Franklin, Cayley was a Renaissance man: he researched and invented in a variety of fields including optics, artificial limbs, theater architecture, unemployment relief, and electricity. However, he is best known as the Father of Aerial Navigation.[3] In 1799 Cayley made what is probably the key discovery for aviation: he observed that air flowing over the top of a curved, fixed wing produces more lift than when air flows over a flat surface. He also calculated that the bigger the wing and the faster the airflow over that wing, the more lift will be produced.

Combining these findings, Cayley discerned that a vehicle could fly if it had the proper weight, shape, and surface area, plus some type of power.[4] In 1808 he attempted unsuccessfully to accomplish flight by supplying a glider with a lightweight gunpowder engine.[5] Finally, he recognized that a flying vehicle would need some type of tail device to have lateral (side to side) and vertical (up and down) control, the theory behind steering rudders and rear elevators (discussed in chapter 2). These surface controls are also integral to the airplane. It is no wonder that in 1909 Wilbur Wright credited Cayley with "carr[ying] the science of flying to a point which it had never reached before and which it scarcely reached again during the last century."[6] How did Cayley discover so much about flight? He flew a kite, of course!

Cayley's Kites and Gliders

Since Leonardo da Vinci's day, people have believed that human flight could occur by the ornithopter approach, or an individual's mimicking the birds' flapping power for successful flight (see figure 1.2). Although most students of flight focused on birds' wings, Cayley was also studying kite wings. In 1796 Cayley built a kite that resembled a helicopter; in fact, it looked somewhat like da Vinci's ornithopter. He later modified and improved upon this device and published his results in 1809. This led directly to the development of the helicopter which will be discussed in chapter 4.

Using his knowledge of kites, Cayley constructed in 1804 what "is honoured rightly as the first modern-configuration aeroplane [sic] in history."[7] As shown in figure 3.3, it was actually a 5-foot-long, kite-winged *glider*—a powerless airplane carried by air currents. To make this, he attached near the front of the rod a 154-square-inch flat paper kite, with the surface or cover of the kite functioning like wings. At the rear of the rod he fastened a tail made of two flat kites intersecting at right angles; the tail could be adjusted to determine the glider's flying direction, thus acting like a rudder. Referring to this glider, the great British aviation historian, Sir George Harvard Gibbs-Smith, praised Cayley's contribution to the development of the airplane, reminding us of the relationship among kites, gliders, and airplanes: "The kite—which is really a tethered glider—... is the true ancestor of the aeroplane [sic], and has played an important part in the history of flying. The kite was first to take part in aeroplane flight when it formed the wing of Cayley's first model glider of 1804."[8]

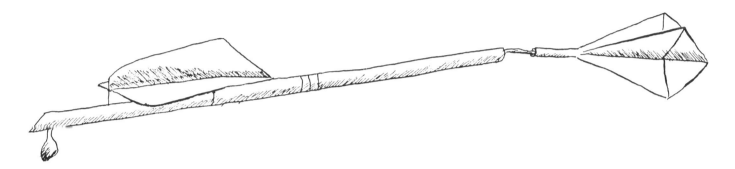

Fig. 3.3. Cayley's glider.

In 1809 Cayley built a full-sized glider with a wing area of 200 square feet; whether or not it actually carried anyone is uncertain. However, the important outcome of this creation was that he discussed it in his ground-breaking article, "On Aerial Navigation," the first publication (1810) on aerodynamics. This and other writings by Cayley influenced all subsequent research in the field.

Building gliders throughout his life, Cayley recounted in 1853 how in 1849 he had constructed a large glider with stacked *triplane wings* (three sets of wings stacked vertically) and two tails that reportedly carried a ten-year-old boy. However, if the youngster was, in fact, carried by the glider, he certainly did not pilot it. Furthermore, the glider was simply that—a glider carried by air currents and not powered by an engine as an airplane is. Yet, at a time when the public largely regarded human attempts at flight with either laughter or scorn—despite passenger-carrying balloons sailing overhead—Sir George Cayley did much to give, in his own words, "a little more dignity" and a great deal more knowledge to the search for the secrets of flight in heavier-than-air aircraft.[9]

WHAT ARE "RENAISSANCE PERSONS"? ARE THERE ANY TODAY?

- Library research, language arts, oral communication, acting, social studies, critical thinking

- Intermediate and advanced

In Chapter 1, Leonardo da Vinci was described as a "Renaissance man." America's Benjamin Franklin and Britain's Sir George Cayley certainly deserve that title, too. Have the students do a research report on Franklin's contributions to science and other areas (as an educator, a postmaster, printer, diplomat, and politician). Beginning students can read the classic Robert Lawson book, *Ben and Me* (see bibliography). Senior high school students might want to read Franklin's famous autobiography. There are also several good biographies of Franklin, as well as a twenty-five-volume edition of his *Papers* (see bibliography) plus other smaller collections of his writings, including a compact edition by Peter

Sharo. Advanced students should also investigate the work of Cayley. Students can prepare written and oral reports on the various facets of these Renaissance men's talents.

Students also might want to role play these characters, creating dramatic vignettes about them and perhaps even designing costumes. Franklin, especially, lends himself to a one-person show. Different students also could be the many "Ben Franklins," personifying his numerous interests. A skit might be called, "Will the Real Ben Franklin Please Stand Up?"

Advanced and intermediate students might wish to speculate on this question: Is the Renaissance man (or woman) a phenomenon of the past? In our contemporary world of narrow specialization, is it possible to be a Renaissance man or woman? Who might be considered as such in modern times? (Perhaps the late president of Yale University, literary scholar, and baseball commissioner, A. Bartlett Giamatti or the late American composer and conductor, Leonard Bernstein?) Have students research these figures and any others they might suggest.

Otto Lilienthal and Bernoulli's Principle

The first human being to fly through the air with some control in a glider was the German, Otto Lilienthal (1848-1896), known as the Father of Gliding. Meticulously studying the anatomy and function of birds' wings, Lilienthal applied what he learned to human flight. Particularly important was his understanding that a wing with an upward-curved surface would give more lift than a flat wing, producing less drag against it as it went through the air. Recall that Cayley, too, had observed that a curved surface gives more lift than a flat surface. Thus, modern airplane wings are flat on the bottom, but curved on the top. This relates to a law of physics called *Bernoulli's Principle*, demonstrated in the following Aerospace Magnets.

WING SHAPE AND BERNOULLI'S PRINCIPLE

- Science (physics)

- General

As discussed, Cayley and Lilienthal observed that an upward-curved wing gives more lift than a flat wing when moving through the air. This concept is so important that it underlies airplane wing design even today. The underlying principle was articulated over two centuries ago by a Swiss scientist named Daniel Bernoulli (1700-1782). He found that the faster air (or any fluid) moves over an object, the less the air presses on the object. Conversely, the slower the air moves over an object, the more it presses on the object. (This is the simplified verbal equivalent for a complicated equation that an advanced placement physics teacher may wish to explore.) This became known as Bernoulli's Principle. You can demonstrate the principle using the following straightforward method with students ranging from kindergarten through college.

Materials: Lightweight paper (notebook or newspaper), scissors, paper clips.

Procedure: Cut a strip of lightweight paper about 2 inches wide by 10 inches long. Hold one end of the paper and set it just below your mouth against your chin. Then blow over the top of the paper strip. You can produce the same effect by holding one end of the paper strip and running about the room. See how many paper clips you can lift by adding them to the end of the paper strip you are blowing on (opposite the end you are holding below your mouth).

Result: The paper strip is lifted by air blowing over the *top* of the paper because there is less air pressure on the top side than there is underneath the paper. This is Bernoulli's Principle, the same one behind the lift of a kite (discussed at the beginning of this chapter).

As noted, Bernoulli's Principle relates to wing shape. A curved wing causes the air to move faster over its surface than a flat wing. Again, this is why modern airplane wings are shaped flat on the bottom and curved on top: to give lift. Wings with this shape are called *airfoils* (see figure 3.4). An airfoil is a surface designed to keep an aircraft up or regulate its movements by obtaining a specific reaction from the air through which the surface moves; wings and propeller blades are examples of airfoils. The following Aerospace Magnet will help students understand how an airfoil works.

The faster air moves, the less the pressure.

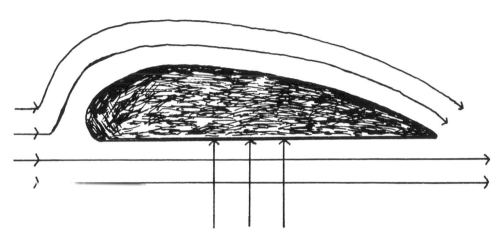

The slower air moves, the more the pressure.

Fig. 3.4. An airfoil.

UNDERSTANDING AN AIRFOIL: HOW WINGS ATTAIN LIFT

- Language arts and science (physics)

- General

First, have students add *airfoil* to their aerospace terms dictionaries. Then, to simulate the effects of an airfoil, do this simple demonstration that will show what Cayley and Lilienthal figured out about curved wing surfaces (see figure 3.5).

Materials: Spoon, fast-running water in your classroom sink (turn the faucet all the way on).

Procedure: Ask students what they think will happen if you (or one of them) hold(s) the convex, or outward bulging, bowl side of the spoon against the edge of some running water.

Conclusion: Although you and your students might have speculated that the water would have pushed the spoon away, the water actually sped up as it flowed over the convex (back) side of the spoon, thus creating an area of less water pressure. The spoon was then sucked into the water. This is another demonstration of Bernoulli's Principle. How do a spoon and running water relate to an airplane's wing and lift? Just as the water sucked the curved side of the spoon in and towards the water, so the air on

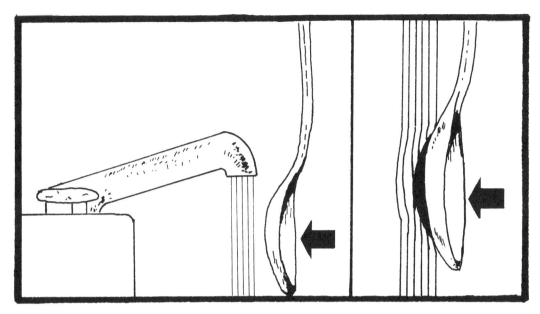

Fig. 3.5. Bernoulli's Principle.

top of the airfoil (e.g., the wing) sucks the wing up and, simultaneously, the air below the airfoil pushes up. Thus, the wing attains lift.

Lilienthal built his first successful fixed-wing glider (a powerless airplane) in 1891, and from then until his death five years later he constructed five types of *monoplane* (having one set of wings) and two types of *biplane* (having two sets of wings, one above the other) gliders, almost all of which he patented. Why make a glider with two sets of wings? It was thought that the large wing area provided by the extra set of wings would provide greater lift. Recall that Cayley had constructed a triplane glider in 1849.

WHAT'S A PATENT?

- Social studies
- Intermediate and advanced

Lilienthal patented his gliders and the Wright brothers faced many obstacles in applying for a patent for their 1902 glider. What is a patent? How does an inventor secure a patent and why? For a detailed discussion of patents, a sample patent application, and related activities, an excellent source is Jerry Flack's *Inventing, Inventions, and Inventors*, pp. 92-96 (see the bibliography to the introduction).

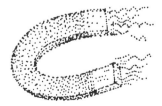

AEROSPACE TERMS

- Language arts
- General

Add the following terms to students' aerospace dictionaries: *patent, monoplane, biplane, triplane*, and *glider*.

In 1893 Lilienthal built two powered gliders, but they failed to fly. His successful gliders were all unpowered and made as light as possible. What they enabled him to grasp was a rudimentary knowledge of pilot control: by shifting his airborne body, he tipped his glider from side to side, moved the nose up and down, and turned the glider to the right or left. Lilienthal was actually introducing the three basic movements of airplanes: they *roll* (tip or lean from side to side); they *pitch* (move the nose up and down or climb and descend); and they *yaw* (turn left or right).

Lilienthal not only kept detailed written records of his over 2,000 glider flights and investigative work, which he published prolifically, but also recognized the truth of the old adage, "a picture is worth a thousand words." Cognizant of recent advances in photography, Lilienthal usually had a cameraman ready to photograph his glider flights. Picture Lilienthal—his outstretched arms attached to his rigid-winged glider, running into the wind, hurling himself off a hill he had built near Berlin, Germany, and gliding through the air as high as 65 feet above the ground, sometimes for distances of hundreds of feet, and once for a record 1,000 feet from where he began![10] He was doing a rudimentary version of hang gliding (see figures 3.6 and 3.7). Unfortunately, Lilienthal's passion to fly finally killed him: on August 9, 1896, strapped to his glider, Lilienthal hurled himself off a hilltop, soared into the air, went nose down at 50 feet, and crashed. He died the next day of a broken neck. The stories and photos about Lilienthal were an inspiration to many, including Wilbur and Orville Wright who, while sitting in their bicycle shop in Dayton, Ohio, read about him and gazed at his photographs in the September 1894 illustrated issue of *McClure's* magazine.[11]

Fig. 3.6. Otto Lilienthal gliding.

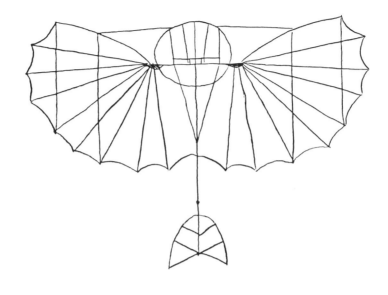

Fig. 3.7. Otto Lilienthal's gliders.

MAKING AND FLYING PAPER GLIDERS

- Science; after-school club

- General

You and your class can make and fly paper gliders without throwing yourselves off hills! All you will need are enough sheets of 8½"x11" paper for all students to have one sheet (they can even tear a sheet from their notebooks) and enough paper clips for each student to have one.

Demonstrate how to fold the paper to make a glider, according to the folding pattern shown in figure 3.8. When the glider is completely folded, use a paper clip to hold it together at the bottom. Move the clip up or back as needed to get proper balance. Take the students outside and have competition flights to find out, for example, which glider can fly the farthest or stay in the air the longest.

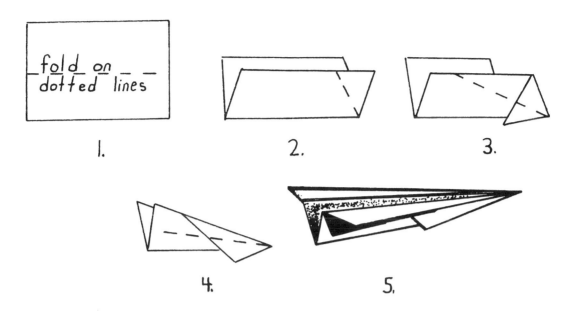

Fig. 3.8. Making a paper glider

Depending on the ability level of your students, you may ask them to design their own model gliders. Students will especially enjoy making *ring wing* (having a circular shape) and polystyrene gliders, which can be found in *The Sky As Your Classroom: Teacher's Aerospace Workshop Resource Book*, available from NASA by written request to the resource center listed in the appendix. Other resources on how to build and fly paper airplanes include Churchill's *Instant Paper Airplanes*, Simon's *The Paper Airplane Book*, Kaufmann's *Flying Hand-Launched Gliders*, Abrams' *Throw It Out of Sight: Building and Flying a Hand-Launched Glider*, and Kawami's *Cut and Make Space Shuttles* (see bibliography). An excellent resource for prefabricated gliders is the "Whitewings" series of model gliders, available in many book stores and hobby shops. Materials for making gliders are available from AG Industries, Inc., 3832 148th Avenue N.E., Redmond, WA 98052.

One second-grader, after taking a Saturday morning gifted and talented class on aerospace taught by one of the authors, devised and taught a model glider after-school club. Each week the children made three or four different gliders and flew them in the school's gymnasium. The class attracted about twenty children from first to fifth grades, becoming the most popular after-school club at the school!

Gliders Today:
Sail Gliders and Hang Gliders

Although the Wrights were interested in gliding for its technical importance to inventing an airplane, people today enjoy gliding as recreation. Nowadays, there are two types of gliders. *Sailplanes* look like airplanes without motors or propellers. A regular airplane tows the sailplane up into the air. Then, when the towline is released, the sailplane flies on currents of rising air called *updrafts*, which keep the sailplane flying. For this phenomenon to occur, sailplane flyers find areas where they can fly on rising warm air currents: hot flat areas from which warm air rises and the wind currents go upward after hitting a hill.

The other type of popular, contemporary sport gliding is the type performed by Otto Lilienthal: *hang gliding*. The hang-glider apparatus looks a lot like a triangular kite with a harness underneath to attach it to the person (pilot) doing the gliding. Like Otto Lilienthal, the pilot runs down a hill or leaps from a cliff to get airborne and the wind lifts the glider—sometimes as high as a single-story house. Little did Lilienthal realize, as he flew over the German countryside attempting to discern the principles of flight, that he was creating a popular sport for the late twentieth century. However, he would have been even more gratified to know that his work would help the Wright brothers invent the airplane.

Lawrence Hargrave and the Box Kite

While Otto Lilienthal was leaping off German hilltops, Lawrence Hargrave (1850-1915) was working on the other side of the world, "down under" in Australia, on box kites. A great humanitarian, Hargrave envisioned a brighter future through aviation. Spending more than thirty years doing *aeronautical* research, he made many futile attempts at powered flight. However, he pursued his research and in 1893 invented the generic kite form that he named the *box kite* (see figure 3.9). Ultimately, the American Wrights' successful *Flyer* combined around-the-world expertise—the glider research of the Englishman Cayley and the German Lilienthal and the box-kite form of the Australian Hargrave.

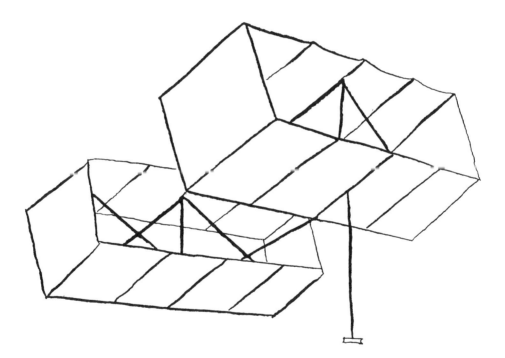

Fig. 3.9. Hargrave's box kite.

MORE SITES OF AEROSPACE HISTORY

- Social studies

- General

On the large wall map of the world, have students locate Berlin, Germany; Australia; and Dayton, Ohio and Kitty Hawk, North Carolina, both of which will figure in the discussion of the Wright brothers. Continue to use colored push pins. Students may even make little tags to identify the event associated with the site, such as "Berlin: Lilienthal Leaps."

FLIGHT PIONEERS' HALL OF FAME

- Library research, social studies, language arts, oral communication, art

- General

Your students can add to the list of persons who contributed to flight: Clement Ader of France; Hiram Maxim, Samuel Henson, and John Stringfellow of England; Percy Sinclair Pilcher of Scotland; and Samuel Langley (Massachusetts) and Octave Chanute (born in Paris, but who lived largely in Chicago and Miller, Indiana, where he and his crew experimented with gliders on the shore of Lake Michigan). Students can present short oral reports about these inventors or use illustrated written reports to create a "Flight Pioneers' Hall of Fame" for the classroom, library, or hallway. Tie in this activity with the previous Aerospace Magnet, asking students to locate on the map the geographical spots associated with these pioneers.

The Birth of Modern Aviation: The Wright Brothers

This chapter has discussed the kite, the glider, and the brave and sometimes fatal efforts of aviation pioneers. All of this work culminated on December 17, 1903, at Kill Devil Hill, near Kitty Hawk, North Carolina, where the begoggled Orville Wright became the first person to pilot a self-powered heavier-than-air aircraft, the Wrights' *Flyer*—which by some error of historical transmission has come to be called the *Kitty Hawk*. It was constructed primarily of wood covered with a cotton (linen) fabric, a piece of which Neil Armstrong would take with him on board the *Apollo XI*'s flight to the moon in July 1969, thus acknowledging the astronauts' debts to the Wrights' experiments of sixty-six years earlier. The *Flyer* took off under its own power (a twelve-horsepower, four-cylinder gasoline engine weighing about 200 pounds) and remained in sustained flight under the pilot's control.

Piloting the first flight, Orville stayed aloft for twelve seconds and traveled 120 feet; he also piloted the third flight of the day. Wilbur flew the plane on the second and fourth flights, with the latter the last and longest flight of the day: he flew 852 feet in fifty-nine seconds, the same amount of time it would take the *Apollo XI* in 1969 to cover 413 miles in its journey to the moon![12]

The Wrights' success grew from their natural curiosity. When Orville (1871-1948) was still a teenager and Wilbur (1867-1912) was twenty-one years old, they built a working printing press based on research in books and parts scavenged from junkyards. The brothers were intrigued with how machines of all types worked. In 1892, with the growing popularity of the bicycle, the Wrights, avid cyclists themselves, opened the Wright Cycling Company in Dayton, Ohio, which grew to be a thriving business and supplied the bicycle chains that went into making their *Flyer*.

After the Wrights read the 1894 magazine story about Lilienthal's glider experiments, the flight bug bit them both. This time they scavenged not junkyards, but libraries, searching for information about flight. When Lilienthal crashed and died, they wanted to know why his glider went nose down. Realizing that their local library had insufficient information about flight, Wilbur wrote to the Smithsonian Institution in a letter dated May 30, 1899, that is preserved today:

> I have been interested in the problem of mechanical and human flight ever since [I was] a boy.... I am about to begin a systematic study of the subject in preparation for practical work to which I expect to devote what time I can spare from my regular business. I wish to obtain such papers as the Smithsonian Institution has published on this subject, and if possible a list of other works in print in the English language. I am an enthusiast, but not a crank in the sense that I have some pet theories as to the proper construction of a flying machine. I wish to avail myself of all that is already known and then if possible add my mite to help on the future worker who will attain final success.[13]

Within a few days the Smithsonian replied, and Wilbur and Orville set to work reading and analyzing the work of their predecessors.

THE COLLABORATIVE NATURE OF RESEARCH

- Library research, language arts, oral communication, social studies, science

- Intermediate and advanced

With the research methods of the Wrights in mind, emphasize to your students the collaborative nature of scientific investigation and the importance of writing things down so that others may benefit from a researcher's successes and errors. Ask your students to look in current magazines (especially magazines with a scientific emphasis, such as *Scientific American, Discover*, and the *Air and Space Magazine*) and newspapers for articles about scientific research; they should pay special attention to accounts that tell how current investigators are using the work of their predecessors. The library media specialist may be able to secure some actual, current research periodicals for students to examine from a college or university library through interlibrary loan. Students should be able to summarize in writing the articles they encounter and also present to the class short reports about what they have read.

LEARNING ABOUT THE SMITHSONIAN INSTITUTION

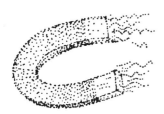

- Library research, social studies

- General

Wilbur Wright wrote to the Smithsonian Institution in Washington, D.C., which today consists of a complex of museums and galleries. Ask students to do some research about the Smithsonian. How and when did it begin? How did it get its name? Of what is it composed today? Have any of your students visited it? If so, do they have photos, booklets, or postcards from the Smithsonian that they would be willing to share with the class? Of special interest will be the National Air and Space Museum, which is part of the Smithsonian's complex. If you don't have the opportunity to visit this wonderful museum, consider purchasing or having the school library purchase C. D. B. Bryan's *The National Air and Space Museum*, a big, beautiful, illustrated book including most of the major exhibits at the museum (see bibliography for more information about the book).

Studying the work of Lilienthal and others, the Wrights decided that the German hang glider was on the right track. However, they wanted to explore further wing shape and its influence on control in flight. In particular, Wilbur had been observing buzzards, which he noted maintained control and balance by twisting the tips of their wings as they few.[14] From watching these birds, Wilbur developed an idea called *wing-warping*, or twisting, which could give the flying object better lateral (side to side) control than Lilienthal had achieved by shifting his body weight.

To test the idea during the summer of 1899, Wilbur built a model kite that resembled Hargrave's box kite. It was a biplane kite with a 5-foot wingspan, its curved wings each measuring 1 foot in width. Wires connected the two sets of wings, which were operated from the ground with lines attached to the wingtips while the kite was in the air. Flying the kite in a field just west of Dayton, Wilbur managed to have good lateral control of the kite by warping the wings and thus altering their wind resistance with the strings he held in his hands. However, suddenly and inexplicably, the kite plunged downward, causing the little boys who were watching the huge kite to panic and throw themselves on the ground. Wilbur controlled the kite and it merely sailed over them. Nevertheless, the Wrights felt ready to take a big step: build a glider in which a person would fly.

Knowing from Wilbur's kite-flying experiment that wing-warping provided better lateral control than Lilienthal had achieved, the Wrights built a cradle-like structure on the lower wing on which the pilot lay prone facing forward. He would move his body in this cradle to twist or warp the wing tips. The wings were also warped by wires. Furthermore, the brothers added to their glider a concept they termed the *forward horizontal rudder*, but which we call today the *elevators*. On a modern plane (see figure 3.10), the elevators are attached to the horizontal section on each side of the tail in the *rear* of the plane; the elevators make the plane ascend (climb) or descend (dive). On the Wright's aircraft, the elevators were attached to the *front*, so that the plane, in essence, flew tail first. The Wrights' elevators looked like two hexagonal flat surfaces, one above the other; the pilot controlled them with a lever. This placement was important: in case the pilot, who was on the lower wing lying prone and facing forward, encountered nose down pressure, he could adjust the lever and go nose up.

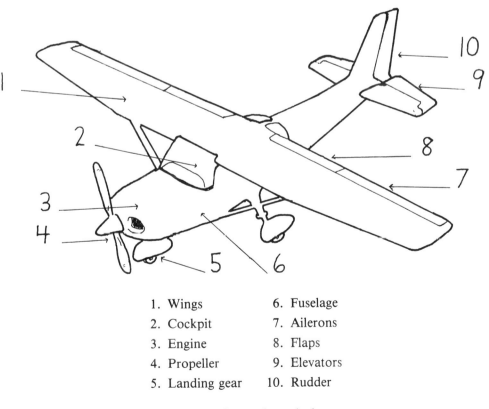

1. Wings	6. Fuselage
2. Cockpit	7. Ailerons
3. Engine	8. Flaps
4. Propeller	9. Elevators
5. Landing gear	10. Rudder

Fig. 3.10. Parts of a modern airplane.

The Wrights spent two seasons, 1900 and 1901, testing their two gliders at Kill Devil Hill, near Kitty Hawk, North Carolina. They went to the desolate sand dunes there on the advice of the U.S. Weather Bureau, whom they had contacted in search of winds that would provide sufficient lift. The two Wright gliders looked and worked like big box kites with two men running on either side of the wings holding the wingtips. When the glider picked up sufficient speed, the two men would let go, and the pilot would actually control the glider. Although the glider flights lasted just a few seconds at a time and covered only short distances, the control achieved by the pilot proved that the Wrights' design worked. By autumn 1902, they had built a third glider on which they made nearly 1,000 successful controlled flights, setting a distance record of 622½ feet and a duration record of twenty-six seconds.[15] With a masterfully designed glider that they planned to patent, the brothers were eager to get the aircraft off the ground under its own power. For this, it needed an engine and propellers.

Orville tells his and his brother's story in "How We Made the First Flight," which first appeared in the December 1913 issue of *Flying* and *The Aero Club of America Bulletin* and which has been reprinted by the FAA (see address in appendix). In Orville's words: "Immediately upon our return to Dayton, we wrote to a number of automobile and motor builders, stating the purpose for which we desired a motor, and asking whether they could furnish one that would develop eight-brake horse power, with a weight complete not exceeding 200 pounds."[16] The request proved futile, and so the Wrights, with the help of their friend Charles E. Taylor, were back in their bicycle shop designing and building their own twelve-horsepower airplane motor, which was placed next to the pilot on the lower wing. This was an *internal combustion engine*, an engine that burns fuel within the engine.

THE INTERNAL COMBUSTION ENGINE

- Science

- General

A physics teacher or car mechanic can demonstrate a simple internal combustion engine. In physics class, students can make their own simple internal combustion engine. What are some other machines that use this type of engine? (Cars, lawn mowers, etc.)

In addition to making their own engine, the Wrights developed a satisfactory *propeller*, a rotating blade (like a fan) nowadays attached to the motor in front of the plane. The engine or motor turns the propeller, which, in turn, normally *pulls* the plane through the air by a screwing-type motion (see figure 3.10). The Wrights, however, put their propellers, which turned in opposite directions, at the *rear* of their plane, attaching them to the engine by bicycle chains. The Wrights' propellers moved air backward, thus causing their *Flyer* to be *pushed* forward. To steer the plane in flight, the *Flyer* had twin rear rudders in the modern sense of the term. The *rudder* is a moving part attached to the vertical section of the tail; when the rudder is moved, the plane turns to the left or right (see figure 3.10).

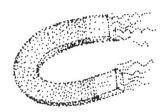

PARTS OF A PLANE

- Science, language arts, art

- General

You are familiar by now with terms like wings, elevators, propellers, and rudders. Figure 3.10 shows how they all fit in terms of a modern airplane and the following list describes the parts of a plane and their functions. Notice that the definitions are numbered to correspond to figure 3.10. Using this illustration as a guide, students can draw and label their own airplanes. They can add as many of the terms as you think necessary to their dictionaries of aerospace terms.

1. *Wings*: The wings give lift and support the weight of the plane while in flight.

2. *Cockpit*: The cockpit is where the pilot sits and contains the plane's instruments and controls.

3. *Engine*: The engine provides the power to move the propeller.

4. *Propeller*: The propeller, or airscrew, is a rotating blade normally attached to the engine in front of the plane. It pulls the plane through the air.

5. *Landing gear*: The landing gear is the wheels and, on some planes, the equipment to raise and lower the wheels.

6. *Fuselage*: The fuselage is the body of the plane to which the wings, tail, engine, and landing gear are attached.

7. *Ailerons*: Ailerons are moving parts connected to the back outside edges of the plane's wings that help the plane tilt or roll and have lateral control.

8. *Flaps*: Flaps are moving parts connected to the back inside edges of the plane's wings that help the plane slow down for takeoff and landing. The flaps can help provide lift on takeoff.

9. *Elevators*: The elevators are attached to the horizontal section on each side of the tail in the rear of the plane. The elevators make the plane ascend or descend.

10. *Rudder*: The rudder is a moving part attached to the vertical section of the tail. It makes the plane turn left or right.

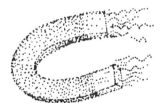

THE FOUR FORCES OF FLIGHT ON AN AIRPLANE

- Science

- General

Figure 3.11 shows how lift, gravity, drag, and thrust relate to an airplane. Students can copy this into their notebooks.

Lift is the upward force that makes a plane fly. Lift is created by the difference in air pressure above and below the wings and the angle of the wings into the wind.

Thrust is the force produced by a power source that moves the aircraft forward.

Drag is a force by which an object resists forward movement.

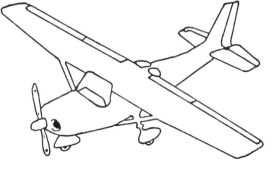

Gravity is the force that pulls objects to the ground (earth).

Fig. 3.11. Four forces of flight.

The Wrights Are Ready

During the summer of 1903, the Wright brothers built their powered aircraft, the *Flyer*. By late September 1903, they were headed back to Kitty Hawk with the airplane. Looking similar to their 1902 glider, the *Flyer* was a biplane with a 40-foot, 4-inch span and a wing area of 510 square feet. Eager to test it, the Wrights were plagued by mechanical and weather troubles, as well as by Wilbur's pilot error on December 14 that damaged the *Flyer* at take off.[17]

Finally, on December 17, 1903, "all systems were go." With five local persons and a camera to witness the events, Orville assumed the pilot's position and took off at 10:35 a.m. History was made: he flew for twelve seconds, going about 120 feet at approximately 30 miles per hour. As Orville writes, this flight was "the first in the history of the world in which a machine carrying a man had raised itself by its own power into the air in full flight, had sailed forward without reduction of speed and had finally landed at a point as high as that from which it started."[18] The Wrights' diligence, mechanical know-how, and imagination enabled them to synthesize the work of others, add their own ideas, and send humans into the air in a self-powered, heavier-than-air aircraft that was controlled by the pilot in sustained flight.

Surprisingly, however, the Wrights' achievement went almost unnoticed in their own country at the time. The great French-born engineer and glider designer, Octave Chanute (1832-1910; his last name is pronounced "Sha-*noot*"), who had encouraged the Wrights in their work and spent time with them at Kitty Hawk during their 1901 and 1902 glider flights, popularized their achievements in Europe. He presented illustrated lectures, thereby promoting aviation research, which had slowed down in Europe after Lilienthal's fatal crash. Meanwhile, in America, the Wrights failed to secure sought-after contracts to produce their aircraft. Turned down by American investors, including the U.S. government, for support in selling their invention, the Wright brothers turned to investors in France and other European countries, but there, too, met discouragement. In addition, even though the Wrights had applied in 1903 for a patent on their masterpiece 1902 glider, they had to challenge their competitors' patent infringements, delaying the granting of the patent until 1906. This only added to their frustration and reluctance to publicize their work and thus delayed the development of aviation.

After developing their *Flyer II* in 1904 and *Flyer III* in 1905, the Wrights ceased to fly or allow anyone to see their airplanes for two-and-a-half years. Finally, in 1909, already celebrities in France largely because of Chanute's lectures, the Wrights received their desired contract to build the first heavier-than-air aircraft for the U.S. Army. That same year they also received the recognition they deserved at home: on June 10 at the White House, President Taft honored the Wrights with the Aero Club of America's gold medals. This event was immediately followed by more medals and parades from Congress, the state of Ohio, and their hometown, Dayton.[19] Six years after making their historical flights, the bicycle-makers-turned-flyers were international heroes for discovering the secrets to heavier-than-air flight.

The Wrights continued to be involved in aviation research, forming the Wright Company, which manufactured and marketed planes. After Wilbur died of typhoid fever in 1912, Orville carried on alone, closing the Wright Company in Dayton in 1917 and starting the Wright Aeronautical Laboratory. He tested new aircraft and taught flying. However, his troubles were not over. In the words of the Wrights' biographer, Harry Combs, in 1914 the Smithsonian Institution "became involved in a shameful plan to discredit the Wrights" by endorsing a statement that Professor Samuel Langley, who was then secretary of the Smithsonian, " 'had actually designed and built the first man-carrying flying machine capable of sustained flight' " a year before the Wrights.[20] Consequently, the insulted Orville refused to give the *Flyer* to the Smithsonian. Instead, he placed it in storage and then, in 1928, sent it to the Science Museum in London for exhibition. Twenty years and a big apology later, on December 17, 1948—the forty-fifth anniversary of the history-making flights at Kitty Hawk—the *Flyer* was officially presented to the Smithsonian, where today it hangs in the National Air and Space Museum. Unfortunately, Orville did not live long enough to witness this: he died on January 30, 1948. The Wrights had finally won their rights. As the FAA observes on its reprint of Orville's account of the events at Kitty Hawk on December 17, 1903, "What the Wright brothers started ... has led to space flight and in the process, changed life on earth forever."[21]

Glenn Curtiss: From Motorcycles to Airplanes

While the Wright brothers, cyclists turned inventors, pilots, and entrepreneurs, were trying to sell their aircraft, Glenn Curtiss (1878-1930), was racing motorcycles. In 1907 he was known as the Fastest Man on Earth for setting a motorcycle speed record of 136 miles per hour.

Because Curtiss' motorcycle engines were lightweight yet powerful, balloonist Thomas Baldwin asked him to design and build an engine for an airship. This resulted in Baldwin's airship becoming the first powered dirigible in the United States. After building engines for several other airships, Curtiss soon turned his attention to building airplanes. He was joined by Alexander Graham Bell (1847-1922), the inventor of the telephone, who since 1898 had manifested an avid interest in flight by building elaborate kites. Together they founded, in 1907, the Aerial Experiment Association, which designed and built aircraft, including the first *seaplane* — an airplane with floats at the bottom instead of landing wheels, enabling it to land on water — to be flown in the United States. The association also made the first American aircraft equipped with ailerons, which Curtiss invented in 1911. Ailerons, as noted in the Aerospace Magnet showing the parts of a modern airplane (figure 3.10), are moving parts connected to the back edges of the plane's wings that help the plane tilt or roll and have lateral control. Ailerons replaced the wing-warping method used by the Wrights for lateral control.

UNDERSTANDING THE USE OF THE PROPELLER AND THE AIRPLANE'S CONTROL SURFACES: RUDDER, ELEVATORS, AND AILERONS

- Science

- General

Now that the class is familiar with the parts of the airplane and the four forces of flight (figures 3.10 and 3.11), following are some demonstrations that illustrate the workings of the propeller and three control surfaces.

Understanding the Propeller

The propeller drives an aircraft forward through the air, or provides the force of thrust. In most airplanes the propeller (turned by an engine) pushes the air backward and is consequently pushed forward, moving the entire plane forward. This is an example of Newton's third law — for every action, there is an equal and opposite reaction — which will be demonstrated in the next chapter by an Aerospace Magnet related to jet engines. At this point, the teacher can conduct a simple experiment that will enable students to understand the function of the propeller.

Materials: Small electric fan with a long (about 20 or 30 feet) extension cord, wagon or skateboard.

Procedure: Set a small electric fan with a long extension cord *firmly* on a wagon or skateboard. The fan acts as the propeller for a plane and the skateboard or wagon as the body of a plane. Plug the fan in and turn it on. What happens?

Conclusion: The blades of the fan, acting as the propeller, propel the air in front of the fan. This action drives the fan (propeller) and skateboard or wagon (body of plane) backward.

Understanding the Use of the Rudder, Elevator, and Ailerons

Explain to the students that just as the driver of a car sits in the front seat behind the steering wheel and controls the car, the pilot sits in the cockpit and controls the airplane. Of course, a car can only go right or left or forward or backward. A plane, however, is capable of three basic movements: yaw, turning left or right; pitch, climbing and descending; and roll, tipping or leaning from side to side.

These movements are made by an airplane with the help of the control surfaces on the wing and tail of the airplane. First, review with the class the parts of the airplane—ailerons, rudder, and elevator—that control the way it moves. For a demonstration, use a model airplane with movable control surfaces. A suitable plastic model airplane is available from Cessna Aircraft Company (see appendix for address). To demonstrate the function of the control surfaces, you can also assemble a balsa glider (available from toy or hobby shops) and glue on pieces of lightweight paper to make a rudder, elevators, and ailerons. Then perform some of the following experiments.

Understanding the Use of the Rudder

Materials: Scissors, paper (4"x6" index cards can simply be cut in half, the long way, for this activity), hole puncher, paper clips.

Procedure: Cut paper into 2"x6" strips (or cut the index cards) and punch a hole with a hole puncher at one end of each paper strip. Give each student a paper clip and one of the paper strips, which students are to imagine is an airplane. The students are to put the paper clip through the hole and fold the other side of the paper 2 inches from the end. They should hold the clips so that the folded end (the rudder) of the paper is opposite their mouths so they can blow on it.

To simulate the movement of yaw for an airplane, ask students to fold the rudder to the left and blow on the paper to find out what direction the plane turns. Why? Then follow the same procedure with the rudder folded to the right.

Conclusion: Folding the paper works like an airplane's rudder. When you fold the paper to the left, air hits the rudder and pushes the tail of the airplane to the right. Simultaneously, this points the nose of the airplane to the left. Thus, for an airplane to have yaw, or turn left, the pilot turns the rudder left. The converse is true when the rudder is turned right.

Understanding the Use of the Elevator and Ailerons

Materials: Basic paper glider (see the Aerospace Magnet earlier in this chapter on "Making and Flying Paper Gliders," accompanied by figure 3.8), scissors.

Procedure: Using the basic glider you made, cut the tail of the glider up 1½ inches from the end on both sides, starting at points 1 inch from the inner fold. (A glider that will not require cutting for this activity appears in the booklet, *History of Flight*, p. 32, offered by the National Air and Space Museum at the address in the appendix.) To simulate an elevator for an airplane, fold both cut sections of the glider up and throw the glider. Do the same with both sections folded down. What happens? To simulate the ailerons for an airplane, fold the left section down and the right section up and throw it. Then fold the right section down and the left section up and throw it. What happens?

Conclusion: Regarding the elevators of an airplane: when you threw the glider with both sections (elevators) folded up, air pushed the tail down and the nose went up; consequently, the glider climbed. When you threw the glider with both sections folded down, air pushed the tail up and the nose went down; consequently, the glider descended. Remember, the climbing and descending movements of an airplane are called pitch.

Concerning the ailerons of an airplane: when you threw the glider with the left aileron section folded down and the right aileron folded up, the left wing was pushed up by air (the air hitting the downward left aileron) and the right wing was pushed down by air (the air hitting the upward right aileron). In turn, the glider rolled to the right. A pilot reverses the procedure for a left turn.

New Uses for Airplanes

In 1910 a Curtiss biplane flew from Albany to New York, and from New York to Philadelphia and back. Keep in mind the world situation around this time. In particular, the German empire was aggressively seeking ways to expand on land as well as on sea by challenging England's naval superiority; World War I (1914-1918) was hovering. Consequently, some persons were investigating the potential of using airplanes in warfare. Curtiss, himself, carried out bombing tests by flying his plane over a lake where the shape of a battleship had been marked out by flagged buoys and dropping dummy bombs. In 1910 pilot Eugene Ely, flying a Curtiss biplane, made the first flight from a ship, the cruiser *Birmingham*. Two months later, in January 1911, he landed his biplane at sea on a wooden platform on the deck of a warship, the USS *Pennsylvania*, marking the first time an airplane ever landed on the deck of a ship. After landing, he took off again from the *Pennsylvania* and safely returned to San Francisco. For his contributions to the use of the airplane at sea, Curtiss has been called the Father of Naval Aviation.[22]

European Advances in Aviation

Although Glenn Curtiss was experimenting with the airplane's utility as a weapon, most Americans were classifying the airplane in the same category as they were balloons and kites: as a toy. This attitude adversely affected America's place in the development of aviation. By 1911, America ranked only sixth in the world in terms of numbers of trained pilots. The manufacturing of American aircraft was equally dismal: America's airplanes were still largely handmade and rapidly becoming obsolete. Across the Atlantic, however, the aircraft industry thrived as European engineers were developing more streamlined planes that offered stability, ease of flying, and utility for military warfare. In 1911 a Frenchman named Robert Esnault-Pelterie built the first fully enclosed fuselage airplane.[23] As noted earlier, a fuselage is the body of the plane to which the wings, engine, landing gear, control surfaces, and tail are attached. The fuselage accommodates the crew, passengers, and cargo (see figure 3.10). Unlike the pilot of the Wright *Flyer* who had to lie prone on the wing, the pilot could now sit upright in a cockpit—yet unenclosed—containing the instruments and controls. Ironically, the nation that had given birth to aviation was falling behind the rest of the western world in developing the airplane, particularly in terms of its potential military uses. In contrast to the present-day reliance on air power in war, America initially thought little of the plane's military uses at the outbreak of World War I.

READY-MADE QUIZZES, PUZZLES, AND WORKSHEETS ABOUT AEROSPACE

- Language arts, social studies, math

- Beginning and intermediate

Teachers who wish to do so can give students worksheets and/or quizzes on which they match famous aviation events, inventors, achievements, and dates. Some sample sheets are in a thirty-three-page packet by John Hartsfield and Shirley Norlem called *History of Flight: Activities for the Primary Students*, produced by and available from the Aerospace Education Services Project, NASA Lewis Research Center (see appendix for address). The pamphlet also includes aviation-based crossword puzzles, word problems, and sample letter-number games.

On the Brink of War

An outstanding long-distance flight occurred in 1909 when the French aviation pioneer, Louis Blériot, became the first to fly across the English Channel in his monoplane, the *Blériot XI* (figure 3.12). Another notable long-distance flight occurred in 1911, when Cal P. Rodgers made the first airplane crossing of the United States: flying from Long Island, New York to Long Beach, California, he covered 4,251 miles in eighty-two hours and two minutes of in-flight time over eighty-four days. Only forty-nine of the eighty-four days involved flying time. Crashing nineteen times, flying once into an eagle and once into a tree, Rodgers covered a maximum of only 133 miles in a single sustained flight. When he made his final landing in Long Beach, he had to hobble on crutches from his plane, which had been virtually rebuilt several times in the eighty-four days it took him to make the trip. In fact, it was amazing that he found Long Beach because for navigation he used what was called *the iron compass*—railroad tracks.

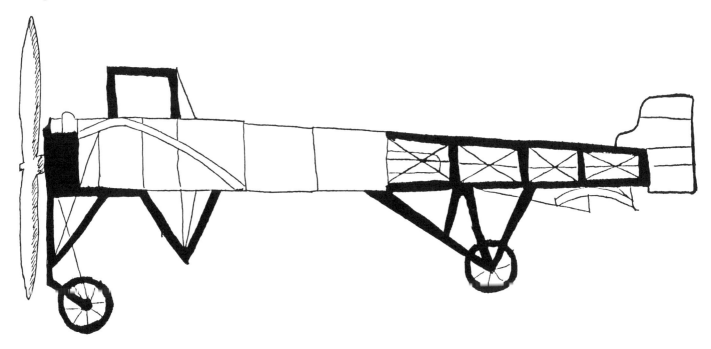

Fig. 3.12. Blériot's airplane.

AEROSPACE PROBLEMS

- Mathematics

- General

Using the numbers in the Cal Rodgers anecdote, ask your class to calculate how many miles per hour he flew if he was able to cover 4,251 miles in eighty-two hours. Likewise, mathematics problems at all levels can be created within an aviation context, such as, how long will it take to fly from point A to point B, traveling at X miles per hour? How much fuel will be used if the tank holds Y number of gallons? The more advanced the students, the more challenging the high school math teacher can make the problems.

Women Flyers

Women also took to the air in the early days of the airplane. Nine years before women won the right to vote in America, Harriet Quimby became the first woman to earn a pilot's license in this country in 1911. A year later she became the first woman to fly alone across the English Channel. As a licensed pilot, Quimby was preceded internationally by Raymonde de la Roche, a French baroness, who in 1910 became the first woman in the world to earn a pilot's license.

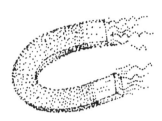

FAMOUS FIRSTS IN EARLY AVIATION

- Library research, social studies, language arts

- General

Students can uncover famous first facts in early aviation (who made the first nonstop flight across America? etc.). Students can also research the role of women in aviation and write reports about their achievements. A good source is the U.S. Air Force ROTC's *Aerospace Science* (see bibliography). Even more accessible is the *Information Please Almanac*, which lists many "firsts" in aviation; students would be wise to familiarize themselves with this handy reference tool. The free education packets from the Smithsonian and especially the Civil Air Patrol (CAP)'s "Falcon Force" teaching kit include information and pictures about people and events; write to the CAP at the address given in the appendix.

A Concise Background to the "Great War"

While Europe was plunged into World War I in 1914, America maintained its isolationist position towards European affairs. However, the United States could not long remain neutral in light of Germany's 1915 sinking of the British passenger liner *Lusitania*, which resulted in the deaths of more than 100 Americans, and Germany's pursuit of unrestricted submarine warfare, which torpedoed and sank foreign ships bound for American ports. On April 6, 1917, the United States entered the war on the side of the Allies, composed of the British Empire, France, Russia, Japan, and Italy, against the Central Powers, consisting of Germany, Austria-Hungary, Turkey, and Bulgaria. A war that drew in the United States mainly because of aggression at sea turned into a war that advanced the development of airplanes, bringing war into the skies.

THE GREAT WAR

- Social studies

- General

Teach your class about World War I (the "Great War," 1914-1918), its causes, its changing the face of Europe, and its leading to the formation of the League of Nations. Locate on a map the countries involved in the war and note how boundaries changed after the war.

The Role of Aviation in World War I

At the outset of World War I, Germany had about 200 aircraft in its air force, while France and England possessed about 450 aircraft. More important, however, these countries had the industries to manufacture more aircraft. When the United States entered the war in 1917, it had no combat-worthy aircraft and only one really productive aviation manufacturer, Curtiss Aircraft.

Initially, the primary wartime role of aircraft was the same as that of the balloon during the American Civil War: reconnaissance. Planes, either one- or two-seaters, were fitted with radios and cameras. For example, the British *B.E. 2C*, with its ninety-horsepower engine (the Wright's *Flyer* at Kitty Hawk had a twelve-horsepower engine!) was built to be speedy (flying up to 75 miles per hour), quick-climbing (ascending 10,000 feet within forty-five minutes), and self-sustaining (remaining in flight three hours and fifteen minutes without refueling).[24] Airborne fighting consisted of the pilots' taking lateral potshots with their pistols or rifles at enemy pilots.

It is an ironic truth that science and technology make some of their greatest strides forward when nations are trying to annihilate each other. During World War I, engineers, particularly English and German, were working on such problems as adding additional and heavier engines to planes; mounting machine guns onto the aircraft that would not fire into the vehicle's own propeller, which was on the front of the plane; improving wing sections for higher lift and lower drag; and carrying and dropping bombs. When World War I began, planes were still largely constructed of the same materials used by the Wrights in 1903: a wooden framework covered with fabric. By 1917, however, the German, Professor Hugo Junkers, developed a metal fuselage.

The First Bombers and Fighters

Early in World War I (January 1915), Germany began supplementing air reconnaissance with an offensive use of aircraft by using its airships, the famous zeppelins (described in chapter 2), for bombing raids on French and English cities. Although the zeppelins proved highly accurate as bombers, they were also highly vulnerable to antiaircraft fire because, being filled with hydrogen, they were highly flammable. The Germans knew that a replacement was necessary. In 1917 the replacement for bomb-dropping dirigibles came in the form of a large twin-engine bomber, the *Gotha IV*, which dropped tons of bombs on English cities and factories. By the end of the war, both the Allies and the Central Powers had specially designed first-generation bombers capable of carrying up to 6,000 pounds of bombs. The bombers were slow moving, but especially horrifying.

Along with bombers, agile fighter planes were developed. The French coined the term *ace* for a fighter pilot who shot down five enemy aircraft. The British and Americans adopted the same number, whereas Germany required ten. The term *ace of aces* was the name given to the pilot from each country who shot down the most enemy aircraft during World War I. These included the American Edward "Eddie" V. Rickenbacker (twenty-six downed aircraft) and the German Manfred von (Red Baron) Richthofen (eighty downed planes).

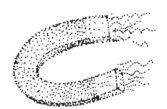

WORLD WAR I AIRCRAFT

- Library research, reading, writing, and art

- General

Having heard of "Snoopy and the Red Baron" and the *Sopwith Camel* from the "Peanuts" comic strip, many students of all ages have an interest in World War I aircraft. They can go to the library to look up some famous World War I planes such as the *Sopwith Camel* (figure 3.13), *Gotha, Fokker, Spad, Nieuport, Albatross*, and others. Bryan's *National Air and Space Museum* and Matricardi's *The Concise History of Aviation* are descriptive, colorful books for starting such research. Students can draw the planes and write short reports about their key features and feats.

Fig. 3.13. *Sopwith Camel*.

WORLD WAR I FLYERS

- Literature
- Advanced

Even a cursory look at the World War I military planes listed in the previous Aerospace Magnet attests to how rickety those planes were. Imagine what it was like to fly one. Read aloud William Butler Yeats's poem, "An Irish Airman Foresees His Death" and discuss the poet's meaning of "fate" and the tone of the poem in terms of the speaker's attitude about his work. How would you feel in the same situation? Two other poems about World War I are Wilfred Owen's "Sonnet: On Seeing a Piece of Artillery Brought into Action" and "Anthem for Doomed Youth."

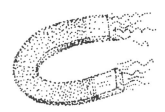

THE AMERICAN ACE OF ACES

- Library research and language arts
- Beginning and intermediate

Have the students research and write about the American ace of aces, Edward (Eddie) Rickenbacker (1890-1973), the only living American to receive the Congressional Medal of Honor during World War I. You can request the Civil Air Patrol's free activities booklet, geared to beginning students, about Eddie Rickenbacker by writing on school letterhead to the CAP at the address in the appendix.

Planes Go Faster and Higher; Pilots Increase Skills

From the beginning to the end of World War I, the average flying speed increased, with some fighter planes going as fast as 155 miles per hour at a low altitude and up to 140 miles per hour at 10,000 feet, to which they could climb within ten minutes. Likewise, the maximum height at which an airplane could fly under normal conditions—known as the *ceiling*—more than doubled, with some fighters soaring as high as 25,000 feet.[25] Monoplanes, biplanes, and triplanes (for example, the German *Fokker DR-1*) flew. Planes, some now having metal fuselages, also increased in maneuverability and stability. To meet the increasing sophistication of the airplanes, pilot training was enhanced, thereby improving pilots' flying skill and control for the now-famous aerial battles called *dog fights*, one-on-one fights between two pilots and their planes. Pilot control and plane construction had come a long way from the days of Lilienthal and the Wrights.

Most of the major aviation advances during the war came from English and German scientists and engineers. Although the American Congress had voted funding to construct wartime aircraft, America lacked sufficient aeronautical engineers and aeronautical industry to play a major role in aviation. Consequently, "not a single American-designed combat aircraft saw action" in World War I; instead, Americans built wartime planes designed by the British.[26]

International progress in aviation would change the way warfare would be executed in the future. For many people, World War I underscored the airplane's capacity for destruction. Between the end of World War I (1918) and the outbreak of World War II (1939), however, this attitude towards the airplane would change, especially in America, as aviation history entered the Golden Age of Flight.

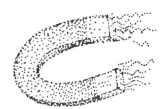

ATTITUDES ABOUT AIRCRAFT

- Social studies, language arts, oral communication, critical thinking

- General

First, add *ceiling* and *dog fight* to students' dictionaries of aerospace terms. Then discuss with the class, in light of our nation's current heavy reliance on aircraft in war, how they feel about airplanes. Does our modern familiarity with airplanes as a commonplace method of transportation make aircraft seem less formidable or destructive? How did they feel about aircraft when they watched all the planes taking part in the air attacks on Iraq? Does the B-2 *Stealth Bomber* arouse the same feelings as a Boeing 747?

The Golden Age of Flight

In American aviation history, the decades between World War I and World War II are called the Golden Age of Flight. The name is derived from the public's growing interest in aviation events, wherein pilots made many record flights and American engineers developed classic aircraft, thereby paving the way for the planes we know today as well as for the beginning of airway systems.

By the end of World War I, not only had most Americans never seen an actual airplane, but what they had heard about planes—that they carried bombs and were capable of massive destruction—made them fearful and even disapproving of them. Then, along came the air races and the barnstormers. Air races got their start in the United States when a newspaperman, Ralph Pulitzer, wanted to see American aircraft win the European air races. To promote the development of high-speed aircraft in America, he helped establish the Pulitzer Trophy Race, the first held in 1920 at Long Island, New York. Pulitzer's efforts to increase American airspeed did not go unheeded. As the annual races continued during the next five years, the winner's speed increased by nearly 100 miles per hour. The popularity of the Pulitzer Trophy Race escalated, and in 1924 it was renamed the National

Air Race. By the late 1920s and early 1930s, the National Air Race was the prime sporting event of the nation, far surpassing in popularity and attendance today's major sporting events. Racing pilots were national heroes, some more famous than modern football and baseball superstars.

Barnstormers

The barnstormers also helped promote aviation and, like the air race pilots, they enjoyed America's adulation. Most barnstormers were ex-military aviators who flew World War I-surplus aircraft over towns to attract attention and then landed on a nearby field. Attracting the attention of the townspeople who had come out to the field to see the plane, the pilot would offer them rides for a small fee. For example, Wilbur Wassaw of Colorado Springs, Colorado, recollects seeing his first airplane in 1926 when a barnstormer came to town; Wassaw paid him five dollars for a plane ride.[27]

Barnstormers also gave flying exhibitions. The acrobatic pilots sometimes performed as a "flying circus," thrilling their audiences with death-defying tricks including loop-de-loops, where the plane turned upside down in circles, performed high above the ground. Among the most daring of these barnstormers was Charles Lindbergh (1902-1974). His most dangerous stunt was standing upright on the upper wing of a biplane as the pilot flew a series of loops. Lindbergh's secret was that his feet were strapped to the wing, and he was steadied by invisible wires going from his belt to the plane's wing. However, "Lucky Lindy," as he would soon be known, had much yet to accomplish in the pilot's seat.

MAKE A BOARD GAME: "THE BARNSTORMING DARE-DEVILS FAME GAME"

- Library research, math, social studies, art, working in a group

- Beginning and intermediate

Materials: Posterboard, paper plates, big U.S. map, crayons and felt markers, pack of 3"x5" index cards, corks from bottles (optional), push-through brass paper fasteners.

Procedure: Have students create a large board game in which the game pieces are cut out from cardboard or cork to form models of famous World War I planes. The pieces move according to a throw of the dice or the number struck on a cardboard spinning wheel, made from a paper plate with numbers from one to six listed around the circumference and with a cardboard dial or arrow fastened to it with a brass paper fastener so the dial can spin. The playing board can be a large U.S. map students draw on poster board with states, cities, mountains, bodies of water and—depending on the students' sophistication—longitude and latitude marked on it. The map will have various coast-to-coast routes marked by an *identical* number of 1" square boxes on each route. The routes can include typical board game delays and bonuses. For example, the playing piece can land on a "PERFORMANCE-DELAY" box, where the player must draw from a stack of "DELAY" cards (made from a package of 3"x5" index cards). A typical DELAY card might read, "Your partner accidentally left his balancing wires for standing on the wing at your last stop; go back there for this turn and remain until your next turn—and don't be so forgetful!"; or "Congratulations: Your wing-walking act is so successful that you stay another day to perform again; lose this turn." Similarly, for landing on a PERFORMANCE-BONUS box, the player may draw from this stack of cards a card saying, "The Sheriff has run you out of town because your loop-de-loops have scared the cows grazing in the field; so, you hastily pack up and fly all night without sleep, moving two towns ahead—and out of the Sheriff's jurisdiction—on your route." Teachers and students can use their imaginations and design all types of board games relating to different facets of aviation and space science: "Balloon Races: Beat the Montgolfières"; "Blimps from Berlin to Boston"; "Zipping in a Zeppelin"; "Shuttling to Mars."

Lindbergh and the Spirit of St. Louis

In 1919 a New York hotel owner, Raymond Oertig, offered a $25,000 prize to the first aviator to fly nonstop between Paris and New York in either direction. Although this was an era of record-breaking flights, the Oertig Prize went unclaimed for some time simply because no existing aircraft engine could withstand the distance and duration of a nonstop flight across the Atlantic. On May 9, 1926, Commander Richard E. Byrd (1888-1957) and his pilot, Floyd Bennett, made the first flight over the North Pole, taking sixteen hours and using three 200-horsepower, air-cooled Wright Whirlwind engines, manufactured by the Wright Aeronautical Corporation, which had evolved from the original Wright Company. (By this time, however, Orville, the surviving Wright brother, was no longer involved with the business.) This flight proved the engine's dependability and endurance over long distances.

Meanwhile, the Oertig Prize was still waiting for the right person to accept the challenge of crossing the Atlantic nonstop. Charles Lindbergh stepped forward to do so. By 1926, when the twenty-four-year-old Lindbergh heard about the Oertig Prize, he had returned to the pilot's seat from the wing of the plane on which he had performed stunts and was flying mail through all kinds of weather for an aircraft corporation in St. Louis, Missouri. Having logged over 2,000 hours of flying experience, Lindbergh understood navigation and was thoroughly familiar with airplanes. Most important, he was determined and persuasive, so persuasive that he secured the financial backing for his transAtlantic attempt from a group of St. Louis businessmen who added $13,000 to his own $2,000 to pay for the building of an appropriate airplane.

YOU ARE LINDBERGH'S ACCOUNTANT

- Mathematics

- Intermediate

Create some math problems for your class in which you provide hypothetical interest rates on Lindbergh's borrowed money, divide the loan amount among six different lenders who each give a particular percentage of the total, etc.

Although multiengine planes had been in use since 1911, Lindbergh reasoned that the more engines a plane had, the more chance there would be of engine failure. He convinced his St. Louis backers that a single Wright Whirlwind engine, such as that used by Byrd and Bennett in their polar crossing, was the right machine for the job. When it seemed all available aircraft were too expensive or manufacturers would be unable to build the plane, Lindbergh encountered the relatively unknown Ryan Airlines, Inc., of San Diego, California. Within sixty days of negotiating their contract with the young pilot, the Ryan company built the plane to Lindbergh's specifications. The result was a small, one-seater, silvery monoplane constructed of wood, steel tubing, and fabric, and powered by a 223-horsepower Wright Whirlwind engine driving a two-bladed propeller.

Notice Lindbergh's choice of a monoplane. By the decade after World War I, the monoplane, with its low drag, became the design of choice. This was possible because more powerful engines were now available. Lindbergh's monoplane measured 27 feet, 8 inches in length, and it had a wing span of 46 feet, with a total wing area of 319 square feet. Seated in the wicker pilot's seat, Lindbergh's only forward view during the New York-to-Paris flight would be through a telescope because of extra fuel tanks needed for the long transoceanic crossing placed above the instrument panel. In fact, the plane was really "a flying fuel tank," capable of holding 450 gallons of fuel in its fuselage and wings.[28]

THE *VOYAGER*: ANOTHER FLYING FUEL TANK

- Library research, social studies, language arts, math

- General

Some of your students will remember the feat of Dick Rutan and Jeana Yeager who, in December 1986, made the first nonstop flight around the world (24,986.727 miles) in the *Voyager*, which is now on display, along with the *Spirit of St. Louis*, at the National Air and Space Museum. The trip took two-hundred-sixteen hours, three minutes, and forty-four seconds.[29] Like Lindbergh's plane, the *Voyager* was a flying fuel tank. The aircraft had an extraordinarily long wingspan because the wings were full of fuel and, through their huge surface area, provided superior lift. Have students do some research about the flight, using the *Reader's Guide to Periodical Literature* (the flight occurred December 14-23, 1986) and other reference tools. Students can learn about the flyers' cramped quarters and bodily positions (reminiscent of the Wrights' in their *Flyer*), the plane's speed (much like Lindbergh's when he crossed the Atlantic in 1927), and fuel consumption for reports about the plane's route and math problems. For example, at takeoff the *Voyager* had 7,011.5 pounds of fuel, equaling 72.3 percent of its gross weight. What was the plane's total weight? What would the plane weigh emptied of fuel? If the plane had only 106 pounds of fuel when it landed, how much fuel did it use?[30] A readable and well-illustrated book that includes the *Voyager*'s flight is Don Berliner's *Distance Flights*, which, though it is in the juvenile section of the library, is appropriate for adults interested in learning the highpoints of information and seeing some great pictures.

Lindbergh's Records

On May 10, 1927, Lindbergh flew the new aircraft, which he named the *Spirit of St. Louis*, nonstop from San Diego to St. Louis in fourteen hours and twenty-five minutes, a new record. The next morning he flew to Curtiss Field in New York, establishing yet another record: twenty-one hours and twenty minutes total in-flight time from San Diego to New York. He had made the coast-to-coast flight considerably faster than the ill-fated, ever-crashing Cal Rodgers, but considerably slower than what we are accustomed to today.

Many well-known aviators, including Richard Byrd, were vying for the Oertig Prize. After waiting several days for bad weather to clear, Lindbergh had his plane towed from Curtiss to Roosevelt Field (since converted into a shopping mall) in Long Island, New York, where he would have a longer, smoother runway for takeoff. Finally, at dawn on May 20, 1927, when the weather over the Atlantic had improved, Lindbergh prepared to take off from a rain-soaked, foggy Roosevelt Field.

Lindbergh was facing a number of obstacles. Dead tired from not having slept the night before, Lindbergh was flying a plane that was not only heavily overloaded because of the extra fuel it required for the ocean crossing, but also drenched from the rain; the dampness of the wings' surfaces added weight and reduced lift. Up ahead, at the misty end of the runway, stood a maze of telephone wires Lindbergh would have to clear at takeoff. As Lindbergh wrote in his autobiography, *The Spirit of St. Louis*, about the treacherous takeoff, "The wrong [decision] means a crash—probably in flames."[31] He was not exaggerating; the plane was "a flying fuel tank." Making two futile attempts to takeoff, he finally succeeded on the third after letting "the wheels touch [the ground] once more—lightly, a last bow to earth, a gesture of humility before it."[32] He was off and crossing the ocean, sometimes at an altitude as low as 10 feet and sometimes as high as 10,000 feet, with neither radio nor parachute.

TEACHING ABOUT THE WEATHER AND TYPES OF CLOUDS

- Science (weather), math, language arts, and art

- General

Lindbergh was delayed in New York before his flight because of bad weather (rain) over the Atlantic Ocean. For beginning and intermediate students, use aviation to teach *meteorology*, the study of weather and weather conditions. What is temperature? What instrument do we use to determine temperature? How do we read that instrument? How does the instrument work? What is Fahrenheit? Celsius (Centigrade)? From where are those words derived? If it is X number of degrees Fahrenheit in the morning and Y number of degrees Fahrenheit in the afternoon, what is the difference between X and Y? How would you convert a Fahrenheit temperature to Celsius or Centigrade (the conversion formula is in the Aerospace Magnet below under advanced activities) and vice versa? What is humidity? What instrument do we use to determine humidity? What is wind velocity? What is velocity? What types of clouds exist? What does each tell us about weather? How much rain has fallen? How much snow? How do we measure these quantities? The class can make wind vanes to determine wind direction; the instructions for doing so are in the next Aerospace Magnet.

Have students keep in the classroom a daily weather chart (see figure 3.14 for a sample chart). Each day a student or a group of students can fill in the chart based on reading a portable thermometer in the schoolyard during recess, looking at the weather and the clouds in the sky, and observing a wind vane. Students also can discuss the weather in terms of "good days for flying."

Conditions ↓	← Monday	— Tuesday	Days Wednesday	— Thursday	→ Friday
temperature	64°	58°	54°	69°	60°
sunny	✕			✕	
cloudy		✕	✕		✕
snow					
rain					✕
windy		✕	✕	✕	
wind direction		E	SE	SE	

Fig. 3.14. Sample weather chart.

For advanced students, discuss Charles's law (for a gas held at a fixed temperature, the quotient of volume and temperature is constant) in relation to a weather (air) thermometer; do problems related to Fahrenheit to Celsius (Centigrade) proportions (5/9 = C/F-32); discuss temperature changes with altitude, causes of clouds, causes of weather, dew point temperatures, air movement and pressure (types of barometers), and the influence of atmospheric conditions on airplane functioning (e.g., the effect of "thin air" on takeoff and landing, etc.).

Among the many available teaching aids for weather are the following at the beginning and intermediate levels: Beech's *Aviation for the Elementary Level*; Housel and Housel's *Come Fly with Me!* from the Michigan Aeronautics Commission; and the FAA's *Safety in the Air*. Addresses for requesting them are in the appendix. Films about weather and its causes are available from the *Encyclopaedia Britannica*.

MAKING A WIND VANE

- Science (weather)

- Beginning and intermediate

One weather-measuring instrument students can easily make is a wind vane, which is used for determining wind direction. Introduce this activity by discussing the importance of wind direction as it relates to flying a plane; that is, a plane ideally takes off and lands toward the direction from which the wind is blowing. (Taking off into the wind is discussed early in chapter 4; you may wish to look ahead at the section entitled "Airspeed versus Ground Speed.")

Materials: For each student: straw, straight pin, pencil, tagboard, 12" ruler, cardboard, clay, scissors. For class: one electric fan.

Procedure:
1. Cut tagboard or index cards into 2"x2" squares and 3"x4" rectangles.

2. Cut cardboard into 5"x5" squares.

3. Cut out a pointer (from the 2"x2" squares) and a tail (from the 3"x4" rectangles).

4. Flatten the ends of the straw and staple the pointer and tail to these ends, making an arrow design.

5. Place a small lump of clay in the center of the 5"x5" piece of cardboard and stand a pencil point securely upright into the piece of clay.

6. After determining the center of gravity for the straw, push the pin through the straw and then firmly into the eraser. The straw should move (spin) freely.

Have students observe the movement of the weather vane with an electric fan as the wind source.

Result: The pointer of the straw will face the direction from which the wind is blowing. Students can enjoy this activity daily by recording the wind direction using their wind vanes.

SIMULATE LINDBERGH'S FLIGHT!

- Library research, math, art, social studies

- Beginning and intermediate

Using Lindbergh's autobiography, *The Spirit of St. Louis*, about his first transoceanic flight from New York to Paris, the class can build a mock-up of the plane's cockpit, complete with wicker chair (wicker was chosen because it is light but sturdy), maps, instrument panel, brown-bag lunch, water canteen, flyer's cap, and goggles. Create a flight plan based on Lindbergh's and keep a flight log that includes such statistics as miles per hour traveled, longitude and latitude, and navigational directions of the flight, as well as impressions. What did Lindbergh see when? When was he tired? What was the weather like as he proceeded away from Roosevelt Field in Mineola, Long Island, New York and crossed the Atlantic, over Ireland, and on to Paris? Teachers interested in doing this type of activity for the Lindbergh flight or for any other famous flight will want to see the material about flight charts in the Smithsonian's booklet, *History of Flight for Students in Grades 4-12*, pp. 13-16, available from the Smithsonian at the address in the appendix.

Lindbergh Lands Near Paris

After flying 3,600 miles in just over thirty-three-and-a-half hours, Lindbergh landed safely at Le Bourget Airport outside Paris, which he found without a map: " 'It's a big airport,' " people had told him before his departure, " 'You can't miss it.' "[33] The ecstatic Parisians certainly found Lindbergh. When he landed, they jubilantly pulled the hero from his cabin door and carried him shoulder high. The Oertig Prize, for which he made this dangerous flight, was just one of numerous honors and rewards (including many that were financial) he would receive for being the first person to make a solo, nonstop crossing of the Atlantic by air. New York City threw him a ticker-tape parade down Broadway, just as it would for astronaut John Glenn thirty-five years later for being the first American to orbit the earth (see chapter 5). The U.S. government awarded Lindbergh the first peacetime Congressional Medal of Honor.

An international hero of superstar proportions, Lindbergh, flying the *Spirit of St. Louis*, visited various heads of states of foreign nations and also made a 22,350-mile nationwide tour of the United States. Speaking in seventy-two American cities, he promoted aviation and urged the construction of municipal airports. Lindbergh, the most famous person in the world of his day, was also American aviation's best supporter. His flight remains one of the greatest individual achievements of all time. Amid the space capsules and rockets, the shining *Spirit of St. Louis* continues to attract crowds of admirers in the National Air and Space Museum, where it hangs in a place of honor.

LINDBERGH'S LIFE

• Library research, language arts, art

• General

The library media specialist will be able to point students to many biographies of Lindbergh written for young readers. Intermediate and advanced students can read Lindbergh's *The Spirit of St. Louis*, as well as other books, and familiarize themselves with the record-setting trip and the plane itself. Younger students can draw pictures of the plane or big moments of the flight, including taking off and landing, flying low over Irish fishermen to get directions to France, etc. Some students might want to look for a commercially available model of the plane and build it for display in the classroom or library. (Ask the really ambitious researchers or puzzle-solvers in your class to find out what the letters "RYAN NYP" on the tail of the *Spirit of St. Louis* stand for [Ryan Airlines built the plane, and "NYP" means New York to Paris].)

Individual Endeavor Gives Way to Team Efforts

The Lindbergh flight, as the phrase suggests, is largely regarded as an individual accomplishment. Although Claude T. Ryan, who built the *Spirit of St. Louis*, has also been acknowledged and honored, people remember that Lindbergh made the flight solo in a small one-seater airplane. People regard Lindbergh as "the hero" of the event, and rightly so. In fact, up to the time of Lindbergh, much of the progress in aviation had been accomplished by individuals working alone: Cayley was designing gliders; Lilienthal was designing gliders and leaping off hillsides strapped to them; the Wrights were virtually ignored at Kitty Hawk, and later they kept their work secret because they feared others' infringing upon their ideas. Some of these early aviation researchers wrote about their work so their findings could be passed to the future. However, this research itself was individually based, and the contributions of individuals like Cayley, Lilienthal, the two Montgolfier brothers, the two Wrights, Glenn Curtiss, and Lindbergh, deserve to be remembered.

Near the end of the first third of the twentieth century, aircraft became more complicated, aviation technology more profound, and aeronautical research more rapid than it had ever been. This is why, although we will still celebrate certain individuals as heroes, the whole world of aviation now emphasizes teamwork and team efforts. As C. D. B. Bryan observes: "As each new plateau ... was crossed by the individual or individuals in each machine, the flight technology demanded less and less of the individual and more and more the effort of groups, of teams of scientist-engineers, test-pilot mechanics, astronaut-scholars, physicists, and theoreticians."[34]

Commercial Aviation between the World Wars:
Airmail

When Lindbergh decided to go for the Oertig Prize, he was an airmail pilot for a private aviation company. Airmail was also flying under congressional auspices as early as 1918, with army pilots doing the flying. Other than the manufacturing of airplanes, carrying mail by air marks the first real combination of commercialism and aviation. Congress's passing the Kelly Act in 1925 permitted the U.S. Post Office to offer lucrative contracts for airmail carriers; thus, the Post Office encouraged big business to use airplanes during peacetime in the normal workaday world. For some good photos of early airmail service, see Ivan Rendall's *Reaching for the Skies*, pp. 136-37; the book also includes great photos of famous aviators and aircraft and a readable text written to complement a British television series of the same title.

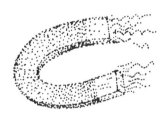

AIRMAIL

- Language arts, social studies, art

- Beginning and intermediate

Are any of your students stamp collectors? If so, ask if they have any airmail stamps they could show the class. Students also can design their own airmail stamps depicting important events in aviation history.

General Aviation

In addition to sending mail by air, Americans—largely inspired by Lindbergh's 1927 flight—became enthusiastic about air travel. Pilot license applications jumped from 1,000 to 5,500 within a year of the Lindbergh milestone. Responding to the growing number of pilots' desires to have small, private aircraft, three men formed a company in Wichita, Kansas in 1925 to build small, light recreational and private planes. These men were Lloyd Stearman, Clyde Cessna, and Walter Beech. They eventually parted to form their own companies. In 1929 G. C. Taylor and William T. Piper formed another company to produce light private airplanes. Piper Cubs, Cessna, and Beechcraft planes are familiar to *general aviation*, flying that is neither commercial nor military, such as in private and company planes.

Both Beech and Cessna have information packets and teaching guides about aviation, some free and some at a low cost, that are available to teachers. You can write to them for information on titles and costs at the addresses given in the appendix. The FAA has a booklet about careers in general aviation, *Take Off for Opportunities: Student Information Guide*; write to the FAA at the addresses in the appendix.

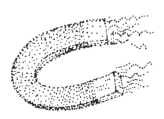

MAP

- Social studies

- General

Beech and Cessna are both in Wichita, Kansas, which has been the light aircraft capital of America since the industry began in the 1920s. Have the students find Wichita, Kansas on their maps.

GENERAL AVIATION

- Library research, language arts, art, oral communication

- General

Learn more about private airplanes and general aviation. Have students find pictures of and information about (speed, size, weight, etc.) Piper Cubs, Cessna, Learjets, and Beechcraft private planes. Students can draw the planes and write short reports about them. Are there any private pilots locally—working for industry or flying for sport? Invite a pilot of a private airplane to class. Have the class write a letter inviting him or her. Interview the pilot in class. Have each student compose and send a thank-you note after the visit. Ask students to find out about securing a pilot's license. The CAP's "Falcon Force" teaching kit includes a packet on general aviation (see the CAP's address in the appendix to request one).

American Commercial Air Travel Begins

To carry civilians who wanted to travel by, but not pilot, a plane, Henry Ford, of automobile fame, created a committee in the mid-1920s to develop a passenger-carrying airplane. The committee designed the Ford *Tri-Motor* (also known as the *Tin Goose*), a tough-looking, all-metal monoplane, almost 50 feet long, with three Wright Whirlwind engines, each driving a propeller, and a corrugated metal skin, which made the wings, spanning 74 feet, look especially thick and durable. This sturdy appearance, along with the familiar Ford name, encouraged potential passengers. Like Lindbergh's *Spirit of St. Louis*, the Ford *Tri-Motor* had wicker seats for its fourteen passengers and could fly as fast as 130 miles per hour. On August 2, 1926, it inaugurated civilian commercial air travel in the United States. A new phase in popular transportation began. For a full first-person account of flying as a passenger in a Ford *Tri-Motor*, see Bryan's *National Air and Space Museum*, pp. 103-5, quoting Ernest K. Gann, *Ernest K. Gann's Flying Circus*.

The Beginnings of the FAA

In the same year as the Ford *Tri-Motor*'s maiden flight, Congress passed the Air Commerce Act, which created the aeronautics branch in what was then called the Department of Commerce (currently the Department of Transportation). The branch's main objectives were to promote and regulate the safety and growth of civil aviation. A series of subsequent congressional acts responded over the years to the growing popularity of aviation after Lindbergh's flight and to the huge surge in civil air traffic and the increasing sophistication of aircraft during and after World War II (1939-1945). Years of legislation culminated in 1967 with the creation of the Federal Aviation Administration (FAA), which became part of the Department of Transportation. The FAA's responsibility continues to be mainly what the aeronautics branch's had been in 1926: to ensure the safety and regulate the growth of civil aviation.

THE FAA

* Library research, social studies, careers

* General

Students can learn more about the FAA, including careers available with it. A good first source is the booklet produced by and available from the FAA simply called *Federal Aviation Administration, Department of Transportation*, which includes sections on "Air-Traffic Control," "Aircraft and Airmen Certification," "Airport Aid and Certification," "Protecting the Environment," and "Civil Aviation Security Program." The FAA also has informative pamphlets in a series called Aviation Careers, which includes *Airline Careers, Airport Careers, Aviation Maintenance, Aircraft Manufacturing Occupations*, and *Pilots and Flight Engineers* (see the FAA's addresses in the appendix). Students may also be encouraged to check newspapers and magazines for news articles about the FAA. Invite someone from the local airport—an air traffic controller, a pilot, a mechanic, a crash investigator, a safety inspector—to talk about aviation careers. Have the class write the person thank-you notes after the visit. The following works deal with aviation careers: the Civil Air Patrol's *Fun in Flight: Exploring Careers in the Aerospace World*; two books by Kimball Scribner, *Your Future in Aviation Careers in the Air* and *Your Future in Aviation Careers on the Ground*; Boeing Aircraft's *Guide to Aerospace Occupations*; Grumman Aerospace's *Your Future at Grumman*; Martin Marietta's *Astronautics Group Careers*; and a number of booklets (e.g., *Women in Aviation and Space* [Flowers]; *Careers in Airway Science*) from this special FAA address: Superintendent of Documents, Retail Distribution Division, Consigned Branch, 8610 Cherry Lane, Laurel, MD 20707. Also see the U.S. Department of Labor's *Workforce 2,000*, available at any library that is a federal depository.

Commercial Scheduled Airlines and Airline Routes

By 1929 aircraft construction and operation had become the country's most profitable investment, leading to the creation of forty-four *scheduled airlines*, which are airlines that arrive and depart at set times. Many of these airlines merged to form major transcontinental systems. For example, Transcontinental and Western Air merged to become the familiar TWA, TransWorld Airlines. By 1930 basic airline routes that are still in effect were created. In that year, a person could take a commercial flight across the United States: it took about forty-eight hours and cost about $352.[35] Three years later, in 1933, Boeing produced the first modern passenger airplane called the *B-247*: a dual-engine, all-metal, low-wing monoplane with *retractable* (able to be drawn into or against the airplane) landing gear that could carry ten passengers and 400 pounds of mail and fly at 189 miles per hour, thus making possible a coast-to-coast flight (with fueling stops) in a single day.

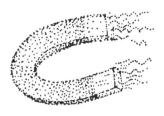

VISIT THE LOCAL AIRPORT

• Social studies, science, field trip

• General (especially beginning, intermediate)

Arrange with the public affairs officer of your local airport for a class field trip there. You can learn about the layout, the control tower, etc. Request an FAA flight plan and study it. Airport visit activities are outlined for students in Housel and Housel's *Come Fly with Me!* (pp. 71-72); Iris Harris's (through the FAA) *Aviation and Space Curriculum Guide, K-3*, pp. 215-230, including instructions and cut-outs for making an airport diorama; and the FAA's *Teachers' Guide for Aviation Education (Grades 2-6)*, p. 3.5, which lists additional resources, such as the FAA's "An Airport Trip," AGA-300-94, for preparing students for an airport excursion. The library will also have materials on this activity.

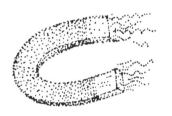

WHY ARE AIRLINES FAILING? HOW DO AIRLINES OPERATE?

• Social studies (economics), library research

• Advanced

Students can analyze past mergers and current failures of airline companies. Follow the stocks of some major commercial carriers and of aircraft builders. Students can also investigate how airlines operate; write for an organizational chart from any major airline. Address the airline's Public Affairs Office, care of the local major airport.

PLANNING A ROUTE

• Mathematics, social studies, art

• Intermediate and advanced

Any of your students who have traveled by plane are familiar with the airline carrier route maps included in the airline's magazine found in the seat pocket. The next time you or one of your students (or their parents) travel by plane, do what the airlines request: take the magazine with you! Then bring it to school and plot the routes shown on a big wall map using colored markers. Using the *Information Please Almanac*'s charts of "Distances between Cities," students can select points of origin and destinations. Find out the miles per hour that specific planes travel and calculate flying times. Information on various planes' average flying speeds is available from the comprehensive data tables in Matricardi's *The Concise History of Aviation* or from the definitive *Jane's All the World's Aircraft* (see bibliography). The classroom teacher and the school library media specialist can collaborate on this project, guiding students in their research. Write to the airlines and request flight maps. Compare their routes with yours.

The DC-3

As the popularity of civil aviation increased, Congress continued to pass legislation dealing with air safety and economics. Commercial airline carriers worked with airplane manufacturers to develop faster, safer, and more efficient aircraft. For example, American Airways contracted the Douglas Aircraft Company of Santa Monica, California, to build a fast, durable, maneuverable plane that could carry passengers in as near to total comfort as possible. This included seating for twenty passengers, which meant that the plane could turn a financial profit by carrying people only (no mail). The result was the Douglas *DC-3*, which C. D. B. Bryan calls the "single most important aircraft in the history of air transportation."[36] First taking to the skies in June 1936, the DC-3 cruised an average 180 miles per hour and was able to climb above *turbulence* (rapid changes in the wind's speed and direction, with up and down currents) to an altitude of 20,000 feet, covering 2,000 miles at 200 miles per hour. The DC-3s proved so popular that by 1939 almost every commercial airline in the world flew them. It was the most successful commercial passenger aircraft in the world, flying travelers until fall 1953. They were so durable and reliable that the U.S. Army flew them as C-47s in World War II, after which General Eisenhower, who commanded the allied invasion of Europe, credited the Allies' victory to the DC-3, along with the jeep, the 2½-ton truck, and the bulldozer.[37] Some are still flying in some parts of the world. Today a DC-3 hangs in the National Air and Space Museum (the heaviest aircraft suspended in the museum); just in front of it hangs a Ford *Tri-Motor*, the first American passenger plane.

INTERVIEWING VETERAN FLYERS

- Research, language arts, social studies, oral communication

- General

Do any of your students' great-grandparents or senior citizen friends or neighbors have memories of flying in a DC-3 or a B-247? If they do, have the class compose a letter inviting them to class. When they come, ask them questions about the flight. How long did it take? Where did they travel? How does the plane's interior compare with planes in which we travel today? Was it roomy? Crowded? Comfortable? What was the check-in procedure like? Did they have to go through a security checkpoint as we do today? Did they have meals on the plane? Did the meals taste good? Were the meals hot? Could they take carry-on baggage? Encourage the students to ask open-ended questions that produce discussion. After the class visit(s), each student should compose and send a thank-you note to the visitor(s).

Contributions of Women and Minorities to Aviation's Early Years

Rivaling Lindbergh in popularity in the 1930s was the female pioneer aviator and one-time teacher, Amelia Earhart (1898-1937). She made the first solo transAtlantic flight by a woman in 1932. In 1935 Earhart piloted a solo flight — and the first flight ever — from Hawaii to California, which is a longer distance than from the United States to Europe. Such flights, as well as Earhart's active involvement with such groups as the "Ninety-Nines," an international organization of women pilots, greatly promoted the public's — and women's — interest in flight. After making a series of successful and record-breaking flights that established her as an international aviation celebrity, Earhart attempted to fly around the world in 1937. After going over two-thirds of the distance, Earhart's plane was apparently lost somewhere between New Guinea and Howland Island. No one knows precisely what happened. However, a recent Associated Press report (January 3, 1991) tells that a metal cabinet, such as navigators formerly used for carrying maps, was found on Gardner Island and could possibly be from Earhart's plane.[38] She was forty years old when she disappeared.

In addition to women flyers, black Americans began contributing to aviation during the 1930s. In 1939 Howard University created a civilian pilot training program. One of its founders was Charles "Chief" Anderson who, with another black flyer, Dr. Albert Forsythe, in 1934 flew from Miami, Florida, to the West Indies. This is now a familiar commercial route, but when Anderson and Forsythe flew it no person had ever flown it before. They did it with just a simple compass to guide them! Another great black flyer was Bessie Coleman, the first black woman to earn a pilot's license. She died in a crash at the age of twenty-seven, after devoting her short life to encouraging young black Americans to fly.

AMELIA EARHART

- Library research, language arts, social studies

- General

Have students explore the life and mysterious disappearance of Amelia Earhart. Have them make a map of her famous flights and trace her final flight as far as they can. Ask them to write reports about her and her flying career. Students may wish to read Earhart's short and touching poem, "Courage," which is reprinted in Blanche Jennings Thompson, *All the Silver Pennies*, p. 190. After reading it, they might be asked to write an essay interpreting the poem. You might also ask students to write poems about Earhart's courage or the courage of any aviator. Intermediate and advanced students may be interested in reading one or more books by Amelia Earhart: *Twenty Hours, Forty Minutes: Our Flight in the Friendship*; *The Fun of It: Random Records of My Own Flying and of Women in Aviation*; *Last Flight*; and *Letters from Amelia, 1901-1937*. Your library media specialist can point to many biographies of Earhart in the juvenile section appropriate for younger readers. Also for beginners, the Civil Air Patrol (CAP) offers a full activities teaching packet, including pictures for coloring, called simply "Amelia Earhart." This comes with the CAP's "Falcon Force" kit (see address in the appendix). This kit includes a map of Earhart's fatal, final flight.

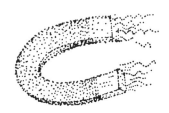

NOTABLE AVIATORS

- Library research, language arts, social studies

- Beginning and intermediate

Have students investigate other notable aviators during this period including James "Jimmy" Doolittle (1896-), a racing pilot and prominent figure in aviation, serving in both World War I and World War II; Wiley Post (1899-1935), an American pilot, who was killed along with Will Rogers in an air crash and who, with his navigator Harold Gatty, flew around the world in 1931 in eight days, fifteen hours, and fifty-one minutes and who, in 1933, repeated the feat solo; Jacqueline Cochran (1912-1980), who set more speed, altitude, and distance records than any other American pilot; and William J. Powell, one of the first black persons to become a licensed pilot. The CAP has an activities packet on General Doolittle (see address in the appendix).

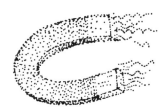

BROADWAY LIGHTS AT SCHOOL

- Music, drama, library research, art, language arts, oral communication

- Beginning and intermediate

Have students write a skit, play, or — with the collaboration of the music teacher — musical about a key figure or some key figures in aviation history. For example, consider a play called "Courage," using Earhart's own words from her poem and her books. Or a skit called "The Flying Brothers" about the Wrights, again using Orville and Wilbur's own words from the documents cited in the section dealing with the Wrights. Use costumes, props, and simple scenery. Perform the skit, play, or musical for other classes and parents. If the class does a play or musical, have students prepare an illustrated program. Videotape the production for your classroom archives.

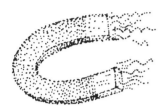

MAKING A TIMELINE

- Social studies, art

- General

Have the students create a timeline of aviation events from Sir George Cayley through the Wrights, World War I, and the "Golden Age of Flight," ending with Amelia Earhart. The timeline can include dates, names, a phrase or two explaining the person's or event's significance, and illustrations drawn by the students. A long roll of white shelving paper works well for this activity.

Timeline of Aviation:
From the Wrights to Amelia Earhart

December 17, 1903: At Kitty Hawk, North Carolina, Orville and Wilbur Wright become the first persons to pilot a heavier-than-air machine, the *Flyer,* which takes off under its own power and remains in controlled and sustained flight.

1904: Frenchman Robert Esnault-Pelterie builds a Wright-style glider and uses ailerons to replace the Wrights' wing-warping flight control technique.

1907: French aviator and inventor Louis Blériot builds and flies first powered monoplane.

1907: American aviation pioneer Glenn Curtiss and Alexander Graham Bell, inventor of the telephone, founded the Aerial Experiment Association. This organization was responsible for building the first American aircraft equipped with ailerons and the first seaplane to be flown in the United States.

1909: The Wright brothers build first Army airplane.

1909: Louis Blériot flies his XI monoplane across the English Channel from France to England. This flight marks the first time anyone has flown across a body of water, as well as the first flight from one country to another.

1911: The Short brothers of England build the world's first multiengine aircraft, the *Triple Twin.*

August 1911: Harriet Quimby, a magazine writer, becomes the first woman in the United States to receive a pilot's certificate and later (April 26, 1912) the first woman to fly solo across the English Channel.

1911: Calbraith P. Rodgers, flying the Wright EX *Vin Fiz,* makes the first American cross-country flight. Leaving September 17 from Long Island, Rodgers arrives in Pasadena, California, eighty-four days later, landing more than eighty times. Total in-flight time was eighty-two hours two minutes.

1914-1918: The need for better airplanes during World War I causes great improvements in terms of speed and safety for the airplane. Not a single American-designed combat aircraft sees action during the war.

May, 1918: The United States begins airmail service between Washington D.C. and New York City, soon expanding throughout the country.

1922: Lieutenant James Doolittle crosses the United States in one day, making only one fuel stop at San Antonio on his Florida to California route.

May 2-3, 1923: Lieutenants Oakley G. Kelly and John A. Macready make the first nonstop flight from the Atlantic to the Pacific, flying across the United States in their *Fokker* T-2.

1924: The first flights to circle the earth completely are made by American army service planes, the *Chicago* and the *New Orleans* (two of the original four army service planes to undertake this flight).

1926: American Lieutenant-Commander Richard Byrd makes first flight over North Pole.

1927: Charles Lindbergh makes the first solo transAtlantic flight from New York to Paris in the *Spirit of St. Louis.* Leaving New York on May 20, he arrives 33 hours and 30 minutes later in Paris, France.

May 20-21, 1932: Amelia Earhart becomes the first woman to fly across the Atlantic Ocean alone in her Lockheed 5-B *Vega.*

1933: Boeing brings out first modern commercial airliner, the B-247.

May 8, 1935: Amelia Earhart becomes the first person to make a nonstop solo flight from Oakland, California, to Honolulu, Hawaii.

May 20-July 1, 1937: Amelia Earhart attempts to fly around the world; lost in the Pacific.

Notes

[1]Benjamin Franklin, *The Papers of Benjamin Franklin*, edited by Leonard W. Labaree (New Haven: Yale University Press, 1961), 4: 367.

[2]All the poetical selections about kites were found under that subject heading in the very valuable work by Dorothy Frizzell Smith and Eva L. Andrews, *Subject Index to Poetry for Children and Young People, 1957-1975* (Chicago: American Library Association, 1977), 518.

[3]George Harvard Gibbs-Smith, *Aviation: An Historical Survey from Its Origins to the End of World War II*, 2d ed. (London: Her Majesty's Stationery Office, 1985), 24.

[4]Walter J. Boyne, *The Smithsonian Book of Flight for Young People* (New York: Collier Macmillan, 1988), 14.

[5]Don Berliner, *Before the Wright Brothers* (Minneapolis: Lerner Publications, 1990), 14.

[6]John W. R. Taylor and Kenneth Munson, *History of Aviation* (London: Octopus Books, 1975), 34.

[7]Taylor and Munson, *History of Aviation*, 34.

[8]Gibbs-Smith, *Aviation*, 3.

[9]Taylor and Munson, *History of Aviation*, 36.

[10]Harry Combs with Martin Caidin, *Kill Devil Hill: Discovering the Secret of the Wright Brothers* (Englewood, Colo.: TernStyle Press, 1979), 54.

[11]Combs, *Kill Devil Hill*, 37-38; Tom D. Crouch, "Engineers and the Airplane," in *The Wright Brothers: Heirs of Prometheus*, ed. Richard P. Hallion (Washington, D.C.: National Air and Space Museum, 1978), 13-14, 131.

[12]Combs, *Kill Devil Hill*, 348; Lyranne Wescott and Paula Degen, *Wind and Sand: The Story of the Wright Brothers at Kitty Hawk* (New York: Harry N. Abrams, 1983), 106-45.

[13]Orville Wright, *How We Made the First Flight* (Washington, D.C.: U.S. Government Printing Office, 1988), 5.

[14]Jason Hook, *The Wright Brothers* (New York: Bookwright Press, 1989), 11.

[15]Gibbs-Smith, *Aviation*, 99.

[16]Wright, *First Flight*, 7.

[17]Gibbs-Smith, *Aviation*, 100; Wescott and Degen, 133, with a photo of Wilbur in the damaged *Flyer*, 134-35.

[18]Wright, *First Flight*, 14.

[19]Combs, *Kill Devil Hill*, 332-33; Roger E. Bilstein, "The Airplane, the Wrights, and the American Public," in *The Wright Brothers: Heirs of Prometheus*, ed. Richard Hallion (Washington, D.C.: National Air and Space Museum, 1978), 42-44.

[20]Combs, *Kill Devil Hill*, 332-33; advanced students with access to the *New York Times* on microfilm might be intrigued to follow the Wrights' legal battles reported in that newspaper, see *New York Times* of 1910, Feb. 12, 1:6; Feb. 18, 16:3; Feb. 20, pt. 3, 5:5; Feb. 25, 8:2; Feb. 27, 8:5; March 5, 5:3.

[21]Wright, *First Flight*, verso of front cover.

[22]Air Force ROTC, *Aerospace Science: History of Air Power* (Maxwell Air Force Base, Ala.: Air University Press, 1986), 1-40. See also Gibbs-Smith, *Aviation*, 155-56.

[23]Air Force ROTC, *Aerospace Science*, 1-39.

[24]Gibbs-Smith, *Aviation*, 172; *Information Please Almanac*, 44th ed. (Boston: Houghton Mifflin, 1991), 355.

[25]Gibbs-Smith, *Aviation*, 174.

[26]Air Force ROTC, *Aerospace Science*, 1-50.

[27]Wilbur Wassaw, interview with author, Colorado Springs, Colo., 24 December 1990.

[28]Taylor and Munson, *History of Aviation*, 149.

[29]Data come from *Information Please Almanac, Atlas and Yearbook*, 44th ed. (Boston: Houghton Mifflin, 1991), 358.

[30]Data on the fuel and weight come from C. D. B. Bryan, *The National Air and Space Museum*, 2d ed. (New York: Harry N. Abrams, 1988), 138.

[31]Charles Lindbergh, *The Spirit of St. Louis* (New York: Scribners, 1953), 186.

[32]Lindbergh, *Spirit of St. Louis*, 187.

[33]Lindbergh, *Spirit of St. Louis*, 487.

[34]Bryan, *Air and Space Museum*, 69.

[35]Air Force ROTC, *Aerospace Science*, 2-12.

[36]Bryan, *Air and Space Museum*, 111.

[37]Ivan Rendall, *Reaching for the Skies* (New York: Orion Books, 1989), 219.

[38]Associated Press, "Crash Site Clues Point to Earhart," *Colorado Springs Gazette Telegraph*, 4 Jan. 1991, p. A-8, col. 1.

Bibliography

Abrams, Lawrence F. *Throw It Out of Sight! Building and Flying a Hand-Launched Glider*. Minneapolis, Minn.: Dillon Press, 1984.

Air Force ROTC. *Aerospace Science: History of Air Power*. Maxwell Air Force Base, Ala.: Air University Press, 1986.

Associated Press. "Crash Site Clues Point to Earhart." *Colorado Springs Gazette Telegraph*. 4 Jan. 1991, p. A-8, col. 1.

Beechcraft Aviation. *Aviation for the Elementary Level*. Wichita, Kansas: Beech Aircraft Corp., 1989. Available from Beech Aircraft (address in appendix).

Berliner, Don. *Before the Wright Brothers*. Minneapolis, Minn.: Lerner Publications, 1990.

_____. *Distance Flights*. Minneapolis, Minn.: Lerner Publications, 1990.

Bishop, Richard W. *From Kite to Kitty Hawk*. New York: Thomas Y. Crowell, 1958.

Boeing Aircraft. *Guide to Aerospace Occupations*. n.p., n.d.

Boyne, Walter J. *The Smithsonian Book of Flight for Young People*. New York: Collier Macmillan, 1988.

Brewton, Sara, and John E. Brewton. *Sing a Song of Seasons*. New York: Macmillan, 1955.

Bryan, C. D. B. *The National Air and Space Museum*. 2d ed. New York: Harry N. Abrams, 1988.
  The current price is $65.

Churchill, E. Richard. *Instant Paper Airplanes*. New York: Sterling Publishing, 1988.

Civil Air Patrol. "Falcon Force: An Aerospace Education Kit for Grades 4-6." Maxwell Air Force Base, Ala.:
  Civil Air Patrol, n.d.
  Available from the CAP and filled with teaching packets; cost about $40. See appendix for CAP's address.

_____. *Fun in Flight: Exploring Careers in the Aerospace World*. Maxwell Air Force Base, Ala.: Civil Air
  Patrol, 1988.
  Activities, pictures, worksheets for beginning students.

Cole, William, ed. *Oh, What Nonsense!* New York: Viking, 1966.

Combs, Harry, with Martin Caidin. *Kill Devil Hill: Discovering the Secret of the Wright Brothers*. Englewood,
  Colo.: TernStyle Press, 1979.

Earhart, Amelia. *The Fun of It: Random Records of My Own Flying and of Women in Aviation*. New York:
  G. P. Putnam's Sons, 1932. Reprint 1975.

_____. *Last Flight*. Edited by George Palmer Putnam. New York: Orion Books, 1937.

_____. *Letters from Amelia, 1901-1937*. Edited by Jean L. Backus. Boston: Beacon Press, 1982.

_____. *Twenty Hours, Forty Minutes: Our Flight in Friendship*. New York: G. P. Putnam's Sons, 1928.
  Reprint 1979.

Flowers, Sandra H. *Women in Aviation and Space*. Washington, D.C.: U.S. Government Printing Office,
  1990.
  Includes addresses and bibliography. Write to FAA for a copy.

Fowler, H. Waller, Jr. *Kites: A Practical Guide to Kite Making and Flying*. New York: Ronald Press, 1953.

Franklin, Benjamin. *Autobiography*. New York: Random House, 1990.
  This is one of several reasonably priced paperback editions currently available.

_____. *Autobiography and Other Writings*. New York: Bantam, 1982.
  This is another reasonably priced paperback.

_____. *The Papers of Benjamin Franklin*. Edited by Leonard W. Labaree (vols. 1-14) and W. B. Willcox (vols.
  15-25). New Haven: Yale University Press, 1961.

Gann, Ernest K. *Ernest K. Gann's Flying Circus*. New York: Macmillan, 1974.

Gibbs-Smith, George Harvard. *Aviation: An Historical Survey from Its Origins to the End of World War II*. 2d
  ed. London: Her Majesty's Stationery Office, 1985.

Glines, Carroll. *The Wright Brothers: Pioneers of Power Flight*. New York: Franklin Watts, 1968.

Grumman Aerospace. *Your Future at Grumman*. n.p., n.d.

Hallion, Richard P. *The Wright Brothers: Heirs of Prometheus*. Washington, D.C.: National Air and Space Museum, 1978.
Essays by Wright scholars; great photos of Wrights.

Halperin, Richard P. *Physical Science*. New York: Barnes and Noble, 1983.

Harris, Iris, and the Alabama State Department of Education. *Aviation and Space Curriculum Guide, K-3*. Washington, D.C.: Department of Transportation, FAA, 1990.
Contact the FAA for a copy; see addresses in appendix.

Hart, Clive. *Kites: An Historical Survey*. New York: Frederick A. Praeger, 1968.

Hook, Jason. *The Wright Brothers*. New York: Bookwright Press, 1989.

Housel, David C., and Doreen K. M. Housel. *Come Fly with Me: Exploring K-6 through Aviation/Aerospace Concepts*. Lansing, Mich.: Michigan Aeronautics Commission, 1983.

Information Please Almanac, Atlas, and Yearbook. Boston: Houghton Mifflin, 1991.
The cost is $6.95.

Jacobs, Leland Blair, ed. *Poetry for Autumn*. Champaign, Ill.: Garrard, 1968.

Johnston, William B., et al. *Workforce 2000: Work and Workers for the Twenty-first Century*. Indianapolis, Ind.: Hudson Institute, 1987. (Prepared for the U.S. Department of Labor).

Kautmann, John. *Flying Hand-Launched Gliders*. New York: William Morrow, 1974.

Kawami, David. *Cut and Make Space Shuttles*. New York: Dover Publications, n.d.
A good buy at $2.95; see address in appendix.

Kelly, Fred C. *Miracle at Kitty Hawk*. New York: Farrar, Straus, and Young, 1951.

Lambert, Mark, Kenneth Munson, and Michael J. H. Taylor. *Jane's All the World's Aircraft*. 81st ed. Surrey, England: Jane's Information Group, 1990.

Lask, Thomas, ed. *The New York Times Book of Verse*. New York: Macmillan, 1970.

Lawson, Robert. *Ben and Me; A New and Astonishing Life of Ben Franklin As Written by His Good Mouse, Amos*. Boston: Little, Brown, 1939.

Levey, Judith S., and Agnes Greenhall. *The Concise Columbia Encyclopedia*. New York: Columbia University Press, 1983.

Lindbergh, Charles. *The Spirit of St. Louis*. New York: Scribners, 1953.

Martin Marietta. *Astronautics Group Careers*. n.p., 1989.

Matricardi, Paolo. *The Concise History of Aviation*. New York: Crescent Books, 1985.

Mitton, Bruce H. *Kites, Kites, Kites: The Ups and Downs of Making and Flying Them*. New York: Drake Publishers, 1978.
Good, detailed instructions for kite making.

Morrison, Lillian, comp. *Sprints and Distances: Sports in Poetry and the Poetry in Sport*. New York: Crowell, 1965.

National Air and Space Museum and National Aeronautics and Space Administration. *Discovery* (n.p., n.d.).
Contact the Smithsonian's National Air and Space Museum for a copy; see appendix for address.

Ninomiya, Yasuaki. *White Wings*. Redmond, Wash. and Osaka, Japan: AG Industries, 1988.
A kit and accompanying book for making rather sophisticated and very beautiful cardboard gliders, including the *Voyager*, the *Amelia* (in honor of Earhart), and many others; for advanced students and teachers.

Rendall, Ivan. *Reaching for the Skies*. New York: Orion Books, 1989.
Written to accompany a British television series; great photos and very readable.

Scribner, Kimball. *Your Future in Aviation Careers in the Air*. New York: Richards Rosen Press, 1979.

_____. *Your Future in Aviation Careers on the Ground*. New York: Richards Rosen Press, 1979.

Shiffert, Edith, and Yuki Sawa, trans. *Anthology of Modern Japanese Poetry*. Rutland, Vt.: Tuttle, 1972.

Simon, Seymour. *The Paper Airplane Book*. New York: The Viking Press, 1971.

Slade, Richard. *Paper Airplanes*. New York: St. Martin's Press, 1970.

Smith, Dorothy B. Frizzell, and Eva L. Andrews, comps. *Subject Index to Poetry for Children and Young People, 1957-1975*. Chicago: American Library Association, 1977.

Smithsonian Institution. *History of Flight for Students in Grades 4-12*. Washington, D.C.: National Air and Space Museum, 1988.
Lots of activities; contact the museum at address in appendix.

Taylor, John W., and Kenneth Munson. *History of Aviation*. London: Octopus Books, 1975.
Many details; great photos.

Thompson, Blanche Jennings. *All the Silver Pennies*. New York: Macmillan, 1967.
Includes Amelia Earhart's poem, "Courage."

U.S. Department of Transportation, Federal Aviation Administration. *Aviation Science Activities for Elementary Grades*. Washington, D.C.: U.S. Government Printing Office, 1983.
Available free from the FAA; see appendix for addresses.

_____. *Demonstration Aids for Aviation Education*. Washington, D.C.: U.S. Government Printing Office, 1987.
Available free from the FAA; see appendix for addresses.

_____. *Safety in the Air*. Washington, D.C.: U.S. Government Printing Office, 1983.
Available free from the FAA; see appendix for addresses.

_____. *Teachers' Guide for Aviation Education, for Use in Grades Two through Six*. Washington, D.C.: U.S. Government Printing, 1990.
Available free from the FAA; see appendix for addresses.

Wassaw, Wilbur. Interview with author. Colorado Springs, Colorado, 24 December 1990.

Wescott, Lyranne, and Paula Degen. *Wind and Sand: The Story of the Wright Brothers at Kitty Hawk*. New York: Harry N. Abrams, 1983.
Using the Wright's own words and numerous wonderful photographs, this book traces the Wright's flying from 1900 to 1903. Great photos.

Wright, Orville. *How We Made the First Flight*. Washington, D.C.: U.S. Government Printing Office, 1988.
Available from the FAA; see addresses in appendix. This is a beautifully illustrated booklet, providing primary source documents in the Wrights' own words.

Wright, Wilbur, and Orville Wright. *The Papers of Wilbur and Orville Wright*. 2 vols. Edited by Marvin W. McFarland. New York: McGraw-Hill, 1953.
Advanced students would enjoy seeing the Wright's correspondence with Octave Chanute included in this collection.

Yolen, Jane. *World on a String: The Story of Kites*. Cleveland and New York: World Publishing, 1968.

4

The World at War and Aviation in Revolution

The Golden Age of Flight gave way to the age of World War II, 1939-1945. Some say that this war was truly a war of air power. History gives as much credit to the builders—many of them women—who constructed the planes quickly and soundly at home as it gives to the pilots and crew who flew them in the European and Asian battlefronts. That this war would be decided by air power was forecast by Brigadier General William (Billy) Mitchell (1879-1936). A World War I veteran, Mitchell advocated the plane as the superior military weapon, particularly in waging *strategic warfare*, or striking at the enemy's military and industrial targets. He worked to convince the government to add funds to military aviation and to create a separate airborne military service. Unsuccessful in these endeavors, he aroused anger when he criticized the American naval base at Pearl Harbor, Hawaii, for being highly vulnerable to air attack. A little over five years after Mitchell's death, the Japanese air force proved that he was correct.

Meanwhile, Germany, under Adolph Hitler (1889-1945, dictator of Germany from 1933 to 1945), not only invaded its neighbors, but also built up its offensive air power by forming the *Luftwaffe* (meaning *air weapon*, the name of the German air force in World War II). These actions prompted President Franklin Roosevelt to call upon Congress in January 1939 to increase the Army Air Corps. Turmoil increased in Europe, with Germany and Italy pitted against the rest of the Continent. However, what brought the United States into war was Japan's devastating air attack on the Pearl Harbor Naval Base on December 7, 1941.

The Biggest Aircraft Buildup in History

When the United States entered World War II in December 1941, the country had fewer than 9,000 airplanes. With American men serving their country in a war fought on two fronts—European and Pacific (or Asian)—American women emerged from the home to work in factories. Working alongside American men, "Rosie the Riveter," as the female factory worker came to be known, helped produce 300,000 aircraft during the war years. A Seattle factory built the Boeing B-17 *Flying Fortress*, 75 feet long with four engines and a 1,420-square-foot wing area, built to carry a ten-person crew trained to drop 6,000 pounds of bombs. The factory turned out eighty-eight planes a week in March 1944. Likewise, America's allies, Russia and Great Britain, were rapidly producing planes. The three nations built 500,000 airplanes between 1940 and 1945—the first and biggest buildup of military aircraft in history. This massive increase in the quantity of airplanes was matched by one in quality. During the war the aviation world also witnessed the perfection of rotorcraft (the helicopter) and the revolutionary jet engine.

WOMEN IN THE WORK FORCE

- Library research, social studies, language arts

- Intermediate and advanced

Do a study with your class on women in the work force, beginning with Rosie the Riveter. How did World War II change the role and perception of women in American society? See if the local public library has magazines like *Life* and *Look* from the 1940s through the 1970s in its bound periodicals collection. What do you learn about this subject from these examples of popular culture? Notice the change from the 1940s to the 1950s, when women were back in the home, until the women's movement of the 1970s. Ask students to do written or oral reports about women in the work force and women's changing roles. Invite to the class some women who work in what were once considered "male" occupations (pilot, police officer, military officer, physicist, college professor, surgeon). What do they have to say about being women in their particular jobs? Advanced students may be interested in reading Beverly Rubik's "Science, A Feminine Perspective" in *Creation*.[1] Dr. Rubik, director of the Center for Frontier Sciences at Temple University in Philadelphia, discusses the changes that women are making in science, which, she says, has traditionally been male based.

Airspeed versus Ground Speed

Planes with more modern designs—streamlined, slender fuselages and elliptical-shaped wings—increased speed and lift. For example, in 1939 a single-engine fighter such as the British *Spitfire*, powered by a 1,000-horsepower Rolls Royce engine, traveled 350 miles per hour; by 1945, *Spitfires* flew at 450 miles per hour. Ceiling heights of fighters went as high as 35,000 to 40,000 feet; likewise, these planes could climb 5,000 feet per minute.[2] Unlike the World War I pilots, flyers now were in completely enclosed fuselages that were heavily armed with machine guns, cannons, and, later, rockets.

A discussion of speed must consider the difference between *airspeed* and *ground speed* and their relation to takeoff. As the names suggest, ground speed means the actual speed of the plane in relation to the ground; airspeed means the speed of the plane in relation to the air. They relate to airplanes in the same way they relate to kite flying.

For example, if you are running with your kite in nonwindy, motionless air, at 4 miles per hour, the kite's ground speed is 4 miles per hour because that is the speed you are running along the ground. Suddenly, a little wind picks up, also blowing at 4 miles per hour. The kite is still moving at a ground speed of 4 miles per hour because you are still running at that rate. However, the windy air, blowing at 4 miles per hour, is now passing the kite at 8 miles per hour (your running speed plus the air's speed as it blows past the kite). You are now out of breath, so you stop running and stand still for a few minutes to enjoy the breeze and feel a little drag on the kite string. The kite's ground speed is now zero because your ground speed is zero (standing still). However, the kite is still affected by the 4-mile-per-hour breeze, so its airspeed is now 4 miles per hour. A plane flying from point A to point B is described in terms of its ground speed, but the airspeed supplies the lift and drag.

Now consider a plane as it taxies down the runway, turned towards the direction from which the wind is blowing (into the wind), which gives the plane some airspeed. The pilot opens the *throttle* (the valve that regulates the amount of fuel vapor entering an internal combustion engine), and the plane goes faster and faster down the runway. Going into the wind, the plane picks up ground speed as well as airspeed and then reaches its *flying speed*, whereupon the lifting force working on the wings helps the plane lift up from the ground as the pilot slightly increases the *angle of attack* (see chapter 3). The pilot controls the plane so that its nose is lifted higher and the plane climbs higher. That is how the plane gets off the ground.

How does the plane fly at an even level? Lift depends on the angle of attack and the speed. When the pilot increases the plane's speed, but keeps the angle of attack steady, the plane goes higher. When the pilot decreases the plane's speed, but keeps the angle of attack steady, the plane loses altitude. In the first instance, when increasing speed, the pilot needs to lower the plane's nose a little to achieve even, level flying. In the second instance, when decreasing speed, the pilot must increase the angle of attack by pulling the plane's nose up a little to achieve level flight. In both cases, adjusting the plane's angle of attack according to the plane's speed will keep the lift and weight equal and the plane will fly evenly.

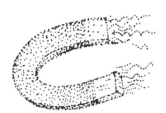

PLANE SPEED, ALTITUDE, AND ANGLE OF ATTACK

- Science

- General

Demonstrate to the class the previous explanation of how a plane takes off (into the wind) and achieves a level flight by using a model plane with movable control surfaces, such as that available from the Cessna Aircraft Company for just a few dollars (see address for Cessna in appendix).

Landing the Airplane

Landing the airplane requires great pilot skill. To slow the plane down, the pilot progressively cuts the engines' power and heads into the wind, if possible. The pilot releases the landing gear, which has been tucked under the plane since takeoff, and closes the throttle. Speed, and thus thrust, is reduced, but lift is maintained by slightly raising the plane's nose, thereby increasing the angle of attack, which keeps the plane's lift equal to its weight—and keeps the plane flying. Doing the landing maneuvers, the pilot uses controls to increase the wings' curves by moving the wings' *flaps* out and down (see figure 3.10). Extending the flaps gives the plane extra lift to keep it up while slowing it down to prepare it for landing. The plane's speed decreases to a minimum, and the plane is no longer at its flying speed. The plane lands as its wheels touch the runway.

Bombs Away

During World War II, the United States began building bombers with 100-foot wingspans. At the outset of the war, a twin-engine bomber could fly between 200 and 270 miles per hour, covering about 1,000 miles carrying a bombload of 1,000 to 1,500 pounds. By 1945, a medium bomber could carry 4,000 pounds of bombs at 400 miles per hour for a round-trip of 1,500 miles. Moreover, the bombs could now be aimed with deadly accuracy by using the *Norden bombsight*, an automatic speed and distance calculator.[3] Some bombers had as many as four engines, replacing the twin-engine planes of the past. For example, the famous B-17, which made its first flight in 1935, had four 1,200-horsepower Wright engines (the Wright's 1903 *Flyer* had a single twelve-horsepower engine).[4] Likewise, it was a Boeing bomber, the B-29 *Superfortress*, that brought the Pacific war to a close in 1945 when it dropped two atomic bombs on Japan, one on Hiroshima (August 6, 1945) and one on Nagasaki (August 9, 1945). (First used in 1944, the B-29 bomber was famous for its speed and range—it could fly 300-350 miles per hour carrying a bombload of 20,000 pounds. See figure 4.1.)

Air and sea operations joined forces in World War II when planes landed and took off from the decks of ships, as Eugene Ely had done experimentally in a Curtiss biplane some thirty years earlier (see chapter 3). Some of the greatest naval battles in the war were fought mainly by airplanes taking off from huge warships called *aircraft carriers*. In addition to flying offensively, airplanes were also used in World War II to save lives. They carried medical and food supplies and equipment, flew the wounded to hospitals, brought entertainment to the troops, and flew rescue missions.

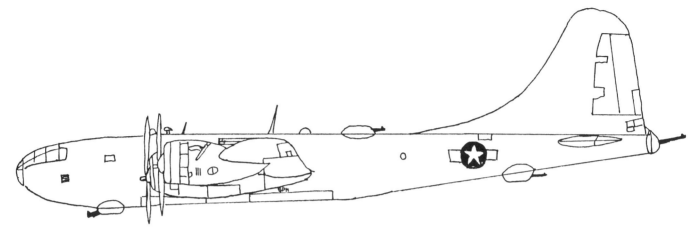

Fig. 4.1. B-29 bomber.

WORLD WAR II FIGHTERS AND BOMBERS

- Library research, social studies, language arts, art

- Beginning and intermediate

Have students research the many World War II fighters and bombers, especially those flown by American, British, German, and Japanese forces. They include the B-17, B-26 *Marauder Flak Bait, Spitfire*, Hawker *Hurricane, Mustang, Lancaster, Messerschmitt*, the shark-mouthed Curtiss P-40 E *Warhawk* flown by the famous Flying Tigers, and the Mitsubishi *Zero*. There are enough airplanes for each student in the class to pick one model, learn some facts about it for a brief written report, and illustrate it. Some students may want to purchase commercially available models of these planes to build and share with the class. Display the drawings or paintings of the planes in the school library. Matricardi's *Concise History of Aviation* is a good source for color pictures and data.

Rotorcraft

Among the many incredible advances in aviation during World War II, three stand out: rotorcraft (the aircraft class to which helicopters belong), the jet engine, and the rocket. This chapter will discuss the first two and chapter 5 will examine rockets.

As discussed in chapter 1, in the fifteenth century Leonardo da Vinci designed a vehicle with a screw-like, aerial propeller that theoretically operated like a helicopter. Helicopters belong to a class of aircraft called *rotorcraft*: aircraft that are lifted and sustained in the air by two to eight rotating blades revolving in a circle around an axis or hub (see figure 4.2).

Although a few forerunners of the helicopter were constructed after da Vinci's day, it was not until 1923, when Juan de la Cierva, a Spanish mathematician working in England, built the first operable *autogyro* (pronounced "au to jīro") that real strides were made toward the helicopter we know today.

A precursor to the familiar helicopter, but not a member of the rotorcraft family, the autogyro has a *rotor* (a set of blades that rotate around a central hub) on top that is turned by the wind as it starts moving along the ground. It also has a propeller on the front and fixed wings at the sides, so it looks like an airplane with a rotor on top. Like an airplane, an autogyro takes off by taxiing along the ground to pick up speed for lift. Autogyros are still flown today, mostly for recreation.

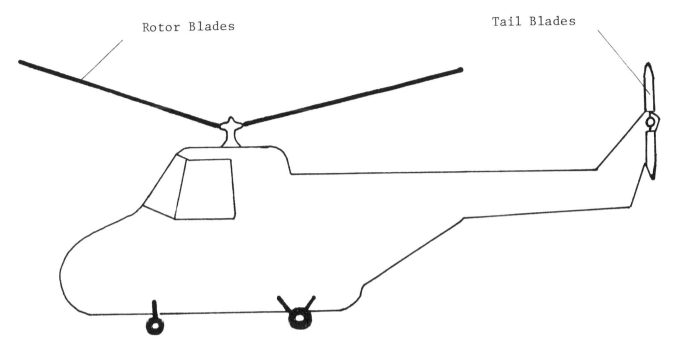

Fig. 4.2. Modern helicopter.

Cierva's autogyro, which was the first aircraft to make use of a rotor, looked very similar to the modern version just described. It could take off with a very short forward run and land nearly vertically.[5] However, although an autogyro has a rotating blade on top—the ultimate perfection of which would lead to a satisfactory helicopter—it works in a different way from a helicopter.

For example, for lift an autogyro has fixed wings on its sides like an airplane; a helicopter, having no side wings, has a rotating blade on top that functions as its rotating wing, providing both lift and thrust. Another difference is that an autogyro's top rotor blade is unpowered; instead of empowering the rotor, its engine drives its front propellers. Its rotor only starts to spin from the flow of air created by the vehicle's moving forward on the ground and then in the air. A real helicopter's rotor, on the other hand, is powered by the engine, and a helicopter has no propeller. Finally, an autogyro cannot move in every direction as a real helicopter can. This is the real advance in the helicopter: it flies straight up (needing no runway for takeoff), straight down, forward, sideways, and backward—every way except upside down. Like a hummingbird, a helicopter also can *hover* (remain at a fixed, nonmoving position at a fixed altitude above the ground); an airplane, with fixed wings that require speedy movement for lift, cannot hover.

BIRD-WATCHING

- Science and nature

- Beginning and intermediate

Ask the class what would happen if an airplane stopped moving in midair. (It would dive to the ground, pulled by gravity.) Ask students if any of them have a hummingbird feeder at home. If they do, ask them to describe how the hummingbird feeds. (It hovers and inserts its beak into the feeder.) Remind them that a helicopter hovers, too.

AEROSPACE TERMS

- Language arts, science

- General

Add *hover, aircraft carrier, rotor*, and *rotorcraft* to the students' dictionaries of aerospace terms.

My First Real Helicopter

In 1937 the Germans were the first to have an aircraft that accomplished all the helicopter's functions, but their helicopter was very impractical because it could not carry much weight. It soon became obsolete because of the work of the Russian-born American engineer, Igor Sikorsky, who was influenced by da Vinci's drawing of an aircraft with a vertical rotating blade.

Originally a designer of multiengine airplanes, Sikorsky worked on the problem plaguing previous attempts at making helicopters: stability and control. The German model was too lightweight for practical use. Other attempts at the helicopter, such as by the Frenchman Etienne Oemichen and the Argentinian Raul Pescara, were shaky at takeoff and unsteady and unreliable once airborne. Between 1939 and 1942, Sikorsky solved these problems by designing a stable and controllable rotating wing (blade) for the top of the fuselage and a smaller balancing rotor (blade) at the tail that kept the helicopter itself from spinning in the direction of its main rotor on top (see figure 4.2). The placement of the two rotors allowed the helicopter to maneuver in all directions without any extraneous motion or spinning by the actual helicopter.

The successive versions of Sikorsky's *VS-300*, built between 1939 and 1942, with a ninety-horsepower engine motorizing the rotors, resulted in the first fully practical helicopter. The Sikorsky helicopter became the premier commercial helicopter in the world. Able to fly and function with much more versatility than the airplane or autogyro, the helicopter would be especially important in the Korean War (1950-1953), the Vietnam conflict, and in everyday life in our own times.

USES OF HELICOPTERS

- Social studies

- Beginning and intermediate

Emphasizing that helicopters are useful in peacetime as well as wartime, ask students to list as many uses of the helicopter as they can. If your local hospital has a helicopter ambulance service, consider inviting the pilot and nurse to the class so students can interview them, or invite a helicopter traffic reporter. Encourage students to ask divergent (open-ended) questions rather than convergent (close-ended, "yes" or "no") questions. Have students write thank-you notes to the visitors.

How does a helicopter work? The rotor on top of the fuselage acts as both wings and propeller, providing both lift and thrust. When the engine starts the rotating blades' circular movement, the airflow that is produced creates lift. The quicker the blades turn or rotate, the more lift they produce. The rotor is angled slightly upward so that the blades "dig" into the air. Likewise, the rotor blade is curved at the top. This is known as an *airfoil*, the part of the aircraft designed to produce lift from the air through which it moves (wings and propellers on an airplane). (Review chapter 3 and Aerospace Magnet demonstrating airfoils and Bernoulli's Principle.) As the wind passes around the airfoil, the air on top sucks the blade up, while the air below it pushes the blade up. When lift exceeds weight (as with an airplane), the helicopter goes straight up into the air.

With a rotating wing or blade, helicopters differ from fixed-wing aircraft (airplanes), which in order to gain lift must taxi or move forward, picking up speed down the runway. Instead of taking off from a runway, helicopters merely lift off from a pad marked "H." Once airborne, the rotating blades also act like propellers, providing thrust. A modern helicopter can fly up to 240 miles per hour.[6]

An airplane turns the same way as Otto Lilienthal turned his hang glider left and right, by banking the wings. (See chapter 3, Aerospace Magnet on an airplane's control surfaces.) Because a helicopter does not have wings to bank, the pilot tilts the helicopter's rotor shaft and turns the whole helicopter. Tilting the rotor alters the direction of the lift, thus pulling the helicopter into a new direction of lift: to the right or left or backward. Because the helicopter can travel in all directions, its cockpit is usually enclosed in a see-through bubble so the pilot has all-around vision.

Although helicopters can descend vertically, they are rarely landed straight down because the downdraft from its rotating blades creates turbulence, making the helicopter wobble. To avoid this turbulence, the helicopter descends at a forty- to sixty-degree angle called the *glide slope*.[7]

MAKE AND FLY A "HELI-PENCIL"

- Science, games

- Beginning

Doing this activity will help students see how a helicopter blade provides thrust and lift.

Materials: A freshly sharpened, full-sized pencil (not a round one; use the hexagonal, flat-sided kind) for each student and enough cardboard or tag board for each student to get one 1"x8" strip of it; a tube of glue for the class to share; an implement to make a small hole in each strip of cardboard (the sharply pointed leg of a geometry compass seems to work well here); enough scissors to go around.

Procedure: (See figure 4.3 for instructions on making the cuts and folds).

1. At dead center of the cardboard strip, make a small hole using the compass leg or other tool.

2. Holding the cardboard strip horizontally (the wide way), first snip off two edges, the bottom left and the top right as you look at that cardboard.

3. Holding the cardboard in the same position, go about 3 inches in from the top left side (the edge not snipped) and make a small, perpendicular cut about halfway down; then cut out a right triangle.

4. Do the same thing on the opposite side (again, about 3 inches in towards the center from the edge not snipped). These triangular cuts allow you to bend the cardboard slightly to form blades.

5. Gently push your pencil, point first, through the little hole in the cardboard.

6. Put a little dab of glue on the hole by the pencil so the pencil will hold in place.

To fly the heli-pencil, hold the bottom (eraser end) of the pencil between two fingers and flick it with a twisting motion: this will give the heli-pencil lift and thrust, just as the rotor blade of the helicopter is supplied with power by the engine. Be sure to do this in an open area, like the gym or the schoolyard.

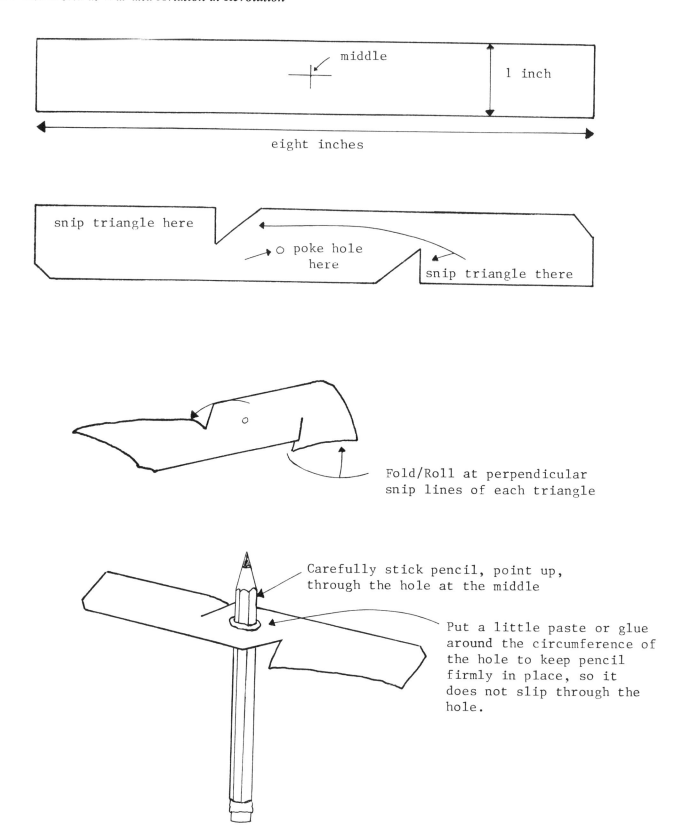

middle

1 inch

eight inches

snip triangle here

o poke hole here

snip triangle there

Fold/Roll at perpendicular snip lines of each triangle

Carefully stick pencil, point up, through the hole at the middle

Put a little paste or glue around the circumference of the hole to keep pencil firmly in place, so it does not slip through the hole.

Fig. 4.3. Making a "heli-pencil."

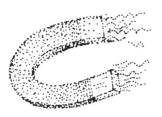

DESIGN A HELICOPTER

- Art, library research, science

- Beginning and intermediate

Students should know that a helicopter requires a rotating, engine-powered blade at the top and a rotor at the tail. With these as the only stipulations, ask students to design their own helicopters. They may wish to do some library research and look at the many types of helicopters flying today, such as the *Chinook, Apache, Sea King, Dolphin, Cobra*, and *Alouette III*.

British Ingenuity: The Jump-Jet

The principles behind helicopter flight have influenced other aircraft, particularly in the military. In 1957 the British Aerospace Corporation began addressing the problem of getting regular aircraft up in the air from a small field, especially near a battle, or from ships with short flight decks. Ten years later they presented the solution, the Hawker *Siddeley T2 Harrier*. Still used today by the Royal Air Force and the U.S. Marines, the *Harrier* is a *jump-jet* or *VTOL* (vertical takeoff and landing) plane. This means that the plane can takeoff vertically, like a helicopter, and then fly like an airplane. This plane has proved so successful that McDonnell-Douglas secured a license from the British to produce it in America and to develop an advanced version, the AV-8 *Harrier*, which reaches speeds of 700 miles per hour and is used by the military today. The *Harrier* is powered by jet engines.

The Jet Revolution

The most important and revolutionary aeronautical advance during World War II was the development of jet propulsion. Whereas the *piston* engine powered the propeller to *pull* the aircraft forward (see chapter 3, Aerospace Magnet on control surfaces), the jet engine *pushes* the aircraft forward. In 1939 the Germans produced the first jet airplane, the *Heinkel He 178*, which flew 435 miles per hour.[8] British (especially the work of Sir Frank Whittle) and American versions followed, although they did not really affect the outcome of World War II. Instead, the jet-powered airplane would rise to prominence, causing a revolution in aviation, in the post-World War II years. There are many more jet airplanes than propeller planes today. With jet engines, airplanes are able to fly at speeds that would have been unthinkable fifty years ago.

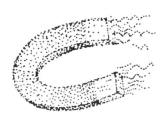

NEWTON'S THIRD LAW

- Science (physics)

- General

Basically, a jet engine works by the principle known as Newton's third law: "For every action there is an equal and opposite reaction." This law was formulated in seventeenth-century England by the same Sir Isaac Newton who articulated the law of universal gravitational pull (see chapter 1).

You can demonstrate Newton's third law easily in class with a simple balloon. When the balloon is blown up and the neck is held shut, the air pressure inside the balloon is equal in all directions and the balloon does not move. Have a student demonstrate this by blowing up a balloon, grasping its neck firmly, and extending his or her arm, holding the balloon out. It does not move. Now prepare to take cover! Have the student release the balloon: it will fly away, moving by reaction to a backward jet of air. In other words, reaction to the air coming out of the balloon will drive it forward quickly. This is Newton's third law at work.

How does the balloon demonstration relate to a jet engine? In a jet engine, the air is sucked in, and a *compressor* (a machine that reduces the air's volume by pressure) pumps it under pressure into a combustion chamber, where it is mixed with fuel and burned. The gases produced by this process come rushing or "jetting" out of the exhaust nozzle at high speed. As with the balloon experiment, this action causes a reaction, which drives the engine and, in turn, pushes the airplane it powers forward. Hence, there is no need for propellers on a jet-powered aircraft. (However, there are propellers powered by jet engines: *turboprops*.)

An excellent, illustrated, nontechnical book that explains jet engines is Julian Moxon's *How Jet Engines Are Made* (see bibliography).

Advanced students can have their physics teacher explain piston (internal combustion) and jet engines in greater detail. For the former, go over the strokes in a piston engine and the function of the carburetor; for the latter, discuss the ramjet engine and its sections (air intake, combustion chamber, and exhaust outlet), as well as the turbojet and turboprop engines; also explain how thrust is measured in jets.[9]

Jet Engines and New Wing Designs

Germany produced the first operational fighter-jet, the *Messerschmitt ME 262*, in 1942. With a wingspan of just under 41 feet and a length of nearly 35 feet, it had low dart-like wings that swept back from the fuselage at an acute angle and jet engines that enabled it to fly up to 541 miles per hour. The swept-back wing design replaced the traditional straight-wing design, in which the wing extends from the fuselage at a right angle. The new wing shape helped reduce drag, thus enabling the plane to go faster. With its advanced aerodynamic design and jet engines, this plane would have been unbeatable in the war. According to aviation historians, Hitler refused to accept advice on how to use the new airplane and so it was largely misused.[10] In addition, many of these new German jets were destroyed by either Allied bombing raids or training accidents caused by inexperienced pilots.

By March 1943, the British had come out with its counterpart, a straight-winged, rather than swept-back winged, jet called the Gloster *Meteor I*, which measured a little over 41 feet in length and 43 feet in wingspan and flew at 420 miles per hour. However, the new jet-powered German and British planes never met in combat. An American jet, the Bell XP-59A *Airacomet*, powered by two British engines designed by Britain's Frank Whittle, appeared in October 1942; its flying speed at 389 miles per hour was comparatively slow. The first wide use of jet aircraft by the military would occur in the Korean War, by which time America would improve its jet design.

CREATE A MURAL

- Art, social studies

- Beginning and intermediate

Share your class's knowledge of the history of flight by having students draw or paint a mural of some of the important events discussed so far. If the class is not concerned with having the mural as a permanent fixture for the classroom or library, they might want to draw it with colored chalk on a section of the cement schoolyard that is temporarily cordoned off.

The Post-World War II "Flying Generation"

Amid the destruction of World War II, the world also had more pilots, more planes, and more aviation technology than ever. As Walter J. Boyne observes, it is no wonder that the post-war years "gave rise to the first real flying generation" and to an America that was, in President Eisenhower's phrase, a "military-industrial complex" of great technological momentum.[11] The jet engine was its main focus.

Just as during the 1920s and 1930s propeller-driven airplanes went from one to four engines to increase power, the new jet-powered aircraft boasted up to eight engines. The great new power that jets gave to airplanes prompted changes in aerodynamic design. Some of these changes were learned from the Germans who, as mentioned, built their jet, the *Messerschmitt*, with swept-back wings.

Whereas the first American jet bomber, the *XB-3* ("X" means experimental) looked like a traditional bomber, with straight wings extending almost at right angles from the fuselage, later models of this plane soon had wings and tails swept back at thirty-five-degree angles in the style of the German jet fighter. This shaped wing, set farther back and lower on the fuselage, would be especially influential in the design of the great military jet aircraft called the Boeing B-47 *Stratojet* bomber. It flew so fast that fighter planes had trouble intercepting it. The B-47 would give way in 1958 to the more famous long-range bomber, the Boeing B-52, also known as the *Stratofortress*. Powered by eight jet engines, this 158-foot-long plane flies at over 600 miles per hour and reaches a ceiling of more than 50,000 feet. Huge B-52 bombers are flown today.[12]

Another military plane, America's F-86 fighter, which theoretically could fly 600 miles per hour, was redesigned after World War II as the F-86 *Sabre* and given swept-back wings and tail surfaces. To ease the handling of the swept-back design at slower speed, aerodynamic engineers added leading-edge slats to the wings. The swept-back design would also improve aircraft performance when reaching the speed of sound, which airplanes were now approaching. (The sound barrier will be discussed in chapter 5, dealing with rockets and flight at supersonic speeds.) The F-86 *Sabre* became familiar to Americans during the Korean War, when it conquered the equally familiar Russian-made MiG-15 jet-fighters flown by the North Koreans. It was not that the F-86 was a better plane; rather, America had more highly trained pilots.[13]

Yet another wing design that become popular with military jets was the delta wing: a triangular-shaped wing seen first in 1955 on the English Avro *Vulcan*, which reached a speed of 640 miles per hour and a ceiling of 55,000 feet and remained in service until 1980.[14] A form of swept-back wing, the delta wing is the type seen on the F-16 fighter jet.

Advances in aerodynamic design combined with new developments in the jet engine to create even more sophisticated aircraft that required increased pilot knowledge and skill. As planes reached higher and higher speeds and altitudes, these designs would change to accommodate new flying requirements, such as flying at the speed of sound.

DESIGN A JET PLANE

- Art and science

- General

Students can design their own jet plane, keeping in mind that although such a plane has jet engines (and thus no propeller-driven engines), it must also conform to regular airplane design, with such familiar parts as wings, elevators, tail, cockpit, rudder, etc. Encourage students to pay special attention to the streamlined fuselage and the wing and tail shapes, which will be swept back at an acute angle rather than extended perpendicularly from the fuselage. Review with the class the reasons for such design and shape and the related idea of streamlining, which we first encountered with dirigibles in chapter 2.

Commercial Jet Travel Begins

Jet-engine aircraft were not to remain the exclusive province of military personnel. In 1952 the British introduced commercial jet service on the deHaviland *Comet 1A*, which cruised at 500 miles per hour at an altitude of 40,000 feet between London and Johannesburg, South Africa, carrying its thirty-six passengers in luxury. The flight took just under 24 hours, with stops. The *Comet* seemed to be the airplane of the day until disaster struck: three *Comets* crashed within weeks of each other in 1953. Investigations showed that, among other factors, the plane's high speed and altitude adversely affected the pressurization of the cabin, causing the fuselage to burst. This is known as *metal fatigue*. For a while it looked to sceptics that the explosion of the *Comets* would do to commercial jet travel what the explosion of the *Hindenburg* in 1937 did to commercial dirigible travel: end it.[15]

PLOTTING AN AIR ROUTE

• Social studies, language arts, mathematics

• Intermediate and advanced

First, add push pins for London and Johannesburg, the key cities on the *Comet*'s route, to the class's world map of aerospace locations. Then plot an air route, first between London and Johannesburg, and then between your hometown and Johannesburg. What are the distances between the places? If the *Comet* flew 500 miles per hour, how long would a direct flight theoretically take? How many students are familiar with Johannesburg and/or South Africa based on all the news stories about that city and/or country? Ask students what they know about them. A beautiful book about life in South Africa in general and Johannesburg in particular is Alan Paton's classic *Cry, the Beloved Country* (see bibliography).

America Reigns in Commercial Jet Travel

Commercial jet travel was not to end with the disasters of the *Comet*. On the contrary, it would proliferate. A major reason was the test flight on June 15, 1954, by pilot Tex Johnston of the *Dash 80* made by Boeing, a company that had learned about making large jet aircraft by producing the B-47 and B-52 for the military. We know this plane as the *Boeing 707* (figure 4.4), the first American passenger jet, for which the Dash 80 was the prototype. Built with engineering advances, the Boeing 707 included extremely thick metal and titanium "tear stoppers" to prevent cracking and thereby avoid the disasters of the *Comet*. It flew 571 miles per hour at a ceiling of over 32,000 feet and could carry from 108 to 165 passengers.[16]

Using Boeing 707s, Pan American World Airways initiated scheduled New York-to-Paris service on October 26, 1958 (recall from chapter 3 the route of Lindbergh's famous flight in 1927). Although the British Overseas Airlines Company (now British Airways), using the redesigned deHaviland *Comet*, had started transAtlantic service from New York to London three weeks earlier (on October 4), Boeing's 707 gave a superior performance. Huge, sleek, and economical in terms of fuel consumption, this four-engined jet became the most popular jet for commercial airlines in all the world.[17] The Boeing 707 did for the flying world in the 1950s and 1960s what the DC-3 had done in the 1930s.[18] By the time Boeing stopped building 707s in the 1980s, more than 800 of them had been made.

Soon after the Boeing 707 appeared, it was rivaled in this country by the Douglas Aircraft Corporation's even larger four-engined jet, the *DC-8*, which went into service in 1959. The companies (Douglas is now McDonnell-Douglas) continue to be two of the world's largest airplane producers.

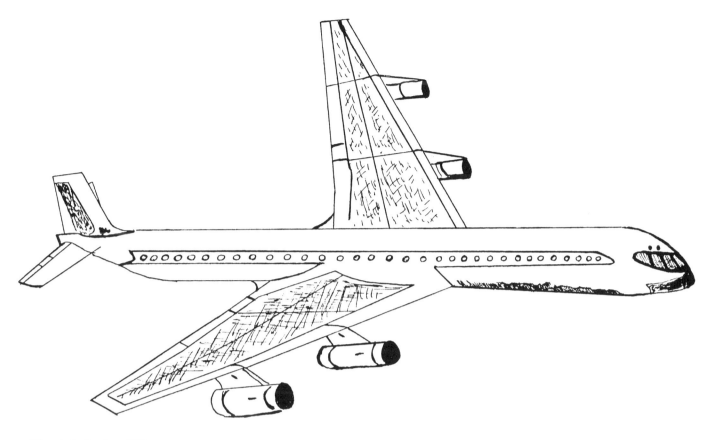

Fig. 4.4. Boeing 707.

The increased public demand for commercial jet travel brought the *Boeing 727* (1967), used for intermediate and short-range flights, and the familiar *737* (1967), which has proved especially popular because it can land at and take off from any airport that could accommodate the reliable DC-3 of the 1930s.[19] It would be as second officer on a Boeing 737 that Emily H. Warner would become the first female pilot on a major U.S. scheduled airline (Frontier) in January 1973.

AUGUST MARTIN

- Library research, social studies, language arts

- General

In 1955 August Martin (1919-1968) became the first black man to become the pilot of a scheduled U.S. carrier, Seaboard World Airlines. Have students find out about this brave and determined man, who was killed in a storm while trying to land a mercy flight to Biafra on July 1, 1968. Students can find Biafra on the map and write reports and illustrate important events in Martin's life. The Civil Air Patrol (CAP) has an excellent activities booklet about Captain Martin suitable for beginning students (see CAP's address in the appendix).

GENERAL DANIEL "CHAPPIE" JAMES, JR., USAF

- Library research, social studies, language arts

- General

Have students research the accomplishments of America's first black four-star general, the late General Daniel James, Jr. (1920-1978). A pilot-hero in the Korean War and Vietnam, he was also a hero in our country, excelling in volunteer work. General James was also an award-winning writer. Ask the library media specialist to locate his essay from 1967, "Freedom—My Heritage, My Responsibility," which won the George Washington Freedom Foundation Honor Medal. Have students try to write an essay on a similar topic. The CAP has an excellent activities booklet about General James, suitable for all levels (see the appendix for the CAP's address).

Jumbo Jets

Increased transcontinental and transoceanic travel, along with a desire for economy, led to the development of commercial jumbo jets or "wide bodies." Capable of carrying up to 400 or so persons, the four-engined *Boeing 747*, at 231 feet long, was the first to appear in 1970. It continues to be the most popular jumbo jet for long-haul flights and may well be so into the twenty-first century. Although not so large as the lighter-than-air dirigibles that flew over sixty years ago (the Hindenburg was nearly 804 feet long), the 747 is the largest heavier-than-air aircraft flying today.

In 1972 the equally well-known McDonnell-Douglas Company's three-engined *DC-10*, able to carry nearly 400 persons, went into service. Another popular wide body, the *Lockheed 1011*, powered by three Rolls Royce jet engines, began service in 1976. With the exception of the Lockheed, which can go 610 miles per hour, the jumbo jets' general speed is about 565 miles per hour. Yet, there are commercial jets that go faster; these appeared in 1981 and 1982.[20]

America has dominated commercial jet aviation, particularly in the jumbo-jet category. However, Europe has competed with its *Airbus 300*, produced by a consortium consisting of aircraft companies from France, Germany, England, Spain, Holland, and Belgium. Two basic models, the A-300 and the A-310, made their respective first flights in 1974 and 1982.[21]

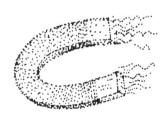

POST-WAR PLANES

- Library research, social studies, language arts, art, science

- General

Have students research post-war military and commercial planes. Each student in the class can select one plane and become the class "expert" on it. Students may write short reports, give brief oral reports, and draw their respective planes. Commercial models of the planes are also available.

INVITE AN AIRLINE CREWMEMBER TO CLASS

- Careers

- General

If you have an airport in your town, invite a crewmember from the commercial airlines to visit the class and be interviewed by the students. Before the visit, review the material in chapter 3's Aerospace Magnet about the FAA, which includes a bibliography of works dealing with aviation careers. Students should be encouraged to ask open-ended questions that will prompt discussion. After the interview, have the class write thank-you letters to the visitor.

CITIZENS OF A SHRINKING WORLD

- Social studies, oral communication, music

- General

As most students know, it is now possible to fly just about anywhere in the world within a day or two in the relative comfort of a jumbo jet. Countries that were once unfamiliar are now brought closer together by advances in communication and transportation. Discuss the advances in both fields in class. How did the advances in aviation, in particular, change the way people think about travel? What do the advances in aviation mean for us as citizens of the world? Intermediate and advanced students may also write essays dealing with some aspects of the suggested discussion questions. For this Aerospace Magnet, beginning students might enjoy learning the popular song, "It's a Small World After All."

People-Powered Flight

Before turning to rockets, the sound barrier, and space travel in chapter 5, we note briefly a certain irony in aviation history. Amid the desire to go faster and faster in bigger and bigger planes, the 1970s saw a return to attempts at people-powered flight in the mode of the mythical Icarus. On August 23, 1977, Bryan Allen was both pilot and engine for the 3-mile flight of the *Gossamer Condor*, designed by a California aeronautical engineer, Paul MacCready. Allen set another record on June 12, 1979, this time for making the longest person-powered flight: 22.3 miles across the English Channel, which took two hours and fifty-five minutes.

Even more astounding was the 74-mile flight that occurred on April 23, 1988. A team of engineers from the Massachusetts Institute of Technology (MIT) built three planes with extremely long wings made of Mylar (a very strong polyester) and polystyrene (a plastic) foam and connected them to a long pole-like structure with a tail and rudder. The designing and building of the planes took three years and cost $1 million. On April 23, Kanellos Kanellopoulos not only piloted but also powered, by pedaling, the 68-pound airplane called *Daedalus* from Crete to the island of Santorini, a distance of 74 miles, which he covered in a little under four hours. A Greek bicycle-race champion, Kanellopoulos pedaled the plane to create .25 horsepower and flew between 30 and 50 feet above the sea. The flight proved that a human being could produce the physical energy needed to fly long distances.[22] It also reminds us that for all the technical advances made in flight, human ingenuity, courage, and strength underlie them all. This is especially true as human beings go out of this world, beyond our atmosphere, past the speed of sound, and into space.

Notes

[1]Beverly Rubik, "Science, A Feminine Perspective," *Creation* (November-December 1990): 6-7.

[2]George Harvard Gibbs-Smith, *Aviation: An Historical Survey from Its Origins to World War II*, 2d ed. (London: Her Majesty's Stationery Office, 1985), 208-9.

[3]Gibbs-Smith, *Aviation*, 209. See also C. D. B. Bryan, *The National Air and Space Museum*, 2d ed. (New York: Harry N. Abrams, 1988), 292.

[4]John W. R. Taylor and Kenneth Munson, *History of Aviation* (New York: Octopus Books, 1975), 306.

[5]Gibbs-Smith, *Aviation*, 190.

[6]Ian Graham, *Helicopters* (New York: Gloucester Press, 1989), 15.

[7]Graham, *Helicopters*, 18.

[8]Gibbs-Smith, *Aviation*, 197.

[9]See also Aimee Dye, *Aviation Curriculum Guide for Middle School Level, Secondary School Level* (Washington, D.C.: Department of Transportation, FAA, n.d.), 36-37.

[10]Taylor and Munson, *History of Aviation*, 342-43.

[11]Walter J. Boyne, *The Smithsonian Book of Flight for Young People* (New York: Collier Macmillan, 1988), 91, 93.

[12]Data on the aircraft are from Paolo Matricardi, *The Concise History of Aviation* (New York: Crescent Books, 1985), 230-31.

[13]Ivan Rendall, *Reaching for the Skies* (New York: Orion Books, 1989), 253.

[14]Matricardi, *Concise History of Aviation*, 153-54, 230.

[15]For more on the *Comet*, including pictures, see Rendall, *Reaching for the Skies*, 276-77, and Boyne, *Book of Flight*, 97-98.

[16]Matricardi, *Concise History of Aviation*, 226-27.

[17]*Information Please Almanac, Atlas, and Yearbook* (Boston: Houghton Mifflin, 1991), 357.

[18]Rendall, *Reaching for the Skies*, 280.

[19]Bryan, *National Air*, 306.

[20]Data on the jumbo jets and the newer, faster jets come from Matricardi, *Concise History of Aviation*, 232-33.

[21]Data on the Airbus 300 come from Matricardi, *Concise History of Aviation*, 192, 236-37.

[22]Information about these people-powered flights comes from the *Information Please Almanac*, 357; Bryan, *National Air*, 133-35, 138 (includes photo of *Gossamer Condor*, 134-35).

Bibliography

Air Force ROTC. *Aerospace Science: History of Air Power*. Maxwell Air Force Base, Ala.: Air University Press, 1986.

Boyne, Walter J. *The Smithsonian Book of Flight for Young People*. New York: Collier Macmillan, 1988.
Readable and well illustrated.

Bryan, C. D. B. *The National Air and Space Museum*. 2d ed. New York: Harry N. Abrams, 1988.
Comprehensive and beautifully illustrated: an armchair trip to the museum.

Civil Air Patrol. *Falcon Force: An Aerospace Education Kit for Grades 4-6*. Maxwell Air Force Base, Ala.: Civil Air Patrol, n.d.
Available from the CAP for about $40 and contains dozens of excellent teaching packets; see appendix for CAP's address.

Dye, Aimee. *Aviation Curriculum Guide for Middle School Level, Secondary School Level*. Washington, D.C.: Department of Transportation, FAA, n.d.
Available free from FAA; see addresses in appendix.

Gibbs-Smith, George Harvard. *Aviation: An Historical Survey from Its Origins to the End of World War II*. 2d ed. London: Her Majesty's Stationery Office, 1985.
A definitive study by one of the world's foremost aviation historians.

Graham, Ian. *Helicopters*. New York: Gloucester Press, 1989.

Halperin, Richard P. *Physical Science*. New York: Barnes and Noble, 1983.

Harris, Iris, and Alabama State Department of Education. *Aviation and Space Curriculum Guide, K-3*. Washington, D.C.: Department of Transportation, FAA, 1990.
Contact the FAA for a copy; see addresses in appendix. Be sure to work out the activities given before you try them with the class because many of the procedures are sketchy.

Housel, David C., and Doreen K. M. Housel. *Come Fly with Me: Exploring K-6 through Aviation/Aerospace Concepts*. Lansing, Michigan Aeronautics Commission, 1983.

Information Please Almanac, Atlas, and Yearbook. Boston: Houghton Mifflin, 1991.

Lambert, Mark, Kenneth Munson, and Michael J. H. Taylor. *Jane's All the World's Aircraft, 1990-91*. 81st ed. Surrey: Jane's Information Group, 1990.
The definitive work on the topic.

Matricardi, Paolo. *The Concise History of Aviation*. New York: Crescent Books, 1985.
    Contains scale color drawings of aircraft and statistical tables; good for showing all the planes from World War I and World War II, as well as all commercial aircraft.

Moxon, Julian. *How Jet Engines Are Made*. New York: Facts on File Publications, 1985.
    Clear enough for the nonphysicist to gain a basic understanding and well illustrated enough for the specialist to use with students.

Paton, Alan. *Cry, the Beloved Country*. New York: Charles Scribners, 1948.
    Available in paperback in a 1987 edition with a new prefatory statement by the author.

Rendall, Ivan. *Reaching for the Skies*. New York: Orion Books, 1989.
    Good, readable history and great photos; published to complement a British television series.

Smithsonian Institution. *History of Flight for Students in Grades 4-12*. Washington, D.C.: National Air and Space Museum, 1988.
    Lots of activities; contact the museum at address in appendix.

Strickler, Mervin K., Jr. *A Model Aerospace Curriculum Based on August Martin High School* [in Queens, New York City]. Washington, D.C.: Department of Transportation, FAA, n.d.
    Available free from the FAA; see addresses in appendix; great turnaround story for this high school through adopting an aviation curriculum.

Taylor, John W. R., and Kenneth Munson. *History of Aviation*. London: Octopus Books, 1975.
    A thorough and beautifully illustrated book from people associated with the definitive *Jane's All the World's Aircraft*.

U.S. Department of Transportation, Federal Aviation Administration. *Aviation Science Activities for Elementary Grades*. Washington, D.C.: U.S. Government Printing Office, 1983.
    Available free from the FAA; see appendix for addresses.

_____. *Demonstration Aids for Aviation Education*. Washington, D.C.: U.S. Government Printing Office, 1987.
    Available free from the FAA; see appendix for addresses.

Vision. Seattle, Wash.: Boeing Aircraft, n.d.
    Poster giving various "firsts in flight"; good data and illustrations.

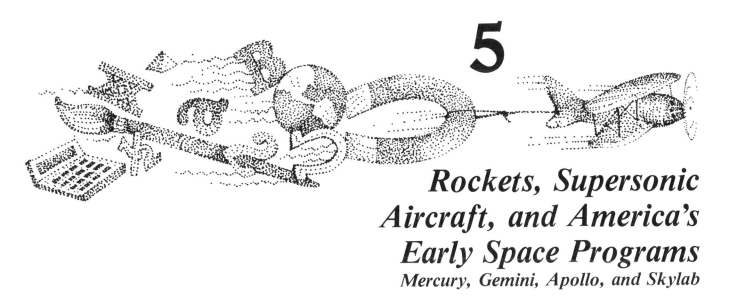

5

Rockets, Supersonic Aircraft, and America's Early Space Programs
Mercury, Gemini, Apollo, and Skylab

When Francis Scott Key watched the British bombard Fort McHenry, near Baltimore, during the War of 1812, he was struck by the sight of "the rockets' red glare"—indeed, so struck that he proceeded to write about them in the poem that would provide the lyrics for our national anthem, "The Star-Spangled Banner." What he saw were rockets developed by an Englishman named Sir William Congreve (1772-1828), who had probably heard of the rockets invented by the Chinese as early as 1000 A.D. and, more recently, those used in India in the 1700s as incendiary weapons against English soldiers.

What is a *rocket*? A rocket is a container, usually cylindrical, with a combustible substance inside which, when ignited, produces gases that escape through a rear vent or nozzle, thereby driving the container forward (see figure 5.1). The container is the combustion chamber. The rocket operates by the principle of reaction articulated in Newton's third law (see chapter 4's discussion of a jet engine): for every action there is an equal and opposite reaction. A rocket is, therefore, sometimes called a *reaction engine*.

Rockets work in terms of Newton's third law. When the fuel inside the cylindrical rocket's combustion chamber burns, it makes gases that expand with explosive force. These gases zoom out of a small hole, the *throat*, at the back of the chamber. In fact, scientists learned that making this hole even smaller causes the gases to zoom out even faster, creating more thrust. At the bottom of the throat is a cone-shaped nozzle that causes the gases to go still faster; in addition, the nozzle helps guide the rocket. As the gases zoom out of the chamber through the small hole and then through the nozzle, they propel the rocket forward with great (equal) force. This is how the rocket takes off. Of course, the rocket began in primitive form, but the operating principle remains the same.

REVIEWING NEWTON'S THIRD LAW

- Science

- General

Teachers may want to review with the class the balloon demonstration in the "Newton's third law" Aerospace Magnet under jet engines in chapter 4. Remind students that although the balloon's thrust is uncontrolled, thereby causing the balloon to fly erratically around the room, the rocket's thrust is controlled and directed so the rocket can stay on course.

---

solid fuel rocket   liquid fuel rocket

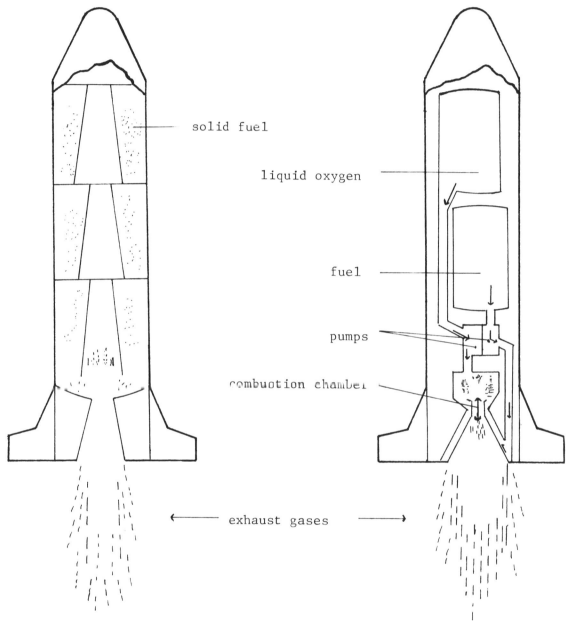

solid fuel

liquid oxygen

fuel

pumps

combustion chamber

← exhaust gases →

Fig. 5.1. Rockets.

Early Rockets

To make their rockets, the Chinese packed gunpowder and charcoal into a piece of bamboo, which naturally has a tube-like or cylindrical shape; placed a conical, pointed structure on the top; and attached to the tube a stick or arrow to serve as a fuse, which was then lit. These rockets had a range of about 100 to 300 feet. The Chinese army used them to frighten the enemy, especially their horses. As with the balloon and the kite, the rocket had at least part of its beginnings in recreation or entertainment: the Chinese used rockets in fireworks displays. In India, soldiers launched rockets that were tied to long bamboo guidesticks that helped balance them in flight. These rockets were quite effective against the English in battle during the eighteenth century.

Sir William Congreve improved upon the Chinese and Indian rockets, making rockets with metal cases that had a range of almost 2½ miles. With gunpowder in their heads, Congreve's rockets blew up when they hit something. However, the advances Congreve made in using the rocket as a weapon were not immediately pursued because, by the early nineteenth century, effective artillery had been developed. After the War of 1812, rockets were used mainly for lifesaving at sea. Congreve rockets with ropes attached were fired off a ship's deck to stranded persons. Rockets were also used for entertainment in fireworks shows. Not until 1926 would *rocketry* — the science of rocket design and flight — be used as we know it today: to launch objects into space. An American physicist, Robert H. Goddard (1882-1945), called the Father of Modern Rocketry, was responsible for this. He designed and launched the first liquid-fuel rocket, a great advance over the rockets of Congreve, the Chinese, and the Indians, all of which were solid-fuel rockets. What the Wright brothers did for aviation, Goddard did for space travel.[1]

Using Rockets for Space Travel

Goddard was inspired to design rockets not as incendiary weapons but as a way of reaching space, particularly the moon, after reading H. G. Wells's *War of the Worlds* and Jules Verne's *From the Earth to the Moon* during his childhood (see bibliography).[2] In Verne's novel, three men (one dressed in a velvet suit and leather gaiters) are fired to the moon in a cone-shaped projectile, which is launched by a 900-foot-long cannon, the *Columbiad*, loaded with 200 tons of guncotton, a nitrated, highly explosive substance.[3] Although in reality the launch method would have killed Verne's fictional moon travelers at takeoff, the novelist was correct in recognizing that great *velocity* (speed) would be needed to escape the earth's atmosphere and thus reach space.

What Is Space?

Our planet earth is surrounded by a thin layer of gases called the *atmosphere*. The higher we rise above the earth, the thinner the atmosphere gets. Above about 60 miles, there is hardly any atmosphere at all. The region beyond the first 60 miles of the earth's atmosphere is officially called *space*. Not only is the atmosphere very thin at that point, but the temperature is extremely changeable: out of sunlight it can descend to -400 degrees Fahrenheit, while in sunlight it can rise to nearly 500 degrees Fahrenheit. Temperatures can fluctuate by hundreds of degrees within minutes. Because there is no gravity in space, astronauts experience the condition called *weightlessness*. Finally, there is no air in space. Although there are meteors and various heavenly bodies "out there," *space*, as the word suggests, is a *vacuum*, a place empty of air.

The conditions of space help to account for a rocket's shape. Because space has no air or wind, a spacecraft does not deal with aerodynamic forces. Thus, a rocket does not need airfoils for lift and flight: the rocket engines' tremendous thrust provide the lift. Nor does a rocket need to be streamlined to overcome drag, for there is no drag. However, because rockets are launched from the earth, where there is dense air near the surface, rockets have streamlined, conical noses at the top. Some rockets even have wing-like structures at their base to help keep the rocket on course as it soars through the earth's atmosphere, heading for space.

WHY DO PEOPLE WANT TO GO TO SPACE?

- Science, critical thinking, language arts

- General

Now that your class knows something about the conditions of space—extreme temperatures, no air, and no gravity—ask them why they think human beings want to go there. Would they? These questions can be discussed in class and then used for a writing topic, involving an expository essay, a short story, or a poem.

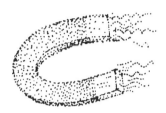

BELIEFS ABOUT THE MOON

- Library research, oral communication, language arts, social studies

- General

Robert Goddard became interested in rocketry because he wanted to make possible travel to the moon, which fascinated him. Our lunar neighbor has long intrigued humanity. Many attribute crazy behavior (lunacy) to the moon's influence, see a "man in the moon," or have superstitions about a full moon. Using the library, students can investigate some of these folk beliefs and superstitions and report on them to the class.

AEROSPACE TERMS

- Language arts, science

- General

Add the words *rocket, rocketry, space,* and *vacuum* to the students' aerospace dictionaries.

Today scientists know that to overcome gravity, which pulls all objects to the earth, and launch an object into space, the object must travel at a very high rate of speed, about 17,000 miles per hour. This far exceeds the speed capability of even the fastest jets, which go about 2,000 miles per hour. Therefore, something more powerful than a jet engine is needed to reach the velocity (speed) required for space travel: a rocket. Rockets can exert a thrust of more than 7 million pounds, sufficient to send something zooming into space. How rockets that could do this came into being is a fascinating story.

The First Modern Liquid-Fuel Rocket

Robert H. Goddard, a physics professor at Clark University in Massachusetts, was looking for a device that would travel fast enough to escape the earth's atmosphere. In 1919 he published through the Smithsonian Institution (which also gave him a $5,000 grant to pursue his research) a monograph called *A Method of Reaching Extreme Altitudes.* It dealt with the liquid-fuel rocket, propelled by a combination of liquid hydrogen and liquid oxygen. Goddard built and finally launched on March 16, 1926, the world's first working liquid-fuel rocket. Reaching 60 miles per hour, the 50-pound rocket went 41 feet high and traveled 184 feet from the launch site. The "rocket age" had begun at a farm in Massachusetts!

Although Goddard's early efforts met ridicule in the press, Goddard continued to design, build, and launch rockets in an effort to gain the velocity they would need to escape the earth's gravity. In 1929 Charles Lindbergh helped him secure additional funding from the Guggenheims for his work, which the Smithsonian and Carnegie Foundation also aided.

Among Goddard's subsequent pioneering achievements in rocketry were methods for steering and pumping the fuel, as well as designs for the nozzle and combustion chamber. Working for the U.S. Navy after World War II, Goddard saw the rockets made by German scientists, particularly Wernher von Braun's (1912-1977) huge *V-2* ("Vergeltungswaffen," meaning "vengeance weapon"), the world's first large liquid-fuel rocket with a range of about 220 miles (figure 5.2).[4] Another term for the V-2 is *guided missile*. A *missile* is a spear-shaped object that can be thrown or fired as a weapon at a target. A guided missile is a self-propelled, unmanned air or space vehicle or projectile that carries an explosive charge in its head, called a *warhead*. Such missiles can be powered by rocket or jet engines; the V-2 was rocket powered.

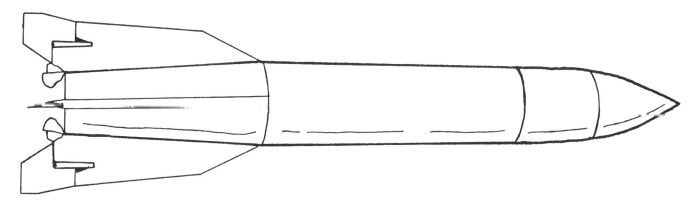

Fig. 5.2. V-2 rocket.

Although the V-2, weighing 12½ tons including fuel, was much larger than even Goddard's latest efforts, he saw that it had systems very much like those he designed. This was not surprising because the Germans used Goddard's patents in their V-2 research. (Patents are discussed briefly in an Aerospace Magnet in chapter 3.) Five years after Goddard's death, von Braun, then working in America and later as an administrator at the National Aeronautics and Space Administration (NASA), lauded the American physicist's achievements, saying, "Until 1936, Goddard was ahead of us all."[5] In 1962 NASA named its Greenville, Maryland space center for Goddard.

GRANTS

• Library research, oral communication, science, language arts

• Advanced

Goddard's experiments were funded mainly by the Guggenheim and Carnegie foundations and by the Smithsonian Institution. Have students find out how scientific research, as well as most other types of research, is funded by grants. What, for example, are the Guggenheim and Carnegie foundations? What are some of the recent research projects they have funded? An index to the *New York Times* might be a readily available source for finding out; another option is to write to these foundations, requesting an information booklet. The library media specialist can direct you to the *Grants Register* for addresses. If your town has a nearby university or other research institution, such as a hospital, as well as an industrial research site (designing microchips? automobiles?), invite researchers from the different sectors to class and have students interview them about the "business" of research.

How do the experiences of researchers working for industry differ from those of researchers at universities or hospitals? Many of today's gifted students will be tomorrow's researchers. Have the students write thank-you letters to the researchers after the visit.

AEROSPACE TERMS

- Language arts

- General

Add *missile, guided missile*, and *warhead* to the students' dictionaries. The war in the Persian Gulf will probably already have familiarized most students with such terms.

The Rocket and Liquid Propellants

As noted, Goddard launched the first liquid-fuel rocket in 1926; the Germans launched the V-2 liquid-fuel rocket during World War II. However, as early as 1903 a Russian teacher, Konstantin Tsiolkovsky (1857-1935), postulated that a rocket could use liquid oxygen and liquid hydrogen as propellants. The liquid oxygen is needed because in space there is no air and thus no oxygen. This is yet another reason why a jet engine could not work in space: jets need oxygen from the air to burn their fuel. This is also why a solid-fuel rocket could not do the job: like the jet engine, a solid-fuel rocket needs some oxygen from the air to burn its fuel. Furthermore, in the past, even if one could get oxygen into solid fuel, the fuel—like Jules Verne's guncotton—would explode. That is why a modern solid-fuel rocket uses a specially mixed propellant (e.g., aluminum powder packed with ammonium perchlorate powder) that provides the oxygen for the aluminum's combustion which, once ignited, cannot be turned off. The solid-fuel rocket is used mainly as a booster and is attached to the main engine. We will examine the solid rocket booster when we look at the space shuttle in chapter 6. (See figure 5.1 for solid-fuel and liquid-fuel rockets.)

For space travel, the pioneers of rocketry turned to a liquid-fuel rocket that carries the oxygen it needs to burn its fuel. The rocket uses an *oxidizer* (a source of oxygen for the fuel burned in rocket engines when in the vacuum of space), usually liquid oxygen (LOX), in its combustion chamber. The oxygen is the oxidizer and the liquid hydrogen is the fuel; together they are the *propellants* (oxidizer plus fuel). Even so modern a spacecraft as the space shuttle has a main engine that uses pressurized liquid oxygen and liquid hydrogen.

LIQUID OXYGEN (LOX)

- Science

- General

Liquid oxygen is the most commonly used oxidizer in rocketry. Invite a high school chemistry teacher to class to explain how oxygen, a gas, is liquefied by cooling it and pressing it. LOX needs to be kept in extremely cold tanks, at -220 degrees Centigrade (Celsius), to prevent it from boiling under the earth's normal atmospheric pressure. This is why in photos of rocket launches we can see ice forming on the LOX tanks.

The German V-2: Wernher von Braun

During the pre-World War II years, renewed interest in rocketry prompted the formation of rocket societies in Germany, Austria, England, Russia, and America. A member of one such society, Hermann Oberth (1894-1989), had been influenced, like Goddard, by reading Jules Verne's science fiction as a child. During World War II, he worked at the 10,000-person elite German rocket research center at Peenemünde, where the V-2 was built and launched on October 3, 1941, under the technical direction of Wernher von Braun. While acknowledging Goddard's great achievements in rocketry, aviation historian Sir Charles Harvard Gibbs-Smith observes of the V-2: "This remarkable weapon marked the most decisive step taken towards the conquest of space. [It] provided the pivotal achievement in practical rocketry, and was to confront the world for the first time with the reality of space travel."[6]

The V-2 rocket in its regular performance soared 60 miles up in the air, traveling 3,600 miles per hour (more than six times faster than the contemporaneous Messerschmitt jet) and landing at approximately 2,000 miles per hour at a location up to 220 miles from the launch site in five minutes of flying time.[7] It carried a 2,000-pound warhead. The Germans used the rocket as a weapon, as the Chinese had done nearly a thousand years earlier. Between September 1944 and March 1945, the Germans fired 4,320 V-2s; their targets were London and cities on the Continent. Their effect, when they hit their target, was devastating. For all of its destructiveness, however, the V-2 would set the standard for rockets after the war, when German engineers and scientists worked on rocketry in the United States and Russia.

TODAY'S MISSILES

- Science and current events

- General

In light of the outbreak of war in the Persian Gulf on January 16, 1991, students are undoubtedly familiar with terms like Scud missiles and Patriot missiles. The *Patriot* is an antimissile missile manufactured by Martin Marietta. It is 17.4 feet long and 16 inches in diameter, weighing about 1 ton with about 1,000 pounds of fuel. The Soviet-made *Scud-B* liquid-fuel missile is 37 feet long, 3 feet in diameter, and weighs 7 tons at launch. Students can see photos and drawings of these missiles in newspapers and magazines dated within two weeks from the outbreak of hostilities. They should note that the basic structure of these modern missiles has not changed since Goddard and the V-2.

The Speed of Sound and X-Planes

While Germany was launching rockets that flew 3,600 miles per hour, American, German, and British airplane pilots, flying jets at several hundreds of miles per hour, were noticing that as they approached 600 miles per hour at about 40,000 feet they seemed to encounter an invisible force or "barrier" that caused many problems. For example, the planes' control would go opposite to the way they normally operate, and some planes vibrated so much that they literally shook apart.[8] Although they did not know it, the pilots were traveling close to the speed of sound. At sea level, sound travels at a faster rate, 760 miles per hour, than it does at higher, colder altitudes. The speed of sound is known as *Mach 1*; twice the speed of sound (1,520 miles per hour at sea level and 1,320 miles per hour at 40,000 feet) is *Mach 2*, etc. The speed of sound or Mach number varies with temperature and altitude. The word *Mach* is derived from the name of an Austrian physicist, Ernst Mach (1838-1916), who did research in *ballistics* (the science of the motion of projectiles in flight). Speeds one to five times the speed of sound are called *supersonic* speeds; five times the speed of sound or greater is *hypersonic* speed.

In 1945 the Army Air Force decided to attack the control and stability problems both in the laboratory and in the air. Working under contract to the government, the Bell Aircraft Company built the *X-1* (X = experimental) to investigate the problems of high-speed flight.[9] To begin testing supersonic flight, the X-1, powered by rocket engines, made its first flight in January 1946. The following year, the X-1 was ready for the big test at the so-called *sound barrier* encountered by jet pilots. On October 14, 1947, a B-28 bomber flew over California's Mojave Desert carrying the X-1 under its bomb bay to an altitude of 20,000 feet. There it was launched and piloted to 42,000 feet by its test pilot, Air Force Captain Charles "Chuck" Yeager, who had nicknamed the plane *Glamorous Glennis* after his wife. No one knew what would happen at the transition from subsonic to supersonic flight.

Yeager ignited the rocket engines and accelerated. Reaching 660 miles per hour (Mach 1), the X-1, with straight, stub-like wings and bullet-like fuselage, started to shake. However, when it exceeded the speed of sound, the vibrations stopped. The plane reached 670 miles per hour at 42,000 feet and 700 miles per hour (Mach 1.06) at 45,000 feet.[10]

What Is the "Sound Barrier"?

As a result of this test flight, scientists and engineers recognized what happened at the "sound barrier," which is really no barrier at all, but a transition point. A flying plane causes pressure waves that move at the speed of sound. Flying at less than the speed of sound (below Mach 1, called *subsonic speed*), the plane is behind these waves. As the plane approaches the speed of sound, it starts to reach those pressure waves that were ahead of it. (Another way of saying this is that the plane at Mach 1 catches up with its own waves and produces drag and turbulence.) The pressure waves grow into a shock wave that puts the aircraft under great stress, causing the phenomena mentioned earlier. This shock wave is the "sound" barrier that the plane must cross or "break." When this happens, the pressure change produces a *sonic boom*. Flying faster than Mach 1, the plane crosses or "breaks" the "sound barrier," leaving the shock wave behind it. There is no literal barrier; rather, the speed of sound is a transition point for a plane in flight.

As a result of this famous test, engineers designed planes that could pass through Mach 1 more easily: planes with swept-back wings, slender contours, and other special shapes. The X-1 flew test flights until 1956; it now hangs in the National Air and Space Museum.

AN AMERICAN HERO: CHARLES "CHUCK" YEAGER

- Library research, language arts, art, science

- General

Have the class do research on Charles "Chuck" Yeager, who may well be familiar to students through his many television appearances. They can write short sketches of his career and can illustrate the X-1 that made him famous for being the first human being to travel faster than the speed of sound in level flight. Advanced students will enjoy his two autobiographies: Chuck Yeager with Leo Janos, *Autobiography*, and Chuck Yeager with Charles Leerhsen, *Press On: Further Adventures in the Good Life*. Beginning and intermediate students might read Timothy R. Gaffney, *Chuck Yeager: First Man to Fly Faster Than Sound*, or Nancy Smiler Levinson, *Chuck Yeager: The Man Who Broke the Sound Barrier*. Your library media specialist can suggest other titles.

POETRY GOES BOOM!

- Language arts

- Intermediate and advanced

Get a copy of John Updike's short, humorous poem, "Sonic Boom," and read it aloud and discuss it in class. What is the speaker's attitude towards sonic booms? Consider the effect of the "pop"-"drop" couplet with which the poem closes. Have your students ever heard sonic booms? If so, how do they feel about sonic booms? You can find this very teachable poem in several anthologies, including the following: Stephen Dunning, et al., eds., *Reflections on a Gift of Watermelon Pickle and Other Modern Verse*; Sara Hannum and John T. Chase, eds., *To Play Man Number One*; Sara and John E. Brewton and John Brewton Blackburn, *Of Quarks, Quasars, and Other Quirks: Quizzical Poems for the Supersonic Age*; Richard Peck, *Sounds and Silences: Poetry for Now*; and John Updike's *Telephone Poles and Other Poems*. With the exception of Updike's collection, these anthologies are geared to student readers.

"MEET THE FLIGHT PIONEERS"

- Library research, social studies, science, oral communication, problem solving, critical thinking, art

- Intermediate and advanced

A few years ago, entertainer Steve Allen did a show on Public Broadcasting called "Meeting of Minds," in which actors dressed as famous historical figures and discussed subjects of mutual interest. Have your class do a "Meeting of Minds" in which Otto Lilienthal (perhaps wearing one of his gliders), the Wright brothers, Charles Lindbergh, Dr. Robert Goddard, and Chuck Yeager appear in appropriate costumes. Have students script the meeting, in which these aerospace pioneers tell about their respective experiences and what they tried to accomplish. Encourage students also to speculate what their respective characters would think and say about aerospace events that occurred subsequent to their lives. Be sure to have one student prepared to act as moderator; this, too, can be a character—Leonardo da Vinci, the all-time Renaissance man, might work well here. Have students perform this for a school assembly so your class can share its knowledge about aerospace history and maybe turn other students and teachers onto its possibilities!

More X-Planes in the Sky

The X-1 led to the *Bell X-2*, another rocket-powered aircraft, but this time with the swept-back wing design found in jet aircraft.[11] Two such planes were built in 1955 to study the effects of heat when flying at Mach 3. Both X-2s were destroyed by accidents during testing, but not without one of them setting a speed record of 2,094 miles per hour at Mach 3 on September 27, 1956.[12] The thrill of setting this record was dramatically undercut when the plane crashed, killing the test pilot, Captain Mel Apt. Subsequently, the X-2 pioneered advances in pilot safety by developing the first modern pilot rapid ejection systems.

While the X-1 and X-2 were rocket powered, the *Douglas X-3* was to be the first jet-powered aircraft designed to fly supersonically. Although the X-3 made over twenty test flights beginning in October 1952, it had insufficient engine power to fly supersonically. Future jet-powered planes, such as the *F-14A Tomcat*, would have the power to do so.

Up to this writing, over two dozen X-planes have been designed and flown to investigate various aspects of aerodynamic design and engine performance at high speeds and different altitudes. The latest actually to fly is the *Grumman X-29A*, with its unusual *forward-swept wings*; it is capable of flying at Mach 1.8 and made its first flight in December 1984. Probably the two most familiar X-planes date from the 1950s and 1960s: the two *Bell X-5s* and the famous *X-15* manufactured by North American Aviation, Inc., of which there were three.

The Bell X-5, which made its first flight on June 20, 1951, was the first aircraft to use *variable or swing-wing* design. Recall from chapter 4 that the Germans had developed the swept-back wing to reduce drag on its *Messerschmitt* jet. Although swept-back wings, extending at an acute angle from the fuselage, work very efficiently at high speeds and are practically an essential for supersonic aircraft, they produce insufficient lift at low speeds to keep the plane flying.[13] Straight wings are better for the latter. The Bell X-5 was built to have both as a variable-wing aircraft: variable or swing wings can change the angle of the wing setting. One of the test pilots for the X-5 was Neil Armstrong, the first person to walk on the moon (June 20, 1969).[14]

Swing wings are found on the U.S. Navy's famous F-14A *Tomcat*, a supersonic turbojet that flies 1,584 miles per hour and reaches a ceiling of 68,900 feet. Manufactured in 1972 by the Grumman Aircraft Engineering Corporation, it has straight wings for takeoff, landing, and low-speed flight, but for supersonic speeds the wings can be swept back to a delta (triangular) shape to reduce drag.[15] The Tomcat has two turbofan jet engines that give it the power to fly supersonically that the X-3 lacked. In a turbofan jet engine, some of the compressed air goes past the combustion chamber instead of through it.

THE COMPRESSOR; TURBOFAN, RAM-JET, TURBOPROP ENGINES

- Science (physics)

- Intermediate and advanced

Invite a high school physics teacher or aeronautical engineer to explain to the class the function of a compressor and the types of jet engines. A *compressor* is a fan-like device that packs air or gases into the combustion chamber of a jet engine. A *combustion chamber* is that part of an engine into which the fuel is injected, compressed, and exploded. In the *turbofan engine*, some compressed air goes past the combustion chamber; the *ram-jet*, which is the most basic jet engine, has no compressor, so movement pushes or "rams" the air into the combustion chamber; in the *turboprop*, the gases produced in the combustion chamber jet out and empower a propeller. Turbofan engines power the *Airbus-300*, discussed in the section on jumbo jets in chapter 4. An example of a turboprop plane, a less familiar aircraft, is the *Piaggio GP-180*, developed by the United States and Italy in 1985; it flies 460 miles per hour.

The Rocket-Propelled X-15

The most famous X-plane, the X-15, is especially important because it marks the transition from flight within the earth's atmosphere to flight in space—the goal of Robert Goddard when he originally worked on the first liquid rocket. In fact, the work of the early rocket designers and builders contributed directly to the X-15. Although the X-15 has an airplane's traditional aerodynamic control surfaces for flying within the earth's atmosphere, it also has rocket thrusters in its nose and wings so the pilot can control it at high altitudes, particularly at the atmospheric edge of space.[16]

The rocket-propelled X-15 aircraft, which made its first flight on March 10, 1959, was developed to explore flight at extremely high speeds and altitudes—so high, in fact, that pilots who flew the X-15 at altitudes above 50 miles were entitled to "astronaut" wings.[17] An *astronaut* is a space voyager, literally a "star sailor" ("astro" comes from the Greek "astron," meaning star, and "nautes," for sailor). The comparable Russian term is *cosmonaut*, or "universe sailor," derived from the Greek words "kosmos," meaning "universe," and "nautes."

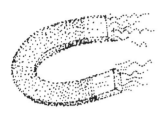

ROOT WORDS

• Language arts

• General

Knowing the roots of the words *astronaut* and *cosmonaut*, students should be asked to come up with as many words as they can with the same roots, such as astronomy, astrology, astrolabe, astrophysics, cosmic, cosmopolitan, cosmology, nautical, nautical mile, etc. In this exercise, remind students how the English language was formed from other languages and how root words function.

The X-15's Records and Contributions to Space Travel

With the exception of the space shuttle, the X-15 has unofficially flown faster and higher than any winged aircraft up to the present day. On October 11, 1961, the world was amazed at the endurance of both people and airplane parts when Major Robert White, USAF, flew the X-15 3,647 miles per hour (Mach 5.21) and reached a maximum altitude of 217,000 feet. Six years and 185 X-15 flights later, Captain William Knight, USAF, piloted the X-15 on October 3, 1967, when it surpassed Mach 6 (flying over 4,500 miles per hour) and climbed to 67 miles—in other words, into space. The official record for airplane speed belongs to Lockheed's *SR-71A/B Blackbird* turbojet, designed for reconaissance and commissioned by the Central Intelligence Agency. On March 6, 1990, it set a transcontinental record, flying 2,404 miles in 1 hour 7 minutes and 53.69 seconds at 2,124.51 miles per hour. Now on exhibit at the Smithsonian, its estimated top speed is Mach 3 + at 78,750 feet.[18] Albeit unofficially, the X-15 flew about twice as fast as the SR-71A/B.

There were actually three X-15s, which altogether made 199 flights before the aircraft was retired from active duty on October 24, 1968. The first X-15 now hangs in the National Air and Space Museum; the second X-15, which holds the unofficial speed record mentioned, is in the Air Force Museum at Wright-Patterson Air Force Base, Ohio; the third X-15 crashed on November 15, 1967, killing the pilot, Air Force Major Michael Adams. The X-15's many contributions to space flight include experiments showing the pilot's abilities to function while experiencing weightlessness and to control a rocket-boosted vehicle as it reenters the earth's atmosphere from space.

On the X-15's flight of March 30, 1961, which set a new altitude record for that time of 169,600 feet, pilot Joe Walker wore for the first time a new full-pressure suit, which would serve as the basic model not only for the astronauts' space suits in the Mercury, Gemini, and Apollo programs, but also for the pilots' pressure suits in many modern supersonic aircraft. (Space suits are discussed later in this chapter, as well as in chapter 6.) The vehicle itself also taught scientists and engineers much about developing sealants and heat-resistant materials to withstand the temperature extremes of space travel and using a wedge tail on the aircraft to alleviate stability problems encountered at hypersonic (Mach 5 and higher) speeds. In all, 700 research documents came out of X-15 flights, many of them directly applicable to space travel.[19] The current X-plane on which scientists and engineers are at work is the *X-30*, the National Aero-Space Plane, which will be discussed in chapter 6.

AERODYNAMIC DESIGN, FRICTION, AND THE HEAT BARRIER

• Science

• General

The X-15 has an especially streamlined design, roughly similar to a cylinder and a cone, to reduce drag and attain supersonic speeds. Likewise, modern aircraft, especially those flying at supersonic speeds (e.g., military fighter planes), are streamlined and made of heat-resistant materials. Flying at high speeds, an airplane creates *friction* with the air through which it is moving. Friction is a force produced by one object or surface rubbing against another and the resistance to that motion of one of the surfaces or objects with respect to the other. How does friction affect aircraft? The greater the drag and the faster the speed of an airplane, the more friction created by that aircraft and the air with which it comes into contact. These factors are especially relevant to supersonic aircraft, which fly at high velocities and thereby create great heat through their friction with the air. In so doing, these planes encounter the *heat barrier*: the minimum temperature at which the structural (metal) parts of an airplane become weakened. The forces of lift, gravity, drag, and thrust that directly affect flight have been discussed. With supersonic aircraft, friction becomes what we might consider a "fifth force" which which the airplane must reckon.

To help the class understand this force of friction and how it produces heat, first have students place the palms of their hands together and rub them rapidly. They are creating friction as the surfaces of their hands rub against each other. If you experience cold weather where you live, your students will probably recollect this is one way they can quickly warm their hands on a chilly day.

The same effect can be achieved by pulling a piece of rope quickly across an opened hand. Again, friction will produce an increase in temperature (rope burn).

Point out to students the smooth aerodynamic design of supersonic aircraft and contrast it with the comparatively bulky shapes of such earlier airplanes as the *Blériot* and the *Sopwith Camel* (see figures 3.12 and 3.13 in chapter 3). The aerodynamic design of supersonic aircraft is relevant to the heat barrier. A simple experiment can illustrate this concept.

Materials: Sandpaper, small board, small but heavy block or piece of smooth wood, thumbtacks, rubber band.

Procedure: To prepare for this experiment, tack sandpaper down securely to cover half a small board to make that half of the board rough. Then put a tack into a small but heavy block or piece of smooth (finished) wood; leave this tack out far enough so you can loop a rubber band around it (see figure 5.3). Ask students what they think will happen when you pull the wood block across the smooth side of the board, as contrasted with pulling the wood block over the side of the board covered with the sandpaper. Why? Then proceed to carry out these activities to find out what actually does happen.

Conclusion: The rubber band stretched more when the block was pulled across the rough side of the board than the smooth side. This indicates that more friction was produced on the rough side because you were using more effort. The rougher the surface, the greater the friction. Supersonic aircraft traveling at high velocities must have the most aerodynamically smooth designs possible to decrease the amount of friction produced and to avoid the damages caused by an encounter with the heat barrier.

Remind students that the X-15's flights showed how excessive heat was produced by the friction created as the aircraft returned from the fringes of space to earth's atmosphere. The space capsules from the Mercury, Gemini, and Apollo programs had special heat shields to deflect heat. When those capsules were retrieved from the ocean, they were charred from the heat produced by friction at the capsules' reentry. The space shuttle has special tiles on parts of the orbiter to handle the high heat of reentry to the atmosphere from space orbit (see chapter 6).

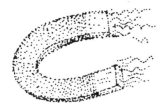

KNOW YOUR X-PLANES

- Library research, science, language arts, oral communication, art

- General

As discussed, there have been many X-planes since the X-1. Advanced students can use a book like Jay Miller's *The X-Planes*, which has a lengthy bibliography, and research their respective contributions, which can form the basis for short written and oral reports. Intermediate students can find accessible information about some of the X-planes in John Gabriel Navarra's *Superplanes*, geared to younger readers. The library media specialist may have other suggestions for sources (encyclopedias, general aviation histories, etc.).

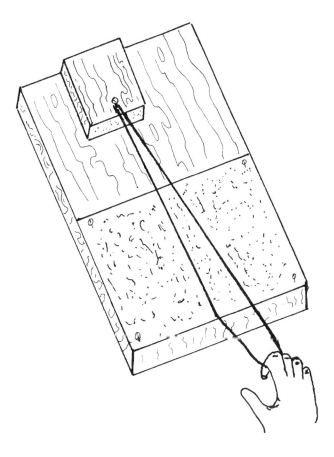

Fig. 5.3. Understanding the heat barrier.

With the help of the library media specialist, intermediate and advanced students can look up newspaper, magazine, and yearbook reports about the X-1, X-2, X-5, and X-15 from the years when they flew and report to the class about popular and/or scientific reactions to the feats these planes accomplished.

Advanced science students should work with their science teachers, especially physics teachers, to understand and be able to explain these contributions to the class. The X-planes are also fun and challenging to draw. All-level students might like to do an illustrated display of X-planes. Remind students that commercially produced models of some of these planes are available for them to purchase and build.

Supersonic Commercial Flight

The daring and sacrifice of the test pilots who flew the X-planes led to many supersonic military aircraft that fly every day. However, the experience of supersonic flight is no longer limited to test and military pilots. In January 1976 Air France and British Airways established regularly scheduled supersonic jet service on their Concorde. With its long, streamlined fuselage, swept-back wings, and droopy nose, the Concorde speedily carries passengers over long distances in comfort and luxury at Mach 2. Although American carriers have not yet offered supersonic travel (SST), some do offer near supersonic speeds. In 1982 United Airlines inaugurated service on the *Boeing 767*, which flies at Mach .8. The following year, Eastern Airlines began offering flights on the *Boeing 757*, which also flies at Mach .8. Both aircraft were designed in response to the energy crisis. Each uses less fuel than the Boeing 727, which is of roughly comparable size. The 757 and 767 are now used by many commercial airlines.[20]

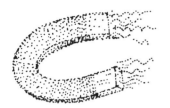

MODERN MILITARY PLANES

- Library research, science, art, language arts

- General

Using the library, students can research some of the modern planes in military service today. These planes exemplify the latest in aerodynamic sophistication. Students can learn about their sizes, speeds, ceilings, and engine type. They might be especially interested in the *B-2 Stealth Bomber*, which made its first flight in July 1989 and is virtually all-wing in design. Equally famous is the *F117A-Stealth Fighter*, used for the first time in December 1989 when the United States invaded Panama. They can also find out about the popular *F-4 Phantom*, the *Tornado*, the *F-111F Bomber*, the A-10 attack plane, the *F-16 Fighting Falcon*, the *Jaguar*, the *A-6 Intruder*, the *Corsair*, and the *Skyhawk*. Students can write and illustrate brief reports about the planes they have chosen. The authoritative *Jane's All the World's Aircraft*, available in the public library's reference section, is the top source for both lay persons and professionals interested in the subject (see bibliography under Lambert).

The Space Age

The X-15 marked the transition from airplane to spacecraft, bringing human beings to the edge of space and into space itself. During the 1940s and early 1950s, scientists and engineers were using the rocketry research of Goddard and others to launch weapons. Soon they were using this knowledge to design and build rockets powerful enough to launch objects into *orbit*: the regular path that one body follows around another body, or, the path followed by one body in its revolution about another body. This path is usually elliptical (see figure 5.4). The objects launched into orbit around the Earth are called *satellites*, from the Latin word *satelles*, meaning "attendant." It means a body that is in orbit around a planet. There are both natural and artificial satellites orbiting around our planet. For example, Earth's natural satellite, the Moon, orbits around Earth; the period required for the Moon to do this is 27 days, 7 hours, 43 minutes, and 11.47 seconds. Our planet is also orbited by many man-made, artificial satellites launched for such purposes as communication, mapping, weather forecasting, and even spying.

There are various types of orbits that satellites and spacecraft may take around Earth (figure 5.4). In a *circular orbit*, the satellite's or spacecraft's distance above Earth is constant. A *geosynchronous* orbit is an *equatorial* orbit—above the equator in a circular orbit—at an altitude of 22,300 miles. The satellite or spacecraft appears to us on Earth to stay at the same spot above us because the satellite or spacecraft is orbiting Earth in the same time period that the Earth rotates on its axis: 23 hours, 56 minutes, and 4.09 seconds. In an *elliptical orbit*, the orbiting object's distance from Earth is not constant. At *apogee*, the object's point in orbit around earth is farthest from Earth; at *perigee*, the orbiting object's point in orbit around Earth is nearest to Earth. Finally, in a *polar* orbit, the orbiting object passes over Earth's poles.

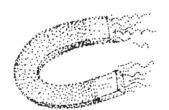

ORBITS AND THE SOLAR SYSTEM

- Language arts, science, art, environmental studies, library research, physical education

- Beginning and intermediate

Have students add to their dictionaries the words *satellite, orbit, elliptical, geosynchronous*, and *polar*. Draw an ellipse on the board. On a map of the Solar System, point out to students the Moon's orbit around Earth. Even better, get one of the commercially available,

circular   geosynchronous   elliptical   polar

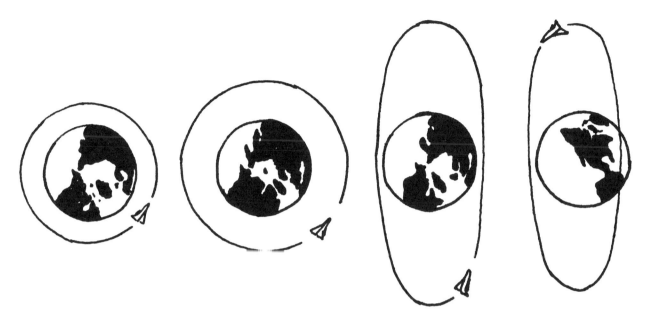

Fig. 5.4. Types of orbits.

reasonably priced three-dimensional models of the Solar System and illustrate the orbit. Students can make model Solar Systems with foam balls, coat hangers, glue, and fishing line. Suspend the mobile Solar Systems from two crisscrossed coat hangers taped into position.

Using library resources, students can find pictures of the planets, Sun, and Moon and draw the Solar System. Drawings of the individual members of the Solar System can be taped in proper order on the classroom ceiling or wall. Students can learn the names of the planets in order from the sun by this mnemonic: My Very Excellent Mother Just Served Us Nine Pizzas—Mercury, Venus, Earth, Mars, Jupiter, Saturn, Uranus, Neptune, Pluto. (Define the word *mnemonic*: a memory device.) Depending on their level, students can find and report on some facts about each planet. Do any of the planets seem habitable? If not, what does this remind us about our responsibilities to our own planet and its environment? In the schoolyard or gymnasium, illustrate the movement of the Solar System by having beginning students take the roles of the planets and the Sun and Moon and act out their respective movements. Have students outline the Solar System on the playground in chalk. Students can do the research for making an illustrated Solar System wall chart for the classroom or library, on which students present such comparative data as each planet's size, period of rotation, number of moons, distance from the sun, etc. Then have the class make the chart.

For beginning and intermediate students, a great illustrated book is Joanna Cole and Bruce Degen's *The Magic School Bus Lost in the Solar System*; if the school library does not yet own it, ask the library media specialist to order a copy. Beginning students will also like Nancy E. Krulik's *My Picture Book of the Planets*.

NATURAL SATELLITES

- Science, language arts

- General

As noted, the Moon is Earth's only natural satellite. Whereas Earth and Pluto each has only one natural satellite, Jupiter has sixteen (also called "moons"), Mars has two, Uranus has fifteen, Neptune has eight, and Saturn—as the *Voyager* interplanetary probe has shown—has at least eighteen. With the library media specialist's help, students can find books and magazines with color pictures of some of these satellites, especially *Voyager 1 and 2*'s pictures of the moons around Jupiter, Saturn, and Neptune transmitted, respectively, in 1979, August 1989, and February 1990 (the last released by NASA in June 1990). Using these for ideas, students can draw their own renditions of the moons/satellites.

Artificial Satellites

Earth now has many artificial satellites in addition to its natural satellite, the Moon. The first man-made, artificial satellite to be launched into orbit around Earth was the Russians' *Sputnik 1*, which went up on October 4, 1957. Looking like a small (23 inches in diameter) shiny sphere with four antennae protruding from it, the 184-pound satellite was boosted into orbit on top of a 96-foot-high military rocket that had nearly 1,125,000 pounds of thrust.[21] (One pound of thrust equals 22 horsepower.) *Sputnik* sent "beeps" back to earth as it flew 18,000 miles per hour.[22] The "space race" was on, with the Soviet Union and the United States vying to win.

America, the home of the Wright brothers, Charles Lindbergh, Robert Goddard, and the X-1 and the world's leading aircraft producer, was stunned. Yet, more was to come. Less than a month later, on November 3, 1957, the Russians launched *Sputnik 2*. This satellite had a passenger: Laika, the world's first living space traveler inside a *space capsule* (an enclosed, detachable compartment designed to hold and protect the occupants of a rocket). Admittedly, Laika was a dog, but she lived orbiting in space for ten days and died before the satellite burned up. Just as lighter-than-air travel had begun with barnyard animals in a hot-air balloon almost 200 years earlier, so now space travel was starting with "man's best friend" as the first cosmonaut. Between 1957 and 1961, the Russians launched ten *Sputniks* carrying seven dogs.[23]

Actually, America had successfully launched a crew of one monkey and eleven mice into space on September 20, 1951, on top of an Aerobee sounding rocket, a smaller liquid-fuel rocket used to carry instruments to the upper atmosphere. However, these animals did not go into orbit; the rocket merely ascended straight up and then fell back to earth.[24] In view of the Russians' orbiting live creatures, America felt pressed to respond.

On December 6, 1957, the United States attempted to launch its first satellite via a Vanguard rocket. It blew up on the launch pad. Number two also exploded, but on the third try to launch a satellite into orbit, success came. A four-stage *Jupiter C* rocket, designed and built by Wernher von Braun and his team using knowledge developed from the World War II German V-2 rockets, launched America's first satellite, *Explorer 1*, on January 31, 1958.[25] This satellite measured cosmic rays and studied other space phenomena, including what would come to be known as the Van Allen belt. America was finally in the space race.

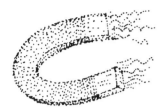

UNDERSTANDING NEWTON'S FIRST LAW

- Science

- General

A satellite stays in orbit around earth when two forces acting on the satellite are in balance: *gravity*, the force that causes an inward pull towards earth and provides the *centripetal*, or inward action force, on a satellite; and *centrifugal force*, the outward pull of objects moving in a circular path. To help enable students better understand how gravity and centrifugal force cause an object to be held in orbit, try this activity.

Materials:

1. Small empty can such as a soda can (with the top and bottom of the can still intact) that has been washed out, drained, and allowed to dry (or, if you can get a comparably sized spool, such as used for wire or thread in factory sewing, you can go right to step two of the procedure).

2. Small rubber ball such as that which comes with a jacks set.

3. About 2 feet of string.

4. Washers (3 or 4) such as those used in plumbing.

5. Piece of old sheet (or other very thin material) that is about three times the size of the ball.

6. Scissors.

Do this activity in an open space, like the gym.

Procedure:

1. Punch a hole dead center in both the top and the bottom of the can and tape down any jagged edges formed.

2. Wrap a small rubber ball in a piece of sheet or other very thin material about three times the diameter of the ball.

3. Tie one end of a string around the corners of the sheet, securing the ball firmly within it.

4. Leaving the end of the string with the wrapped ball attached extending about 12-14 inches, thread the *other end* of the string through the hole in the top of the can (or hole at the top of the spool), downward through the can (spool) and let it extend below the can or spool for approximately 4-6 inches.

5. Run the last inch of this end of the string through three or four washers, stacked one on top of the other, and tie a knot at the very end so the string does not slip through the holes in the washers. Tell students to assume that the wrapped ball is a satellite. Then holding the can in one hand and the washers in the other, start twirling the can (spool) which, in turn, will twirl the ball over your head—otherwise, the ball will hit you in the face! As you do this, gradually loosen your hold on and let go of the washers. Increase and decrease the speed of the ball by adjusting the speed of your twirling of the can. Discuss what happens and how this activity relates to satellites orbiting the earth.

Conclusion: As a satellite is held to the earth by the inner pull of gravity, the ball is held to the can or spool, which represents the earth, by the string. As with a satellite, as you increase the speed of the ball (or satellite), the centrifugal force is increased. The ball then moves farther away from the can (as the force of gravity has been counterbalanced), and the washers move closer to the can. As you decrease the speed of the ball, the centrifugal force is decreased. The ball moves closer to the can (the gravitational effect is increased as there is less centrifugal force), and the washers move further away from the can. When the centrifugal force and gravity are equal, the ball remains in orbit. This is also true with a satellite.

As you are slowly twirling the can, have a student carefully snip the string between the can (spool) and the washers. The ball will fly away in a straight path because of *inertia*, the tendency of an object to keep its current state of motion. Said another way, an object at rest remains at rest unless acted on by an outside force, while an object in motion continues in motion in a straight line at a constant speed, unless acted upon by an outside force. This is Newton's first law.

This experiment works well for all levels of students. Other projects especially for intermediate and advanced students are in Robert Gardner, *Projects in Space Science*.

VAN ALLEN BELT

- Library research, language arts, science

- Intermediate and advanced

What is the Van Allen belt? How did it get its name? What does it cause to happen? Have students research these questions and prepare short written responses. (See the 1991 *Information Please Almanac*, pp. 347-48 for straightforward answers.)

Multistage Rockets

What does it mean when a satellite is launched by a four-stage rocket? To have the power and speed (about 25,000 miles per hour) needed to launch a satellite into space, a rocket launch vehicle contains a number of smaller rockets, joined one on top of the other. We call this a *step-rocket launch vehicle* or a *multistage rocket*. This concept originated with a sixteenth-century fireworks maker, Johannes Schmidlap, who wanted his aerial fireworks to reach greater altitudes.

In a step- or multistage rocket, each rocket fires in sequence, with the bottom rocket firing first to shoot the entire launch vehicle into the air. The rocket is launched so that the satellite or object it carries will fly parallel to the spinning earth and enter into earth's orbit. When this first stage's fuel runs out, it detaches itself and drops away. This makes the launch vehicle lighter. Now the second rocket fires, thrusting the launch vehicle still higher until its fuel is gone, and then it drops away. Each successive rocket or stage functions in this way until the final rocket, now much lighter and thus able to climb faster into space, takes over what remains of the launch vehicle and speeds it into orbit.

As the rocket soars higher and higher beyond earth's atmosphere and gravitational pull, it needs less thrust than it did at its launch point on earth. The satellite or object so launched into orbit will remain in orbit providing it keeps its high speed. As the rocket stages drop away, they burn up reentering the atmosphere. If the satellite in orbit drops in speed, it drops towards earth and, like the rocket stages, burns up reentering the atmosphere. Nowadays, about twenty different types of launch vehicles send human beings, military payloads, and business satellites into space.

If all goes well, the satellite launched by the multistage rockets stays in orbit. As discussed, its forward speed creates an outward force, centrifugal force, that counters the gravity from the earth pulling it back. In a sense, the satellite is falling towards earth, but it is also moving so fast that it can keep going forward. A satellite orbiting 300 miles above earth will complete one orbit in about ninety minutes; this is known as the satellite's *orbital period*. As you can infer, the higher the satellite, the longer the orbital period. It takes twenty-four hours for a satellite 23,300 miles high to complete one orbit. Different types of satellites are put into different types of orbits (see figure 5.4) to carry out their function.

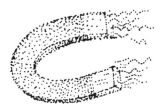

DEMONSTRATING A MULTISTAGE ROCKET

- Science

- General

Materials: At least two regular-sized balloons that you have inflated and deflated a few times and stretched out; at least two 8-ounce polystyrene coffee cups, scissors.

Procedure:

1. Take the polystyrene coffee cups and cut out the bottoms of the cups, as well as the top rims, cutting completely around the lips of the cups about 1½ inches from the top. What you have left is a continuous rhomboid-shaped ring for each cup.

2. Inflate the first balloon (first rocket stage) almost full with air and squeeze its nozzle tight.

3. Pull the nozzle through the small end of one coffee cup rhomboid ring, up through the large end, and drape over the cup so you can hold it with your finger.

4. Extend the front end of the second balloon (second rocket stage) through the large end of the ring, inflate until about half full, and hold its nozzle shut.

   The inflation of the second balloon will hold the nozzle of the first balloon shut by pressing against it. When you're ready to launch, hold your multistage rocket at the last balloon's nozzle and extend it out to the length of your arm. Then let go!

Conclusion: The escaping gas from the second balloon propelled both balloons until it ran out of air. Then the second balloon released the nozzle of the first balloon, which then took its turn at being propelled through the air. If you have fortitude, good finger dexterity, lots of breath, and much patience, try adding more stages to your balloon rocket. Just have as many stretched-out balloons as cut-up coffee cups on hand.

For teachers of beginning and intermediate students, many enjoyable and informative activities about rockets, including a different one on multistage rockets, are in Gregory L. Vogt, *Rockets: A Teaching Guide for a Science Unit with Elementary Students*, available from NASA Aerospace Education Services Project, 300 North Cordell, Oklahoma State University, Stillwater, OK 74078-0422.

ARTIFICIAL OR MAN-MADE SATELLITES

- Science, language arts, library research, art

- General

The *Explorer 1* was America's first space satellite. Since its launch in 1958, the world has seen hundreds of satellites heading into space. Such satellites come in a variety of shapes and sizes, depending on their job. Frequently, a satellite will have antennae and other instruments protruding from all sides, making it look like a junk heap! However, these satellites have important functions. All have communication systems for transmitting messages between the satellite and earth, called *telemetry*. Other communications functions include helping us make overseas phone calls and providing television programs through a satellite "dish" or tracking antenna back on earth. Satellites also provide weather reports (recall the "satellite map" on television weather forecasts) and can be used for spying. Geographers and cartographers (mapmakers) make better, more accurate maps because of satellites like *Landsat*.

First, discuss the role of artificial satellites. Then, have students do some research for short reports about well-known satellites including *Landsat, Intelsat* (telephone), *Meteosat* and *Tiros* (weather), and the famous early communications satellite, *Telstar*. What were and are the satellites' functions? How long have they been or were they in orbit? What type of orbit? Younger students may enjoy drawing one of these satellites. As students will see after finding pictures of the satellites, the satellites do not have to be streamlined like airplanes because they travel in space, where there are no air and wind to cause drag. Students of any age may enjoy creating three-dimensional models of real or imaginary satellites to decorate the room; suspend the model satellites with fishing line, which is strong and nearly invisible. Demonstrate a satellite's orbit by showing a small model satellite orbiting around a globe. For example, *Sputnik* can be made from a foam ball with four toothpicks protruding and can be spray painted silver.

Teachers and students will learn about satellites and enjoy the many pictures of them in Gregory Vogt, *Space Satellites*. Although it is in the library's juvenile section, it is also appealing to adult readers who need the basics on satellites and orbits.

ROCKET FUN

- Art, science, mathematics

- Beginning and intermediate

A Mercury *Redstone* rocket (figure 5.5) and a *Saturn V* rocket (figure 5.6) are pictured. Have students find illustrations of a *Jupiter C*, Mercury *Atlas*, Gemini *Titan*, and *Saturn 1-B*. Students can make paper or cardboard rockets and thereby see the shapes of cylinders, cones, and triangles. The cylinder is the main body (roll construction paper into a cylinder or use the cardboard rolls on which paper towels and waxed paper come); the cone is the nose cone; the triangles are the little wings at the rocket's base. Students can write their names or make up rocket names and insignias and draw them on their rockets. Suspend the paper rockets from the ceiling with fishing line, which is strong and nearly invisible. Or create a space bulletin board scene, complete with planets, moons, and satellites, and attach the rockets onto "space" with sticky-tack so your bulletin board is three-dimensional.

MAKE AND LAUNCH MODEL ROCKETS

- Science, art

- General

Estes Industries' model rockets division offers for sale a good-sized model of the *Jupiter C* that an older student or the hobby-oriented adult could construct and paint. It takes about half a day to build and paint it. The rocket is launchable. Estes makes the engines and wadding and also sells the launch kit, which uses a large dry-cell battery available in any variety or hardware store. Other launchable rockets are also available for purchase, including relatively easy-to-make and inexpensive smaller rockets that first-graders can master. For information on getting either the *Jupiter C* or any other of their many rocket models, contact a hobby shop or write directly to Estes Industries, Penrose, CO 81240 (see appendix). They give an educational discount for orders from schools.

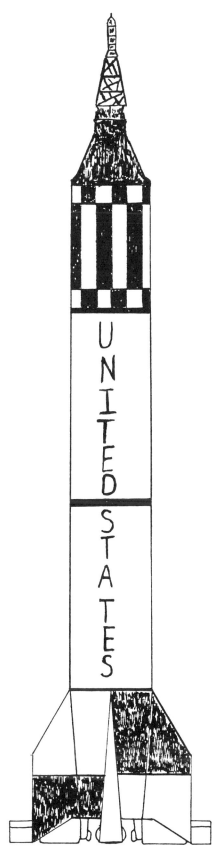

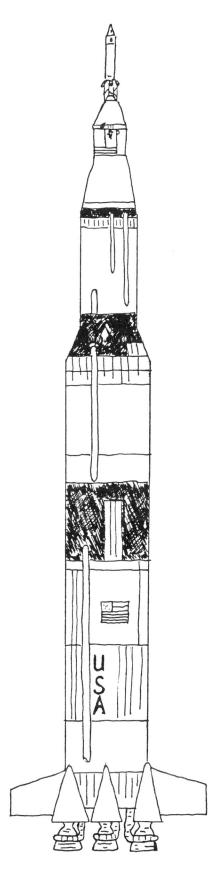

Fig. 5.5. *Mercury Redstone* rocket.

Fig. 5.6. *Saturn V* rocket.

The Creation of NASA

When the *Jupiter C* successfully fired the *Explorer 1* into orbit in 1958, it was the beginning of hundreds of American satellite launches. To coordinate these activities and to surpass the Soviet Union in the space race, President Eisenhower sent a special message to Congress on April 2, 1958, requesting the creation of a civilian agency to direct all government space exploration. On July 29, 1958, Eisenhower signed the Congressional bill that created the National Aeronautics and Space Administration (NASA), which was "devoted to peaceful purposes for the benefit of all mankind."[26] *Aeronautics* literally means "sailing through the air." Officially beginning operations on October 1, 1958, NASA evolved from the National Advisory Committee on Aeronautics (NACA), which had included among its original board members in the 1930s Charles Lindbergh and Orville Wright.[27]

Moon Exploration

In the first years of the space age, both Russia and the United States had successes and failures, with rockets blowing up on the launch pads. Meanwhile, orbiting around Earth over 200,000 miles away, the Moon beckoned scientists, as it had Jules Verne's fictional travelers in *From the Earth to the Moon* and as it had Robert Goddard, the Father of Rocketry. Between 1959 and 1976, Russia sent twenty-four payloads to the Moon, some of them crashing and others sending back the first pictures of the lunar surface and samples of lunar soil.[28] The first American success in lunar probing occurred on March 3, 1959, when the *Juno 2* rocket launched the *Pioneer 4*, which flew by the Moon, measured lunar particles and fields, and then went into orbit around the Sun. (After this mission, the Pioneer program concentrated on planetary probes.[29]) The *Pioneer's* exploration of the Moon was succeeded in the 1960s by a series of *Ranger* and *Surveyor* missions that told us the Moon's surface was hard enough to support a spacecraft and people landing on it.[30]

The lunar probes were spacecraft that had to escape Earth's gravity to reach the Moon. To do this, a spacecraft must go at least 25,020 miles per hour or 6.95 miles per second. This is the Earth's *escape velocity*, the minimal speed required to escape the Earth's gravity. Moreover, because the Moon is orbiting Earth, the probe must be targeted in front of the Moon so the two can meet simultaneously at a certain point in space. Lunar probes took pictures of the moon and, as noted, even landed and secured soil samples from the lunar surface. Sending a planetary probe is even more challenging than sending a lunar probe because the planets are very far away from Earth: our closest planetary neighbor, Venus, is over 40 million miles distant! Extremely powerful multistage rockets are used. The probes carry highly sophisticated equipment, including cameras and communications systems. Probes traveling nearer to the sun, such as to Mercury or Venus, can produce electricity through solar cells to power the equipment. However, probes going into "deep space"—to the outermost planets in the Solar System—are powered by nuclear materials.

THE PROBES

- Science, library research

- General

Students can find basic information about the lunar and planetary probes (especially *Voyager* and *Viking*) in a handy source like an almanac. Encyclopedias and other resources will provide more detailed materials. Ask students to research some of the probes and summarize what the probes have told and continue to tell us.

ESCAPE VELOCITY

- Language arts, mathematics

- Intermediate and advanced

Have students add *escape velocity* to their dictionaries. If the earth's escape velocity is 6.95 miles per second, how many miles per hour is it? (25,020) How many kilometers per second is it? (11.2 kilometers) Kilometers per hour?

A Cosmonaut and Seven Astronauts

On August 7, 1959, the *Explorer 6* satellite was launched into orbit around the earth by a *Thor-Able* rocket and took the first television pictures of our planet, showing humans what earth looked like from space. The first human being actually to see earth from space was the Russian cosmonaut Yuri Gagarin (1934-1968), who later died in a jet crash while training for a space mission. On April 12, 1961, he became the first person to orbit the earth. Inside the *Vostok 1* capsule, launched by an A-1 rocket, Gagarin orbited around the earth once in 108 minutes, after which he was ejected from the capsule to land separately by parachute on the ground. The world was stunned.

By fall 1958, NASA had already begun selecting astronauts for America's first human space program, Project Mercury, whose goal was launching a person into space to orbit the earth. Their criteria included education in engineering, bravery, ability to make split-second decisions, and a height limit of 5 feet, 11 inches because the projected *Mercury* capsule could not accommodate anyone taller in a space suit. The limited size of the capsule was dictated by the size of the *Redstone* and *Atlas* rockets that would boost it.[31] The *Mercury* capsule, manufactured by the McDonnell-Douglas Company, was only 6 feet, 10 inches long (26 feet with its launch escape tower) and 6 feet, 2½ inches in diameter.[32] The press and the American public met the seven Mercury astronauts on April 9, 1959: M. Scott Carpenter, L. Gordon Cooper, Jr., John H. Glenn, Jr., Virgil "Gus" Grissom, Walter "Wally" Schirra, Jr., Alan B. Shepard, Jr., and Donald "Deke" Slayton. The country became fascinated with its new heroes, whose experiences in the early space program have been chronicled by Tom Wolfe in his book, *The Right Stuff*, which later became a popular film.

THE "RIGHT STUFF"

- Library research, language arts, oral communication, physical fitness, career planning, saying "No" to drugs

- General

Criteria for astronauts have changed since the original seven were selected. For example, with the comparatively large space shuttle command module, astronauts can be tall. Likewise, NASA is looking not just for engineers, but for astronaut candidates with training in fields ranging from anatomy and astrophysics to zoology. With the help of the library media specialist, ask students to find the current criteria for becoming an astronaut and report on them. Teachers may wish to order from NASA, at one of the addresses in the appendix, the NASA information summaries, "Astronaut Selection and Training" (Houston, Johnson Space Center: December, 1986), publication number PMS-019, which gives a summary of the history of astronaut selection, shuttle astronaut recruitment and requirements, and other information. NASA also has a flyer, "NASA Careers," in its NASA Facts Series (publication no. JSCO4346REVC).

Discuss in class what type of preparation and education students would need to become astronauts. What kind of college courses (a bachelor's degree is *minimal* education) would they need to pursue? What kind of physical health do they need to maintain and how would they do it? Stress drug awareness in this discussion. Invite the school's physical education teacher to class to discuss the physical fitness aspects of becoming an astronaut. To link physical education with the space activities in your class, ask the physical education teacher — especially for beginning students — to use an astronaut-training motif in gym class (e.g., "Astronauts must be able to touch their toes without bending their knees!"). For beginning and intermediate students, see Kim Long's *The Astronaut Training Book for Kids*, listed in the chapter bibliography. See also chapter 6, including astronaut Captain Dale Gardner's comments about astronaut requirements.

For persons with the enthusiasm and the money, there are various residential camp programs that provide simulated astronaut experiences. Space Voyages, an educational simulation of space travel, can be brought to your school. See the list in the appendix.

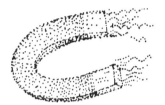

HEROES

- Library research, social studies, oral communication, critical thinking

- General

With the help of the library media specialist, ask students to find newspaper and magazine accounts of the Mercury astronauts' introduction to America and America's reaction to them. Have students report to the class. Back in 1959 and the Project Mercury years, it seemed as though nearly everyone could name the seven astronauts. Teachers might recount to the students their memories of Project Mercury, watching on television Alan Shepard, Gus Grissom, and John Glenn go up and then land at sea. Has the popular attitude towards space flights and those who make them changed today? Has the *Challenger* disaster (January 28, 1986) changed the attitude? Do students have astronaut pictures on their bedroom bulletin boards? What accounts for changes in the popular view of heroism? Who are today's heroes and why? Who were yesterday's heroes? Speculate who tomorrow's heroes will be. Why?

THE ASTRONAUTS' HALL OF FAME

- Library research, language arts, oral communication

- Beginning and intermediate

Ask the library media specialist to help students find biographical books about the astronauts, which are available at all reading levels. Each student can pick one astronaut and research his or her life for a written report and brief oral account to the class. Decide as a class what would be important to include in the written report. As a teacher, you can write, on school letterhead, for free color pictures of astronauts, as well as pictures of rocket launches, shuttle launches, etc., to NASA's teacher centers and distribution centers (see addresses in the appendix). Match each student's written report with a photo and create a bulletin board display of an "Astronauts' Hall of Fame" or "Space Sailors' Gallery" in the hall, classroom, or library.

EXPLORERS THEN AND NOW

- Social studies, science, critical thinking, oral communication

- Intermediate and advanced

With the upcoming 500th anniversary in 1992 of Columbus's voyage, relate the works of the astronauts to Columbus and other early explorers from the Renaissance, a period defined in chapter 1. In other words, how is an astronaut similar to Columbus, Cortez, or DeSoto? Each goes into the unknown, pilots a ship of some type, is searching for something, etc. Teach a

Renaissance unit, linking 1492 and the age of exploration with the 1990s and beyond as the great age of space exploration (see chapter 6).

Americans in Suborbit

Three weeks after Gagarin's history-making orbit of the earth, Navy Commander Alan Shepard, on May 5, 1961, became the first American to be launched into space from Cape Canaveral, Florida. He was seated in a contour seat inside the capsule, *Freedom 7*. As we noted earlier, a space capsule is a closed, pressurized compartment, detachable from the launch vehicle (rocket), in which the astronauts in the early space programs traveled in space. The capsules were vaguely bell-like in shape. A picture of another Mercury capsule, Glenn's *Friendship 7*, is in figure 5.7.

The *Freedom 7* was boosted into space by a 59-foot-high Mercury *Redstone* rocket burning liquid fuel (alcohol and liquid oxygen) to generate 78,000 pounds of thrust on a suborbital flight lasting 15 minutes and 22 seconds and reaching 116.5 miles in altitude. Shepard's flight helped test the spaceworthiness of the Mercury capsule before actually sending it into orbit. A second suborbital flight by Gus Grissom occurred on July 21, 1961; it lasted fifteen seconds longer than Shepard's and similarly tested the Mercury capsule and launch vehicles. The Mercury *Redstone* rockets (figure 5.5) that launched the first two suborbital flights were single-stage rockets but, like the final stage of the multistage rocket, the rocket burned out and fell away after launching the capsule. Meanwhile, the capsule had, of course, separated from the launch vehicle to perform its flight and land at sea, where ships rescued the astronaut and charred capsule.

A spacecraft's reentry to the earth's atmosphere is always dangerous. When satellites or cast-off rocket stages reenter, they travel so quickly (at least twenty times the speed of sound!) that upon reaching the outer layer of the earth's atmosphere there is tremendous friction with the thin air and they burn up. This friction produces 3,000-degree heat. For an unmanned satellite, the intense heat is no problem: its job over, the satellite just burns up. (Review earlier in this chapter, in the section about the X-15, the Aerospace Magnet dealing with friction.) However, for a space capsule carrying human beings, there must be a way to get the capsule and its occupants back to earth safely. From work on the X-15 and other research, scientists and engineers have been able to devise sealants and heat shields able to absorb or deflect this heat.[33] Recall how the Mercury, Gemini, and Apollo capsules were charred when they returned to Earth. In Bryan's *National Air and Space Museum*, listed in the bibliography, are photos (pp. 423-24) of an Apollo capsule that was seared at reentry. In the early days of the shuttle, NASA experimented with various types of protective black-and-white heat tiles glued to certain parts of the shuttle's exterior; 31,000 such tiles prevent the shuttle from burning on reentry[34] (see chapter 6 on the shuttle's tiles). This is a feature that makes the shuttle a reusable spacecraft, unlike the heat-damaged capsules and modules used in the Mercury, Gemini, and Apollo programs.

The returning capsules also must be maneuvered so they reenter the earth's atmosphere at the proper angle; the wrong angle of reentry can mean the capsule will either burn up or bounce back into space out of control. Descending at the proper angle, the capsule splashes into the ocean, where ships and divers, if needed, are ready to retrieve the capsule and rescue the astronauts. Until the space shuttle, all American spaceflights ended with at-sea landings.

Fig. 5.7. *Friendship 7.*

SAVING SPACE

- Language arts, art, oral communication, problem solving

- General

Have students add *space capsule* to their dictionaries and ask them to draw a space capsule. Discuss the confined size of the space capsules used in the first three space programs (Mercury, Gemini, and Apollo). Ask students to speculate about what the confined size would mean to the astronauts; how would it affect living and working conditions? Look ahead at the section on space suits, noting that John Glenn had fingertip lights on his gloves, which enabled him to work during the dark parts of his orbits. The fingertip lights also were "space-efficient," given the confined area of the capsule. Can students think of any other space-saving devices that would have made space travel in the small capsules a bit easier and more efficient? Point out the differences between the living and working conditions for the astronauts in those programs and the astronauts in the far roomier shuttles, discussed in chapter 6.

CAPE CANAVERAL, THE KENNEDY SPACE CENTER, AND THE JOHNSON SPACE CENTER

- Social studies, problem solving, science

- General

Have all students locate on a map Cape Canaveral (CC) on the east coast of Florida. Since 1947 it has been the major launch site for U.S. long-range missiles and, more recently, spacecraft. Between 1963 and 1973, it was called Cape Kennedy; then its name reverted to Cape Canaveral. The Kennedy Space Center occupies over 80,000 acres at CC and is now the main location for space launches. Students can also locate Houston, Texas, where the Johnson Space Center (JSC) is located. JSC is the major center for designing and developing spacecraft to carry people into space and to train astronauts for such flights, as well as for controlling manned space flights. Originally called the Manned Spacecraft Center, it controlled its first flight, *Gemini 4*, in June 1965. It was renamed in honor of President Lyndon B. Johnson in 1973.

Ask intermediate and advanced students why the location of Cape Canaveral was chosen for the main launch site for missiles and spacecraft. Notice its location in the Atlantic Ocean. Spacecraft will not be flying over towns and cities, where people on the ground could be hurt or killed in the event of an accident shortly after lift off (e.g., the *Challenger* disaster). Likewise, when the shuttle's solid rocket boosters (see chapter 6) fall back to earth to be retrieved, refurbished, and reused, they fall into the Atlantic Ocean. Furthermore, because spacecraft are taking off on the far eastern side of Florida, they get an extra boost in speed from the earth's eastward rotation on its axis once every 23 hours, 56 minutes, and 4.09 seconds.[35]

ANGLE OF REENTRY

- Science

- General

To get an idea about the angle of reentry, demonstrate the following. Get three small, flat stones and go to a pond or stream. (Maybe someone will let you throw three small stones in a swimming pool.) To see how the angle of reentry matters in a spacecraft descending to the earth, throw the stones individually into the water according to this pattern: First, throw one stone at a high angle—lob it—and see what happens: it hits the water nearly vertically and goes "plunk." This is the capsule reentering at too steep of an angle and burning up. Throw the second stone into the water with a low, hard hurl, just like you would use for skipping stones. The stone will skip along the surface one or two or more times before sinking. This second stone is the spacecraft coming in at too shallow of an angle and bouncing off the atmosphere back into space, out of control. The third stone should be thrown in between the two extremes just attempted. At that angle, the spacecraft can handle the heat and the speed for a safe reentry.

America Orbits the Earth

With Shepard's and Grissom's flights, America had launched two persons into suborbit; they went up and came down without going around the earth. Meanwhile, about six weeks after Grissom's flight, the Russians sent into space another cosmonaut in the *Vostok II* for just under eighteen orbits. Later that year (November 1961), America worked to catch up by launching a chimpanzee for two-and-a-half orbits. Enos, the chimp, came back fine. NASA gave the go-ahead for a human being to attempt it next.

America's determination to explore space was underscored by President John F. Kennedy in his historic message to the American people at a joint session of Congress on May 25, 1961. He said, "I believe this nation should commit itself to achieving the goal, before this decade is out, of landing a man on the moon and returning him safely to the Earth."[36] In fact, Project Mercury and its Gemini and Apollo successors were all dedicated to that ultimate lunar goal, which was achieved on July 20, 1969 by *Apollo XI*.

On February 20, 1962, Americans young and old were glued to their television sets to see Marine Lieutenant Colonel John Glenn enter his space capsule, the *Friendship 7* (figure 5.7), and become the first American to orbit earth. He orbited three times in a mission that lasted just a little under five hours. The capsule was launched by the one-and-a-half stage Mercury-*Atlas* rocket. It was a little over 67 feet high, and with the capsule and escape tower was just over 95 feet high. Its main engine produced 57,000 pounds of thrust, but it also had two *booster* engines (smaller rockets that are strapped onto the main rocket and then drop away after they burn out) to get it off the ground with an additional 308,000 pounds of thrust. Whereas the first two Mercury flights were completely computer controlled, Glenn was unexpectedly required to pilot the capsule when, near the end of the first orbit, the capsule's *attitude* (position in space) began veering to the right. Consequently, Glenn controlled the capsule's attitude using manual control for the remaining orbits.[37] By reentry, the trouble had disappeared, and the automatic system resumed control.

The nation was jubilant with Glenn's successful flight. After being honored at the White House by President Kennedy, Glenn and his two fellow veteran astronauts, Shepard and Grissom, were showered with ticker tape in a parade in New York City that brought out millions of cheering persons, reminiscent of the parade to honor Lindbergh. The parade was carried nationally on television. Three more Mercury flights were launched in 1962 and 1963, and the number of orbits increased to twenty-two.

Encouraged by the flights, NASA began to enlarge the astronaut corps in 1962 and to look for astronauts with wider training—not only engineers and pilots, but also astronomers, geologists, physiologists, physicians, physicists, and chemists. Meanwhile, in June 1963, Russia launched the *Vostok 6*, carrying the first woman to travel in space: Valentina Tereshkova. NASA's astronaut program did not admit women until 1978. Sally Ride was the first American woman astronaut to go into space on board the space shuttle *Challenger* (STS-7) on June 18, 1983. In October 1984, she returned to space on board *Challenger* (STS-41G) with another female crewmember, Kathryn Sullivan, who was the first American woman to walk in space.

WOMEN ASTRONAUTS

- Science, reading, social studies

- General

Students can read such works as June Behren's, *Sally Ride, Astronaut: An American First* (for beginners); Sally Ride with Susan Okie, *To Space and Back* (for intermediate and advanced); Joanne Bernstein, Rose Blue, with Alan Jay Gerber, *Judith Resnick, Challenger Astronaut* (intermediate and advanced); or other biographies suggested by the library media specialist. They can discuss women's experiences in a program that is male dominated. Female students can consider if they would be interested in joining the astronaut corps, which now as a number of women in it, among them Mary Cleave, Bonnie Dunbar, Anna Fisher (whose husband, William Fisher, is also an astronaut), Linda Godwin, Marsha Ivins, Margaret Rhea Seddon, and Ellen Shulman. Teachers or library media specialists can request updated lists of astronauts from NASA; ask for the "Astronauts Fact Sheet" at one of the NASA addresses in the appendix. NASA also offers an illustrated pamphlet, *Women at Work in NASA*, explaining an array of support positions at NASA held by women.

Next Step to the Moon: Gemini

The success of Mercury gave way during 1965 and 1966 to Project Gemini. Each of Gemini's ten manned missions involved two astronauts making anywhere from 3 to 206 orbits to research effects on people of longer periods in space. The Gemini capsule was twice the size of the Mercury capsule—19 feet long and 10 feet in diameter.[38] Planning to have two persons in the confined capsule for considerable periods of time, up to two weeks, NASA needed to be sure of candidates' abilities to work well with others and cooperate.

With two major propulsion systems provided by an innovative fuel system and a powerful sixteen-thruster maneuvering system, Gemini capsules were far more sophisticated than their Mercury predecessors. They were also designed to give astronauts real control over their flight. Whereas the Mercury capsules were basically controlled automatically—except, for example, when an emergency required Glenn to pilot his capsule—Gemini capsules were designed so that pilots could turn and roll them in all directions, raise or lower their orbits, and operate them during reentry, performing intricate maneuvers that allowed "pinpoint" landings.[39] From the Mercury program, engineers also realized that certain equipment could be located outside the pressurized cabin and could even be left behind at reentry. The Gemini capsules all were launched by Gemini-*Titan* two-stage rockets that produced 430,000 pounds of thrust in stage one and 100,000 pounds of thrust in stage two. The *Titan* was 90 feet high, 109 feet with the spacecraft on top.[40]

WORD ROOTS AND NAME CHOICES

- Language arts, science, mythology, problem solving

- General

Ask students to look up the word *Gemini* and then explain why NASA used it for this project. Ask them to identify Castor and Pollux. Gemini is a constellation containing the stars Castor and Pollux, represented as twins sitting together. In mythology, Castor and Pollux are twins. Twins or the number two have special meanings for Project Gemini: the Gemini missions each had two astronauts on board, involved the docking of two capsules, and were the second series of flights in America's space program.

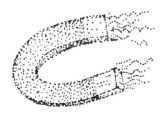

LEARN MORE ABOUT THE U.S. SPACE PROGRAM

- Library research, science, social studies, art, working in a group

- Intermediate

Students can get detailed information about all the American manned spaceflights from an encyclopedia or almanac or from many books devoted to spaceflight. Divide the class into teams (such as astronauts are grouped in the post-Mercury missions) and assign each team (or let each team select) an American space program to research: Mercury, Gemini, Apollo, Skylab, Apollo-Soyuz, and Space Shuttle. In some cases, such as Gemini, Apollo, and especially the Space Shuttle, there are so many flights that each program can be divided among as many as five teams. Students should get the dates and numbers of flights; names of astronauts, launch vehicles, and capsules; data about the flights; and other interesting information. The information from the individual teams can be pooled, and the class can make an illustrated timeline of manned space flights. The teacher can obtain a chart prepared by NASA called "First Americans in Space: Mercury to Apollo Soyuz," which summarizes much of the data about manned flights. NASA's "Information Summaries: U.S. Manned Space-Flight Log" offers similar information. Both are available from NASA's teacher resource distributors (see appendix for addresses).

Two Firsts: A Spacewalk and a Rendezvous

The Gemini program had two major highlights. First, on *Gemini 4* (June 3-7, 1965, making sixty-two orbits in just under ninety-eight hours) astronaut Edward H. White left the capsule and for twenty minutes "walked" in space, moving himself around by "shooting" a "gun" that squirted a jet of gas. He was attached to the capsule by a tether-umbilical cord. This spacewalk — also known as *EVA, extravehicular activity* — proved that an astronaut could survive and function outside the space capsule wearing the appropriate space suit with enough oxygen.

The second Gemini highlight occurred on December 15, 1965, when *Gemini 6* met and matched orbital speed with *Gemini 7*, and the two rendezvoused or docked for twenty hours and twenty-two minutes. This would be a critical procedure for the projected lunar missions, in which the main capsule (command module) would orbit the moon, while a smaller capsule (lunar module) would leave it, land on the moon, and then return to dock with the command module. This is precisely what happened with *Apollo 11* in July 1969: while Michael Collins orbited the moon piloting the command module, Neil Armstrong and Edwin "Buzz" Aldrin took the lunar module and landed on the moon for their moon walk. Gemini had paved the way for the next program: Project Apollo.

Conditions of a Space Flight

As noted in chapter 1, gravity is the force that pulls all objects towards earth. Earth's gravitational force is one g. At blast-off, the Mercury, Gemini, and Apollo astronauts experienced high gravity as much as eight times the normal pull of gravity; on the space shuttle, however, the gravity at launch goes only as high as three. What causes high gravity? When a spacecraft lifts off, it must push against the gravity that is pulling it back to earth. Astronauts feel many times heavier than their normal body weight on earth. To train for high gravity, astronauts are whirled around and around at high speeds in a *centrifuge*, a machine with a model space capsule at the end of a long arm. As the capsule is spun at increasingly high speeds, the more force pushes on the astronaut, who is strapped to the seat inside the capsule, and the heavier the astronaut feels. (To give students an idea of how quickly a centrifuge whirls, tell them it is like the spin cycle on a washing machine.) Astronauts also experience high g's when they reenter the earth's atmosphere from the weightless condition of space. In the early space programs, astronauts sometimes experienced g-forces as high as eleven g's; on today's shuttles, however, astronauts usually experience no higher than three g's.

CENTRIFUGAL AND CENTRIPETAL FORCE

- Science (physics)

- Advanced

Explain Newton's law of acceleration: the force required to give an acceleration is directly proportional to the acceleration. Then discuss the effect of g forces on the astronauts at liftoff and reentry, particularly on pre-shuttle missions, during which g forces were exceptionally high.

Once in space, astronauts experience *weightlessness*, which means there is no gravity; this is also called *zero g*. Weightlessness poses some problems: everything and everyone floats around unless fastened in place or contained. Even water or juice in a container floats out in little spheres. The astronauts themselves float upside down and right side up without any difference because there is no "up" or "down" at zero g. Former space shuttle astronaut Sally Ride describes the feeling: "On Earth being upside down feels different because gravity is pulling the blood toward my head. In space I feel exactly the same whether my head is toward the floor or toward the ceiling."[41]

To train astronauts for life at zero gravity, NASA places them in environments that simulate the condition. For example, to train astronauts for today's shuttle flights (see chapter 6), NASA provides various simulation experiences, including flying the astronauts in a modified KC-135 jet airplane. The plane is flown over the top of a parabolic path, giving the effect of a speedily descending elevator; the astronauts "float" around unstrapped in the padded cabin for about half a minute at a time. For longer periods, astronauts are trained underwater in a special tank, where they experience what is known as *neutral buoyancy*. Some astronauts experience nausea when first encountering weightlessness because the inner ear is affected. Usually, this feeling passes.

WEIGHTLESSNESS

- Science (biology)

- Intermediate and advanced

Explain the physiological effects of weightlessness, especially bone and muscle atrophy and calcium deterioration. Point out that shuttle and space station astronauts are on an exercise program during their mission. On the shuttle, for example, astronauts take a daily walk, while strapped, on a treadmill; air from a duct near the treadmill dries off their perspiration. See also chapter 6 for more on shuttle exercise.

Maintaining the Environment in Space

In the early days of space travel, astronauts' food was in tubes and pouches and they squirted liquids into their mouths. Drinking lots of liquid has always been important, particularly on flights exceeding a few days, because dehydration occurs. However, the ways of carrying and consuming foods and liquids have improved (see discussion of space shuttle in chapter 6).

One thing has never changed, however, and that is the need to supply oxygen and to regulate temperature, pressure, and humidity in the spacecraft so that the environment is earth-like and supports life. Before the space shuttle, astronauts wore space suits for the duration of their missions. Nowadays, however, not all astronauts need to wear space suits. To fully appreciate how far space technology has come, consider the early space suits.

Test pilot Joe Walker's X-15 flight of March 30, 1961, included his wearing a pressurized suit that was the prototype for Mercury, Gemini, and Apollo space suits. Early suits were rigid and made every bodily movement difficult. It took an astronaut over an hour to suit up with the help of another person. A Norman Rockwell painting, *Suiting Up* (1965), depicting the *Gemini 3* astronauts being suited up, illustrates well the complexities involved in dressing for spaceflight in those days.[42] Nowadays, as seen in chapter 6's discussion of the space shuttle, an astronaut can dress in a space suit without assistance even at zero gravity.

Like today's suits, the early suits were pressurized and contained full life support were the capsule systems to fail. They had removable collection assemblies for eliminating bodily wastes. Along with the actual suit, there were boots, gloves, and helmets, all of which were designed to be airtight at the seams and fully pressurized. Made of tear resistant, strong materials, they protected the wearer from radiation and space particles. Within the pressurized helmet the headgear included a microphone and headset for communications with other crewmembers and with mission control on earth, as well as a connection to an oxygen supply. In later suits, the visor on the helmet was tinted to protect the astronaut's eyes from dangerous heat and radiation. Certain mission suits had special features. For example, John Glenn's suit had tiny flashlights attached to the fingers of his gloves so he could work during dark parts of his orbits.[43]

For the Apollo flights, particularly for moonwalking, NASA created a highly complicated but more flexible moon suit to allow greater mobility and to permit the astronaut to leave the command module without being attached to it by the tether-umbilical cord used in the EVAs of Project Gemini.[44] For such activity, the astronauts also wore backpacks holding their portable life support system (PLSS), which supplied oxygen for breathing and also functioned in communicating, maintaining proper suit pressure and temperature, and removing contaminants from the oxygen.[45] Beginning with the Apollo missions, the space suit was white to reflect heat better; for the previous projects, the suits were a silvery color.[46] Although some aspects of the space suit remain the same for today's shuttle astronauts, the current space suit is far more complicated, yet far easier to wear than the old ones — and it is recyclable. The modern space suit and other shuttle apparel are discussed in chapter 6.

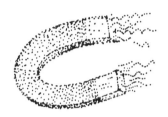

MAKE A SPACE HELMET

- Science, mathematics, art, oral communication, problem solving

- Beginning

Materials: Cardboard boxes that can be cut to fit over the students' heads (boxes from bookstores seem to be a good size), white spray paint, tape, sheets of (amber) cellophane, scissors, razor-type knife, crayons, pencils, string, rulers, newspaper to cover the floor for the spray painting (do in a well-ventilated area).

Procedure: (Note: Only teachers and adult helpers should do the cutting.)

1. Spray paint the box white.

2. After fitting the box so that it goes over the child's head, carefully cut out a square area on one side with a razor; this will be the side for the visor. Students can measure the area and mark the cutting lines with their pencils before the teacher/aid does the actual cutting.

3. Have students draw a flag on the back of the box and/or launch insignias on the sides.

4. Tape a piece of cellophane across the inside of the hole cut for the visor. *Be sure to leave plenty of ventilation holes!*

5. Cut two holes on either side of the "visor" area for a chin strap.

6. Use the string, which students should measure for cutting, to tie the box under the child's chin.

Discussion: Review with students the job of the helmet for real astronauts: protects the head; provides a pressurized environment for the head; contains apparatus for supplying oxygen and filtering out impurities to enable the astronaut to breathe; contains communication units (microphone and headset) so the astronaut can keep in touch with spacecraft and mission control. Then ask students: What are some other activities in which people wear helmets? Who are some persons who wear helmets on the job? (Bicycle and motorcycle riders; construction workers; fighter and bomber pilots; kayakers; fire-fighters; infantry soldiers; football, baseball, hockey players, etc.) Do the students ever wear helmets? (Riding their bikes; playing baseball, football, hockey, etc.)

Apollo Modules

President Kennedy's goal to land a man on the moon by the end of the decade of the 1960s came closer with the Apollo program, for which a manned lunar landing was the specific goal. To do this, it was decided to use a lunar orbit rendezvous, for which the earlier Gemini docking had been a beginning.[47] Using this approach, the Apollo command module would remain in lunar orbit piloted by one astronaut, while two other astronauts descended to the moon in an excursion vehicle and then rendezvoused with the command module to return to earth. Apollo used *modules*, which are separated units within a spacecraft, instead of capsules.

The Apollo vehicles had *service* and *command modules*, based on the Gemini concept of placing equipment not needed for reentry in a special compartment separate from the cabin where the astronauts are seated. Thus, the spacecraft has a command module that holds the crew during launching, flying, and landing and the equipment for life support and communication, as well as for controlling and navigating; it provides oxygen, a regulated temperature and humidity, and removes carbon dioxide. The service module, the unmanned part of the spacecraft, holds equipment and supplies unnecessary for reentry. Only the command module returns to earth. The *Apollo* command module was 10 feet, 7 inches high and a little under 13 feet in diameter. Its service module was 24 feet, 9 inches high by 12 feet, 10 inches.[48]

With the moon as its goal, *Apollo* required a more powerful rocket than had been used for earlier missions. The two-stage *Saturn 1B*, with 1.830 million pounds of thrust, and its successor, the huge three-stage *Saturn V* (figure 5.6), with 9.14 million pounds of thrust, were developed.[49]

AEROSPACE TERMS

- Language arts, science

- Beginning and intermediate

Add *module, command module*, and *service module* to the students' dictionaries.

America's First Human Space Casualties

After several unmanned flights, the first manned mission, with astronauts Gus Grissom, Edward White (the first spacewalker), and Roger Chaffee, was set for *Apollo 204*, later designated *Apollo 1*. The new command module, able to hold three persons, was 10 feet, 7 inches high and 12 feet, 10 inches in diameter. On January 27, 1967, the astronauts entered the command module to perform a preflight launch simulation and test; the actual flight would be in February. Sealed in their cabin, the crew members performed tests with the launch crew on the ground for nearly six hours. Various technical problems irritated the crew. Suddenly, one of the astronauts yelled, "Fire aboard the spacecraft!" Within seconds, the cabin exploded as the fire in the pressurized capsule atmosphere of pure oxygen became an inferno.[50] (Remind students that oxygen is required for combustion; recall the use of liquid oxygen to burn the fuel in the liquid-fuel rocket.) Three astronauts were dead in the cabin, which was a charpit.[51] It looked like the Apollo program was going nowhere, especially not to the moon. Although previous space missions and tests had involved some close calls, the *Apollo 1* disaster reminded everyone of the mortal danger involved in space exploration, even on the ground (see astronaut Captain Dale Gardner's interview in chapter 6).

Apollo Is Redesigned

During the next one-and-a-half years, not only was the *Apollo* command module completely redesigned (including a quick-escape hatch), but safety and manufacturing flaws were corrected. As space historian Neil McAleer emphasizes, the accident and the measures taken to prevent another one like it were viewed by NASA workers as a "team effort" and responsibility.[52] Yet, the memory of three individuals who had burned to death remained with NASA and, indeed, America. On their lunar visit less than two years later, Neil Armstrong and Edwin "Buzz" Aldrin would leave an *Apollo 1* shoulder patch in memory of their dead colleagues.

The first manned flight after the fire was the *Apollo 7* mission of October 11-22, 1968, flown by astronauts Wally Schirra, Donn Eisele, and Walter Cunningham. This flight proved the worthiness of the new command module and support elements. It was launched by the *Saturn 1B* rocket, which stood nearly 80 feet high without the *Apollo* spacecraft and launch escape system, and 224 feet high with them on top. This two-stage rocket had a combined 1.830 million pounds of thrust.[53] The success of this flight led to humanity's first lunar orbit (actually, ten orbits in twenty hours) by the *Apollo 8* in December 1968 by astronauts Frank Borman, James Lovell, and William Anders. The world watched televised pictures from the *Apollo* flight on Christmas Eve 1968. This flight had several other "firsts." For example, it was the first manned capsule to be launched by the huge and mighty *Saturn V* rocket, which would launch all future missions in the Apollo program. Its crew were the first persons to view the entire earth and the back side of the moon. It was also the first manned flight to travel at escape velocity, the minimum speed required to break free of the gravitational pull of a planet — from the earth, it is 6.95 miles per second or 25,020 miles per hour.[54]

Americans Walk on the Moon

The excitement of *Apollo 8*'s lunar orbiting was exceeded only by the actual lunar landing of *Apollo 11*, which followed *Apollo 9* and *10*, proving the ability of the command and service modules to separate from and rejoin with the lunar excursion module (LEM). The LEM was a two-stage module, stored underneath the command and service modules. The historical significance of *Apollo 11* was underscored by the presence of aviation pioneers Charles Lindbergh and T. Claude Ryan, the builder of the *Spirit of St. Louis*, at the launch.[55] Lindbergh's and Ryan's attendance at this launch reminds us how each successive step in aerospace science is built on previous steps, as the "Steps to Outer Space" in figure I.1 illustrate.

What was unique about the lunar landing was that it was a first-in-flight event that the world watched on television.[56] It was one of those few events about which most of us can recall where we were when it happened. For their lunar EVA, the astronauts wore their moon suits and their PLSSs, which weighed 104 pounds on earth, but under 20 pounds on the moon, where there is much less gravity. (See the Aerospace Magnet, "Understanding Gravity's Effects," in chapter 1, where there is a mathematics activity converting gravities: the moon's gravity is .17 of earth's, so the PLSS would weigh 104 multiplied by .17 or 17.68 pounds on the moon.)

On July 20, 1969, at 4:17:40 p.m. EDT, the LEM *Eagle*, carrying Commander Neil Armstrong and Colonel Edwin "Buzz" Aldrin, landed near the dry Sea of Tranquility, with Armstrong declaring, "The *Eagle* has landed."[57] At precisely 10:56:20 p.m. EDT, Neil Armstrong emerged from the *Eagle*, placed his left foot tentatively on the moon's powdery soil and said, "That's one small step for man, one giant leap for mankind."[58] Aldrin followed nineteen minutes later.[59] They spent two hours and thirty-six minutes in extravehicular activity performing various experiments and lifted off at 1:54 p.m. EDT on July 21 to rendezvous with the *Columbia* command module that had been in lunar orbit, piloted by Lieutenant Colonel Michael Collins. The moonwalkers brought back to earth nearly 50 pounds of moon dirt and rock, as well as scores of photographs. They left, among other mementoes, an American flag (stiffened with a brace so that the Stars and Stripes could "wave" in the airless lunar environment) planted in the soil, a plaque saying that the earth persons had come "in peace for all mankind," an *Apollo 1* patch to honor Grissom, White, and Chaffee, and a medal honoring the memory of two dead Russian cosmonauts.

FIRST PEOPLE ON THE MOON

- Language arts, art

- General

Ask students to imagine that they are the first persons to visit the moon. Ask them to write an essay describing what they would leave behind on the moon. Ask them to illustrate their "moon landing." You may wish to look ahead to the end of chapter 6, where the space station *Freedom* is discussed; the station is designed to serve as launch point for future lunar missions.

Ten More Moonwalkers

The Apollo program continued through *Apollo 17* (with *Apollo 13* aborted because of oxygen failure in the service module), which flew in December 1972. In addition to Armstrong and Aldrin, ten astronauts, including America's first astronaut, Alan Shepard, visited the moon. *Apollo 14*, with its command spacecraft named *Kitty Hawk* to honor the Wright brothers, is another reminder of the continuity of aerospace activities from the earliest to the latest. America's dozen moonwalkers came back with a total of 843 pounds of moon rocks.[60]

The last three Apollo missions used the lunar roving vehicles (LRV), popularly known as the *moon buggies*, which could be driven at only 7 or 8 miles per hour (see figure 5.8). They enabled astronauts to make trips and transport equipment several miles from their lunar modules.[61] All were left on the moon—lunar litter!

Fig. 5.8. Moon buggy.

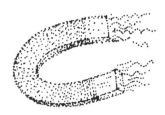

WHAT IS IT LIKE ON THE MOON?

- Library research, science, art, oral communication, language arts

- General

Ask the class to research the conditions on the moon. Could the moon sustain life? What are the craters? What are the "phases of the moon"? How do the moon's "tides" affect our planet? What would we need to do if we created a colony for human beings on the moon? Ask students to investigate these and/or other questions for brief oral and written reports. Students might wish to illustrate their reports with drawings of the moon based on their research; they might draw a moon colony, complete with technical details such as a huge pressurized dome in which persons could function, filtration for air and water, etc. Brainstorm with the class on what would be needed. You may wish to look ahead to the end of chapter 6, where the planned space station *Freedom* is discussed.

ASTRO-POEMS

- Language arts

- General

Ask students to write poems about visiting the moon or a planet. Why would they like to visit the moon or the planet? What would they expect to find there? Would the trip be scary? exciting? fun? boring? too long? What would it be like to be in a capsule at the top of a rocket? What do students feel when they see a rocket or a shuttle launched? Advanced students can read and respond to G. Snyder's poem, "Vapor Trails," in Stephen Dunning, et al., eds., *Some Haystacks Don't Even Have Any Needle: And Other Complete Modern Poems* and in Paul Molloy, ed., *Beach Glass and Other Poems*.

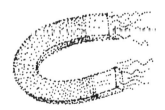

MOON ROCKS AND "LUNATICS"

- Science

- General

Although specimens of moon rocks exist at various museums and collections around the country, it is also possible to show or have shown to your class a lunar sample disc, an acrylic plastic disc containing six lunar specimens. Teachers can take brief workshops sponsored by NASA to become certified as borrowers of the disc; the workshop also gives participants an activities booklet to use with the disc when showing it to students. For information on becoming a certified lunar disc borrower—or, as the NASA Aerospace Education Services Project people say, "a certified lunatic"—or finding if there is a certified borrower in your area who could bring the disc to your school, contact the NASA education or public affairs officer assigned to your state. Their addresses, with their regional responsibility areas, appear in the appendix.

Russian Achievements and Space Stations

While America had been busy having people space walk and moon walk, the first nation to send an artificial satellite into orbit was far from passive. Cosmonauts walked in space (March 18, 1965), rendezvoused, exchanged crews (*Soyuz 4* and *5*, January 1969), and landed a robotic lunar rover (November 10, 1970). However, Russia's major project was launched on April 19, 1971, when *Salyut 1*, the first space station, went into orbit; it was unmanned.[62]

A *space station* is a huge laboratory with living quarters launched into earth orbit for an indefinite period; astronauts travel to it, work and live there in a weightless environment for some time, and then return to earth when other astronauts arrive to take their place in the station. The space station has docking ports so spacecraft can rendezvous with it, leave and accept astronauts, and depart. It is capable of being constantly resupplied with water, oxygen, and other necessities.

Between 1971 and February 1984, Russia launched seven Salyut space stations, with each successive station growing more sophisticated and their occupants spending longer and longer periods in the station. By number six, which remained in orbit a little under four years, there were a water regeneration system and a propulsion system that could be refueled in orbit. The seventh and final space station in the Salyut series went up in April 1982. The first crew to visit it came on the *Soyuz T-5*; two cosmonauts remained on the station for 210 days. In February 1984, three cosmonauts came to the station on the *Soyuz T-10* and remained there for a record eight months.

Without a spacecraft docked, the Salyut space stations were about 43 feet long and 14 feet in diameter; they weighed about 19 tons. The stations could accommodate up to five persons. Occupants performed various kinds of experiments.

America's **Skylab** *Station*

America, too, had its space station, called *Skylab*. This program, consisting of three crews of three astronauts each sent in 1973 and 1974 to the *Skylab* station, succeeded the Apollo program. In fact, the Skylab program literally grew out of Apollo: it was built basically from revamped Apollo materials and the third stage of a Saturn rocket left over from the Apollo days. It was also huge: weighing about 100 tons, it was roughly 118 feet from stem to stern, the size of a three-bedroom house—America's largest spacecraft.[63]

The main objective of the Skylab program was to see the effect of long-term stays in space on human beings. In addition, the crews who lived in *Skylab* performed hundreds of experiments and made the first observations of the sun above the earth's atmosphere, taking about 175,000 photos of the sun.[64]

EFFECTS OF LIVING IN SPACE

- Library research, science (biology), physical education

- General

Using the library, have students first investigate reports from *Gemini 7* about the effects of space travel on the astronauts. These effects, especially due to weightlessness, included physical deterioration: dehydration, loss of muscle tone, loss of calcium, and changes in the cardiovascular system.[65] Ask students to research the experiences of the Russian cosmonauts in 1970 and 1971: the first crew returned from eighteen days in orbit in such a deteriorated state that they had to be carried from their spacecraft on stretchers; in 1971 cosmonauts died mysteriously. What did *Skylab* crews discover about prolonged stays in space? (Leisure time needed to be included in the crew's schedule; daily workouts on an exercycle helped keep muscles toned.) How do the shuttle crews stay fit? To compensate for the lack of gravity, weakening the bones and muscles, the crewmembers exercise on a treadmill fastened to the floor to prevent it from floating in the weightless environment; pull on their wrists with opposite hands; and run in place while pushing against a wall. For beginning and intermediate students, see NASA's two *Living in Space* manuals, which have a section on staying fit in space and include many activities students will enjoy. Teachers and advanced students may wish to read Peter Smolders's *Living in Space: A Handbook for Space Travellers*, which provides information and illustrations about life aboard the shuttle and space stations and looks forward to space colonies. Teachers may wish to work with the school's physical education teacher on this unit.

The three Skylab crews traveled to the space station in a modified Apollo command module launched by a *Saturn 1B* rocket.[66] The *Skylab* itself was launched into orbit about 300 miles above earth by a two-stage *Saturn 5* rocket on May 14, 1973; this was *Skylab 1*. Eleven days later (May 25, 1973), the first crew went up as *Skylab 2* to spend twenty-eight days in the station. The next mission, *Skylab 3*, went up on July 28, 1973, and spent fifty-nine days in the space station. The final crew, in *Skylab 4*, was sent on November 16, 1973, and stayed eighty-four days.[67] Unlike the Russian space stations, *Skylab* was not designed to remain in space indefinitely. In fact, it remained in orbit for an even shorter time than planned.

Skylab's orbit started to decline in 1979, earlier than anticipated because of extremely high sunspot activity.[68] On June 11, 1979, those charred bits and pieces of *Skylab* that did not burn up in the atmosphere fell into the Indian Ocean and onto a farm in Australia. Nobody, fortunately, was hurt by this space debris. Although the space station ended in ashes, the findings of the crews who spent a total of 171 days working and living in it continue to benefit manned space exploration.

WAR AFFECTS SPACE PROGRAM

- Library research, social studies (politics and economics)

- Intermediate and advanced

Discuss with the class what was happening in America and the world during the years of the Skylab missions (1973-1974). Ask students to consult yearbooks, almanacs, and newspapers and magazines on microfilm. How did the United States's involvement in Vietnam affect the space program? How did that war affect the nation's economy and governmental spending decisions? Notice, too, that after the *Apollo-Soyuz* docking during July 1975 (discussed in chapter 6), there is not another manned space launch until the first space shuttle mission in April 1981. In other words, after fourteen years of a busy flight schedule, NASA did not launch another manned spacecraft for nearly six full years.

Cosmonauts and Astronauts Shake Hands in Space

In July 1975 the final mission of the Apollo program was a joint venture between the United States and Russia, the Apollo-Soyuz Test Project (ASTP). The two spacecraft docked in earth orbit on July 18, 1975, and the three astronauts and two cosmonauts visited each other's module, ate together, and remained in space together for four days.[69] Two countries who had long distrusted each other and had been vying for space superiority were literally shaking hands in space. ASTP was a peaceful end to an exciting Apollo program that had included moon orbits, moonwalks, drives in moon buggies, and extended stays in the *Skylab*.

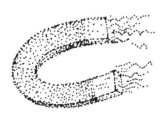

GRAPHING THE ROCKETS AND SEEING PROPORTIONS

- Science, art, mathematics, problem solving

- Beginning and intermediate

The narrative about space flights has included information on the rockets that served as launch vehicles. Their measurements are summarized here, with heights including the space capsule and escape tower mounted on top.[70] Mercury-*Redstone*, 70-inch diameter, 83 feet high; Mercury-*Atlas*, diameter is 16 feet at base tapering to 10 feet near top, 95.3 feet high; Gemini-*Titan*, 10-foot diameter, 109 feet high; *Saturn 1B*, stage one has 21.4-foot diameter, second stage and instrument unit have 21.7-foot diameters, with entire rocket assembly 224 feet high; *Saturn V's* three stages have respective diameters of 33 feet, 33 feet, and 21.7 feet, while diameter of instrument unit is also 21.7 feet, and height of entire assembly is 363 feet.

Using these figures and the drawings of the rockets included in this chapter (figures 5.5 and 5.6), have students:

1. Round off measurements to nearest whole numbers.

2. Create a scale, such as 1 inch equals 1 foot, or use graph paper and have "x" number of boxes equal 1 foot.

3. Do the necessary mathematical conversions from feet to inches.

4. Create a vertical bar graph with the rockets serving as the graph bars so students can understand the different relative sizes of the launch vehicles.

Teachers can also vary this exercise for younger students by simply having the students calculate the differences in height and diameter among the rockets. Review with the class the material about each program such as: What was each program's destination? How far did the rockets have to travel? How many astronauts did each mission per program carry (Mercury, one; Gemini, two; Apollo, three)? Encourage students to speculate why the rockets became progressively bigger. The class may wish to create a mural of the rockets drawn to scale.

Mir: *The Ultimate Space Station*

Building on their experience with the Salyut stations, the Russians launched into orbit a space station called *Mir*, meaning "peace," on February 20, 1986. Weighing 46,300 pounds, it is 43 feet long and 13.7 feet in diameter, and it has six docking ports. On December 29, 1987, a cosmonaut set a single-person endurance record by remaining in *Mir* for just over 326 days. On December 21, 1989, two cosmonauts returned from *Mir* after having spent 366 days in it. Russia holds the world endurance records for extended stays in space.[71] *Mir* is the ultimate space station to date. However, at the end of chapter 6 we will look at NASA's plans for a new U.S. space station, *Freedom*.

After the Apollo-Soyuz mission of 1975, the American space program appeared to be on hiatus: it sent no manned spacecraft until 1981. Add to that hiatus the disintegration and fall of *Skylab* and it certainly appeared as though the American space program, which had achieved so much in so few years, was grinding to a halt. With the Vietnam War at the front of America's mind and budget, space funding was harder to come by. What America seemed to need was a more economical space program, including equipment that could be recycled. America would get this—from reusable space suits to reusable spacecraft—with the Space Transportation System or, as it is popularly called, the *space shuttle*.

Notes

[1]C. D. B. Bryan, *The National Air and Space Museum*, 2d ed. (New York: Harry N. Abrams, 1988), 344.

[2]George Harvard Gibbs-Smith, *Aviation: An Historical Survey from Its Origins to the End of World War II*, 2d ed. (London: Her Majesty's Stationery Office, 1985), 181. See also Bryan, *National Air and Space Museum*, 350.

[3]Jules Verne, *From the Earth to the Moon* (New York: Airmont Publishing, 1969), 116-24.

[4]Gibbs-Smith, *Aviation*, 215.

[5]Bryan, *National Air and Space Museum*, 350.

[6]Gibbs-Smith, *Aviation*, 215.

[7]Data from Gibbs-Smith, *Aviation*, 215.

[8]*Vision*, a poster of twelve "Firsts in Flight" (Seattle: Boeing Aircraft, n.d.), verso side; Air Force ROTC, *Aerospace Science: History of Air Power* (Maxwell Air Force Base, Ala.: Air University Press, 1986), 3-26; Jay Miller, *The X-Planes: X-1 to X-31*, rev. ed. (New York: Orion/Aerofax Books, 1988), 9-11.

[9]Miller, *X-Planes*, 15.

[10]Miller, *X-Planes*, 21.

[11]For complete information and numerous pictures about the whole X-series, see Miller, *X-Planes*. A far less thorough but more readable book about X-planes for beginning and intermediate students is John Gabriel Navarra, *Superplanes* (Garden City, N.Y.: Doubleday, 1979).

[12]Air Force ROTC, *Aerospace Science*, 3-27.

[13]Air Force ROTC, *Aerospace Science*, 3-27.

[14]Miller, *X-Planes*, 65.

[15]Paolo Matricardi, *The Concise History of Aviation* (New York: Crescent Books, 1984), 178, 232-33.

[16]Bryan, *National Air and Space Museum*, 75-76; Miller, *X-Planes*, 113-29, passim.

[17]Miller, *X-Planes*, 122.

[18]*Information Please Almanac, Atlas, and Yearbook* (Boston: Houghton Mifflin, 1991), 359.

[19]Miller, *X-Planes*, 129; Bryan, *National Air*, 76.

[20]Matricardi, *History of Aviation*, 190-91, 236-37.

[21]Bryan, *National Air and Space Museum*, 80. Neil McAleer, *The OMNI Space Almanac* (New York: OMNI, World Almanac Books, 1987), 12.

[22]McAleer, *Space Almanac*, 12.

[23]McAleer, *Space Almanac*, 14-15.

[24]McAleer, *Space Almanac*, 15.

[25]Bryan, *National Air and Space Museum*, 80; McAleer, *Space Almanac*, 210.

[26]Felix Belair, Jr., "Eisenhower Asks New Space Agency," *New York Times*, 3 April 1953, p. 1, col. 5; "Civilian Agency for Space Voted," *New York Times*, 17 July 1958, p. 30, cols. 6-8; "President Hails New Space Board," *New York Times*, 30 July 1958, p. 10, cols. 4-5.

[27]E. John Dewaard and Nancy Dewaard, *History of NASA: America's Voyage to the Stars* (New York: Exeter Books, 1984), 13. "Civil Space Group Starts Operation," *New York Times*, 2 October 1958, p. 37, col. 1.

[28]McAleer, *Space Almanac*, 30.

[29]McAleer, *Space Almanac*, 30. See also *The Information Please Almanac* (1991) for a good summary of lunar and planetary probes, 320-22.

[30]McAleer, *Space Almanac*, 31.

[31]Bryan, *National Air and Space Museum*, 356 n.*.

[32]National Aeronautics and Space Administration (NASA), *First Americans in Space: Mercury to Soyuz* (n.p., n.d.), verso side.

[33]NASA, *First Americans in Space*, recto side.

[34]The shuttle's protective heat tiles are thoroughly discussed and illustrated in *NASA, Space Shuttle News Reference* (Houston, Johnson Space Center: NASA, n.d.), 4.25-4.31. Perhaps more accessible through your school or public library is McAleer, *Space Almanac*, who on pp. 69-70 provides a comprehensive explanation of the tiles' compositions, specific locations on the shuttle, method of custom fitting each tile to the shuttle, etc.

[35]*Information Please Almanac*, 332.

[36]Dewaard and Dewaard, *History of NASA*, 17.

[37]Richard Witkin, "Glenn Orbits Earth 3 Times and Is Picked Up in His Capsule by a US Destroyer," *New York Times*, 21 February 1962, p. 20, cols. 2, 3.

[38]NASA, *First Americans in Space*, recto side.

[39]McAleer, *Space Alamanac*, 22; NASA, *First Americans in Space*, recto side.

[40]NASA, *First Americans in Space*, both sides.

[41]Sally Ride with Susan Okie, *To Space and Back* (New York: Lothrop, Lee and Shepard Books, 1986), 29. Students of all ages will enjoy this book about Ride's first spaceflight; it has great photos, too. See also astronaut Dale Gardner's comments about weightlessness in chapter 6.

[42]See Bryan, *National Air and Space Museum*, 360, for a copy of the painting. Bryan also contains photos of different space suits on display at the National Air and Space Museum.

[43]"The Nation: Space," *Time*, 2 March 1962, 12-14.

[44]Bryan, *National Air and Space Museum*, 352.

[45]Bryan, *National Air and Space Museum*, 353.

[46]Sheila Andrews Birskin and Audrey Kirschenbaum, *Living in Space*, Book 2, Levels D, E, F (Washington, D.C.: U.S. Government Printing Office, 1987), 11; Bryan, *National Air and Space Museum*, 351-53.

[47]McAleer, *Space Almanac*, 31-32.

[48]NASA, *First Americans in Space*, recto side.

[49]NASA, *First Americans in Space*, verso side.

[50]"3 Apollo Astronauts Die in Fire; Grissom, White, Chaffee Caught in Capsule During a Test on Pad," *New York Times*, 28 January 1967, p. 1, cols. 4-8, p. 10, cols. 1-8.

[51]"The Nation: Space," *Time*, 3 February 1967, 13-16.

[52]McAleer, *Space Almanac*, 159.

[53]NASA, *First Americans in Space*, verso side.

[54]"The Nation: Into the Depths of Space," *Time*, 27 December 1968, p. 6, col. 2; McAleer, *Space Almanac*, 54; Dewaard and Dewaard, *History of NASA*, 55-61.

[55]Bryan, *National Air and Space Museum*, 383.

[56]*Vision*, entry for July 20, 1969.

[57]John Noble Wilford, "Men Walk on Moon," *New York Times*, 21 July 1969, p. 1, cols. 7-8.

[58]Ibid.

[59]Ibid.

[60]Bryan, *National Air and Space Museum*, 402.

[61]Bryan, *National Air and Space Museum*, 397.

[62]For a highly detailed account of not only the *Salyut 1*, but all space stations to 1989 and stations planned for the future, see the exceptionally well-illustrated book by Ray Spangenburg and Diane Moser, *Living and Working in Space* (New York: Facts on File, 1989), 5-7, 8, 10, et passim.

[63]NASA, *First Americans in Space*, recto side; *Information Please Almanac*, 322.

[64]*Information Please Almanac*, 322; Spangenburg and Moser, *Working in Space*, 17-19.

[65]Bryan, *National Air and Space Museum*, 414, 422.

[66]NASA, *First Americans in Space*, recto side.

[67]NASA, *First Americans in Space*, recto side.

[68]*Information Please Almanac*, 322.

[69]See Spangenburg and Moser, *Working in Space*, 22-29.

[70]The following data come from NASA, *First Americans in Space*, verso side.

[71]Data about *Mir* come from Spangenburg and Moser, *Working in Space*, 70-74, which includes photos and drawings; *Information Please Almanac*, 323 (includes photo), 325.

Bibliography

Air Force ROTC. *Aerospace Science: History of Air Power*. Maxwell Air Force Base, Ala.: Air University Press, 1986.

Andrews, Sheila Briskin, and Audrey Kirschenbaum. *Living in Space*. Washington, D.C.: U.S. Government Printing Office, 1987.
Two series of manuals at the elementary level—one for grades 1, 2, 3 and another for 4, 5, 6—giving lots of activities related to all aspects of a shuttle mission. One caveat: procedures for activities are sketchy, if given at all, so if you use this series study it well and try some procedures on your own before bringing this into the classroom; also do not be confused by their mixing up flight suits with shuttle crew modulewear!

Behrens, June. *Sally Ride, Astronaut: An American First*. Chicago: Childrens Press, 1984.

Bernstein, Joanne, and Rose Blue, with Alan Jay Gerber. *Judith Resnick, Challenger Astronaut*. New York: Dutton, 1990.

"Biographical Data" sheet on astronaut Dale Gardner. Houston, Johnson Space Center: NASA, May 1986.
NASA has data sheets on all the astronauts.

Bondurant, R. Lynn, Jr. *On the Wings of a Dream: The Space Shuttle*. Washington, D.C.: National Air and Space Museum, n.d.
Readable for intermediate students through teachers; good photos; follows a typical shuttle mission from launch to landing.

Brewton, Sara, John E. Brewton, and John Brewton Blackburn, comps. *Of Quarks, Quasars, and Other Quirks: Quizzical Poems for the Supersonic Age*. New York: Thomas Y. Crowell, 1977.
Includes various poems about technology and space that students of all ages and their teachers will enjoy.

Bryan, C. D. B. *The National Air and Space Museum*. 2d ed. New York: Harry N. Abrams, 1988.
Great photos of exhibits from the museum; great, detailed reading; the school library should own this!

Cole, Joanna, and Bruce Degen. *The Magic School Bus Lost in the Solar System*. New York: Scholastic, 1990.

Dewaard, E. John, and Nancy Dewaard. *History of NASA: America's Voyage to the Stars*. New York: Exeter Books, 1984.
Interesting text and great photos.

Dunning, Stephen, et al., eds. *Reflections on a Gift of Watermelon Pickle and Other Modern Verse*. New York: Lothrop, 1967.

Dunning, Stephen, et al., eds. *Some Haystacks Don't Even Have Any Needle: And Other Complete Modern Poems*. Glenview, Ill.: Scott, Foresman, 1969.

Gaffney, Timothy R. *Chuck Yeager: First Man to Fly Faster Than Sound*. Chicago: Childrens Press, 1986.

Gardner, Robert. *Projects in Space Science*. New York: Julian Messner/Simon and Schuster, 1988.

Gibbs-Smith, George Harvard. *Aviation: An Historical Survey from Its Origins to the End of World War II*. 2d ed. London: Her Majesty's Stationery Office, 1985.

Hannum, Sara, and John T. Chase, eds. *To Play Man Number One*. New York: Atheneum, 1969.

Information Please Almanac, Atlas, and Yearbook. Boston: Houghton Mifflin, 1991.

Krulik, Nancy E. *My Picture Book of Planets*. New York: Scholastic, 1991.

Lambert, Mark, Kenneth Munson, and Michael J. H. Taylor. *Jane's All the World's Aircraft*. 81st ed. Surrey: Jane's Information Group, 1990.

Levinson, Nancy Smiler. *Chuck Yeager: The Man Who Broke the Sound Barrier*. New York: Walker, 1988.

Long, Kim. *The Astronaut Training Book for Kids*. New York: Lodestar Books, 1990.
Lots of information about astronaut training, including details on space camps, museums, etc.

Matricardi, Paolo. *The Concise History of Aviation*. New York: Crescent Books, 1985.

McAleer, Neil. *The OMNI Space Almanac*. New York: OMNI, World Almanac Books, 1987.
Lots of details and photos; fun yet informative reading for teachers and advanced students.

Miller, Jay. *The X-Planes: X-1 to X-31*. rev. ed. New York: Orion/Aerofax Books, 1988.
Loads of pictures and data; for advanced students and teachers, although younger students will love the pictures.

Molloy, Paul, ed. *Beach Glass and Other Poems*. New York: Four Winds, 1970.

National Aeronautics and Space Administration (NASA). *First Americans in Space: Mercury to Soyuz*. n.p.: NASA, n.d.
Lots of data on the missions of those programs and good rocket information; could be used as a wall chart.

National Air and Space Museum. *Discovery*. Washington, D.C.: National Air and Space Museum, n.d.
Museum's collaboration with NASA on aerospace activities for grades K-3.

Navarra, John Gabriel. *Superplanes*. Garden City, N.Y.: Doubleday, 1979.

Peck, Richard. *Sounds and Silences: Poetry for Now*. New York: Delacorte, 1970; rev. ed. New York: Dell-Laurel Leaf, 1990.

Ride, Sally, with Susan Okie. *To Space and Back*. New York: Lothrop, Lee and Shepard Books, 1986.
    Generally easy reading and lots of great photos; the first American female astronaut's own story about a shuttle mission.

Smith, Dorothy B. Frizzell, and Eva L. Andrews. *Subject Index to Poetry for Children and Young People, 1957-1975*. Chicago: American Library Association, 1977.

Smolders, Peter. *Living in Space: A Handbook for Space Travellers*. Translated by Sidney Woods. Blue Ridge Summit, Pa.: AERO (Tab Books), 1986.

Spangenburg, Ray, and Diane Moser. *Living and Working in Space*. New York: Facts on File, 1989.
    Lots of data; good photos.

Updike, John. *Telephone Poles and Other Poems*. New York: Alfred A. Knopf, 1965.

Verne, Jules. *From the Earth to the Moon*. New York: Airmont Publishing, 1969.

Vision. Seattle: Boeing Aircraft, n.d.
    Poster giving various "firsts in flight"; good data and illustrations; good for a classroom wall; Boeing invites submissions for other "firsts in flight" to be used on future posters.

Vogt, Gregory. *Space Satellites*. New York: Franklin Watts, 1987.
    Designed for young readers, but all will enjoy.

Wells, H. G. *War of the Worlds*. New York: Airmont, 1964.
    This is one of several unabridged editions.

Wolfe, Tom. *The Right Stuff*. New York: Farrar, Straus, and Giroux, 1979.
    Intermediate and advanced students who saw the movie will especially enjoy the book.

Yeager, Chuck, with Charles Leerhsen. *Press On: Further Adventures in the Good Life*. Boston: G. K. Hall, 1988, 1989.

Yeager, Chuck, with Leo Janos. *Autobiography*. Boston: G. K. Hall, 1985.

6

The Space Shuttle, the Space Station **Freedom,** and the National Aero-Space Plane

Space Transportation System

The Space Transportation System (STS) is America's most recent manned space program. The spacecraft for STS is the space shuttle, undoubtedly the most familiar space vehicle to today's school students. The shuttle was designed to do just that: *shuttle* or ferry astronauts, satellites, and other cargo between earth and space. Whereas the capsules and modules of previous manned space programs were not reusable, the shuttle is—up to 100 times. Because not only the orbiter, but also the solid rocket boosters are reusable in a short turnaround time, the Space Transportation System was conceived to be less costly than earlier methods of manned spaceflight. Using the shuttle, astronauts can launch, repair, and retrieve satellites, conduct experiments in an orbiting space laboratory, and study earth from that laboratory.

The Space Shuttle

Back to the Future, the title of a hit movie (and series), serves well to epitomize the shuttle's aerodynamic features. Although this extremely complicated, high-tech space vehicle is launched upright on its tail like a rocket, it has wings for lift and control like an airplane; it can be controlled in orbit around the earth like a satellite; and it lands, controlled by the commander and/or pilot, unpowered like a glider, one of the earliest heavier-than-air aircrafts.[1] In fact, on August 12, 1977, the first shuttle to appear in public and be tested, the *Enterprise* (named for the spacecraft on television's "Star Trek,"[2]), was released from its piggyback perch on a NASA-altered Boeing 747 approximately 24,000 feet over the Mojave Desert near Edwards Air Force Base, where it glided in for a landing.[3] The *Enterprise* now belongs to the collection of the National Air and Space Museum and is at Dulles International Airport outside Washington, D.C.

Since the space shuttle's maiden voyage in the *Columbia*'s April 1981 flight, this spacecraft's appearance has become familiar. The world's worst space disaster, the *Challenger* explosion on January 28, 1986, also brought terms like *O-rings* and *solid rocket boosters* into the layperson's vocabulary. A booster leak through an O-ring ignited the fuel seventy-three seconds into the flight, creating the explosion that killed all seven crewmembers, including the first and only teacher in space, Christa McAuliffe.

The space shuttle system actually consists of four parts: two solid rocket boosters, one external fuel tank, and the orbiter—which most people call "the shuttle"—of which there are currently three, the *Atlantis, Columbia*, and *Discovery*. Each is capable of carrying up to eight passengers plus a payload. As of this writing, a fourth orbiter, *Endeavour*, will soon join the fleet. The orbiters compare in length, width, and weight with the McDonnell Douglas DC-9 airplane. The orbiter is about 122 feet long and has an approximate wingspan of 78 feet, weighing between 150,000 and 175,000 pounds; the DC-9 is 119.3 feet long and 93.4 feet in wingspan. The orbiter is just under 57 feet high from the ground to the top of the tail. Its wing configuration is modified delta, the triangular shape used to overcome drag. The orbiter's three main sections are the pressurized crew module up front, the huge payload bay in the middle of the orbiter, and the three main launch engines located at the rear (see figure 6.1).

The crew module in the front of the orbiter has three stories.[4] At the top is the flight deck or cockpit, where the shuttle commander and pilot fly the spacecraft. The commander is in charge of the flight and sits at the front left, "the driver's seat"; the pilot assists the commander and sits in the front right at launch and reentry and may face the back of the deck, towards the payload bay, in orbit. At launch and reentry, the mission specialist(s) can also sit in the flight deck, which can accommodate four persons. These specialist seats, located on both the flight and mid-decks, can be removed without tools and stowed away during orbit and then easily repositioned for reentry. All of the seats have special support and restraint apparatus, including seat belts.

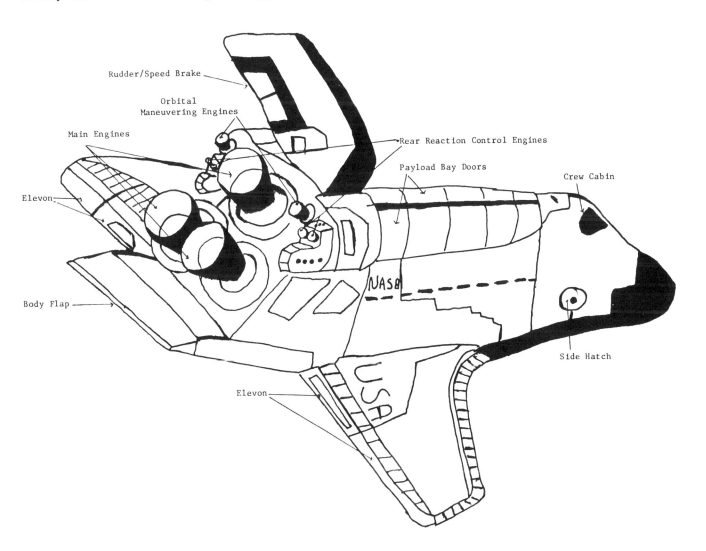

Fig. 6.1. The space shuttle.

At liftoff, the crewmembers sit in their respective seats reclining on their backs, feet above heads—the same position used in the three earlier space programs, Mercury, Gemini, and Apollo. However, although the earlier capsules and command modules were confining, the shuttle's flight deck is comparatively roomy, with six windshields across the front and sides, two overhead windows, and two rearview payload bay windows offering great views. Because there are several backup systems, the flight deck has 2,020 different controls (827 toggle switches alone) and displays—roughly triple the number in the *Apollo* command module—making the shuttle a highly complex aerospace craft to operate. It is no wonder astronauts go through years of training.

From the flight deck, the crew can descend one level through a hatch, which is an airtight doorway, and down a ladder to the mid-deck, where they work and live during the mission. The mid-deck measures 7 feet high by 13 feet long by 12 feet wide in the rear and 9 feet wide in front. There are four sleep stations with sleeping bags; a galley with food trays, water dispenser, water heater, convection oven, and other apparatus; a table for dining and working; and personal hygiene (a handwashing enclosure with soap and hot/cold water dispensers) and waste collection (toilet) stations. Because there is no gravity in space, these accommodations all have special features. For example, the waste collection station has a seat belt, handholds, and footholds, as do other places in the orbiter; the toilet bowl uses air pressure, instead of water, for flushing. The air in the bowl is stirred by a fast-moving centrifuge. Water would float around in space; thus, the astronauts clean themselves with washcloths and towels. The enclosed washbasin has sleeves through which the astronauts push their hands to wash them. (*Skylab* had a hand-held shower apparatus and showering facility that used air pressure to keep the water from flying around in little spheres.)

Limited storage space is available in the mid-deck for the crews' belongings. The crew sleeps for about eight hours daily. In a weightless environment, the crew can sleep in the sleep stations or float and snooze. Crewmembers usually wear earplugs to shut out the noise; they also have sleeping masks to shut out the light.

The lowest of the three stories in the orbiter's crew module is the equipment bay. Along with certain equipment, this level also houses the crews' wet trash. In fact, time is set aside each day for trash collection and removal. Removable floor panels connect the mid-deck and the lower deck.

MID-DECK DESIGN

- Art, mathematics

- Intermediate and advanced

Using a scale such as 1 foot equals 1 inch, design the mid-deck compartment of the crew module in either diorama or drawing form according to the dimensions given in the paragraph describing the mid-deck. Include the equipment and apparatus mentioned. The walls, made of aluminum and fiberglass, are white.

A ROOM OF YOUR OWN

- Social studies, science, language arts, mathematics

- General

As you can tell from the description of the crew's mid-deck quarters, there is not much room for the crew—up to seven persons—to have any real "personal space." First, using chalk and a metal tape measure, measure out on the classroom floor the space available to the astronauts according to the dimensions given in the paragraph describing the mid-deck. Let students get an idea of how confined this space really is. Then, let students assume the roles of group behavior specialists, in which they discuss and write about what they would advise a shuttle crew to do during their mission time to avoid getting on each other's nerves. Two of the psychological criteria NASA looks for in potential astronauts is the ability to get along well with other people and an absence of claustrophobia.

Shuttlewear

Shuttle crewmembers have at least two "costume" changes; and for those astronauts embarking on EVA (extravehicular activity), there is a third costume, the space suit. For liftoff and reentry, the shuttle astronauts wear their one-piece, jumpsuit-styled flight suits and boots; their "Snoopy caps" (like the close-fitting one Snoopy wears when he fights the Red Baron in the "Peanuts" comic strip) equipped with microphone and headset; their visored safety helmets connected to an oxygen supply; and their escape harnesses, vests with rings and ropes that would allow the astronauts to slide from the orbiter to the ground in an emergency during launch and landing. Preparing for reentry, the shuttle travelers put on their *g-suits*, which help their bodies meet the high g's encountered on reentry. These antigravity suits actually consist of pants that the wearer can inflate with oxygen, causing the pants to press on the wearer's legs and abdomen to prevent the blood from rushing from the head (brain) to the lower part of the body, which would cause the astronaut to black out.[5]

After the launch, the crewmembers remove and store away for reentry their helmets, Snoopy caps, boots, and flight suits and wear their "shirtsleeve"-style clothing. The shuttle astronauts do not wear space suits all the time because the orbiter's pressurized crew module provides a "shirtsleeve environment." Nevertheless, the astronauts' in-flight clothing does have special features for spaceflight.

The in-flight shuttle wardrobe consists of navy blue cotton-knit polo shirts; cobalt blue lined jackets and pants, both having many pockets with Velcro® and zipper closures (to keep things from flying out at zero g); one pair of gloves; and cotton or wool socks with special footwear that has suction devices to help the astronauts stand still while weightless. (During the shuttle's flight in space, however, the astronauts tend to float around shoeless because they want to avoid accidentally kicking another crewmember in the head with heavy shoes.) The clothing is made of lightweight, natural fibers and is comfortable and close fitting (so as not to catch onto anything or inadvertently turn on switches). The jacket has a pleated back that allows the wearer to move easily and expands to compensate for the astronauts' "growing" about an inch taller in the weightless environment. A person's spinal column expands in a weightless environment because of the absence of gravitational force on the soft tissue of the vertebrae. (When they return to earth, they return to their normal heights.) The clothing is fireproof and unisex. Astronauts preparing for a shuttle flight simply take their allotted clothing off the rack at the Johnson Space Center.

Pressurized space suits and portable life support systems (PLSS) are also used for certain aspects of today's space shuttle missions. When in the unpressurized payload bay of the orbiter or engaged in EVA, the shuttle astronauts put on their space suits. Considerably advanced from the Apollo lunar suits examined in chapter 5, the shuttle space suits have several layers, are modular, and are reusable on successive missions by different astronauts. Moreover, an astronaut can suit up without assistance in just a few minutes.

First, the astronaut puts on a spandex liner, which looks like long johns with circulating plastic tubing carrying water to help keep body temperature cool in the heat of space. Underneath the liner is a urine collection device. The inner clothing has an interior drinking bag, allowing the astronaut to drink up to 21 ounces of water while in the space suit. The astronaut also dons a Snoopy cap with its communications assembly. For the feet, the astronaut wears special socks and boot inserts. Outfitted from head to toe with the first layer, the astronaut is ready for the outer layer.

The actual space suit is an insulated, multilayered pressure suit that comes in modular parts: a hard upper torso with an aluminum shell and a hard waist ring; a lower torso, also with a hard waist ring, with the boots attached to the leg assemblies; connecting gloves; and a helmet to which is snapped an EVA visor assembly to protect the astronaut from various types of radiation. The entire suit is made of Mylar plastic and unwoven Dacron; it is covered with a layer of Teflon and tear-resistant materials to protect the astronaut from heat and meteorites. The suit is so made at the joints that bending, twisting, and leaning can all be performed quite freely—a vast improvement over previous suits' rigidity. Instead of zippers, hard snap-ring connectors fasten the various modules so that all seals are absolutely "airtight." A modular PLSS is built into the suit's upper torso section. It provides oxygen, eliminates impurities from the "air," includes a tiny computer to warn the wearer of problems, and has a water purifier so the astronaut, who also has a food stick, can sip water while wearing the helmet. Except for the helmet that comes in one size only, the suit's modular units (separate upper torso, lower torso with pants and boots in one piece, and glove modules) come in various sizes that can be coordinated for different astronauts on different shuttle missions. Once a suit is used on a mission, it is simply cleaned, dried, and reworn on another shuttle flight. This, too, is a vast improvement over the suits from the preshuttle days, which had to be custom made for each astronaut and could be worn for only one mission. The shuttle carries only two space suits to be worn by the mission specialists whose job it is to work in the payload bay or to perform EVA.

Because the shuttle carries only two space suits, students may wonder what would happen to the rest of the crew if the shuttle broke down in space. The orbiter is equipped with personal rescue systems, consisting of inflatable, gastight, thermal-protected spheres, each 34 inches in diameter, into which each non-space-suited crewmember would go while the space-suited astronauts assisted in transferring them to a waiting rescue vehicle.

The Payload Bay and the Airlock

The midsection of the orbiter is the payload bay. It measures 60 feet long, about 17 feet wide, and 13 feet high. Up to 65,000 pounds of cargo can be transported for orbital launch and up to 32,000 pounds of cargo can be carried back from space. Once the shuttle is in orbit, the crew must open the payload bay's two doors, which support the orbiter's radiators, to rid the orbiter of heat. This is necessary to prevent the equipment from getting excessively hot, thus mandating an early return to earth. At reentry, the doors are closed and locked.

Unlike the crew module, the payload bay is not pressurized, but crewmembers can work with the payload from the rear of the pressurized flight deck, where they have not only controls, but also windows and a television screen for viewing the interior of the payload bay. If, however, they need to enter the payload bay, they must put on their pressurized space suits. The astronauts don their space suits and enter the payload bay through the *airlock*, a hermetically sealed chamber connecting modules of different air pressures. The airlock is shaped like a cylinder, 63 inches in diameter and 83 inches long, and functions as the dressing room for astronauts who need to don their space suits either to enter the payload bay or to leave the orbiter and space walk. After they are in their space suits, the astronauts empty the airlock of air to test the suits' systems.

If everything is satisfactory, the astronauts can either proceed out a hatch and go into space, or go through a hatch to the unpressurized payload bay. While working in the bay, the crewmembers are tethered to restrict their movements; likewise, unless they are using the manned maneuvering unit (MMU), a one-person propulsive backpack, astronauts working in space outside the orbiter are tethered to the spacecraft. Returning through a hatch to the airlock, the astronauts can repressurize it and remove their space suits. For EVA, the astronauts' tools are tethered to their suits so they do not float away; likewise, the helmet visor has two lights attached to it, and the astronaut carries a tethered flashlight for working in the dark.

The payload bay contains the remote manipulator system (RMS), which is made in Toronto, Canada. Controlled from the flight deck (and thus not requiring the controller to wear a space suit to enter the bay), this 50-foot-long "arm" lifts cargo in and out of the payload bay. It has a clawlike "hand" and assists the astronauts with the movement of bulky or awkwardly shaped cargo, which, remember, is weightless in space. This is why one or two astronauts can do such things in space as move and retrieve satellites, which would require heavy machinery to move on earth.

A versatile part of the orbiter, the payload bay can also carry *Spacelab*, a scientific laboratory funded and built by the European Space Agency (ESA), pooling the resources of eleven European countries, but launched and operated by NASA. Spacelab consists of a pressurized cylindrical module, 23 feet long by 13 feet wide, where the astronauts can work in their ordinary shuttle attire, and unpressurized platforms or racks called "pallets," where the astronauts must wear pressurized space suits. To go from the crew module to Spacelab within the payload bay, the astronauts proceed through a pressurized tunnel. Inside the pressurized Spacelab module are all types of laboratory equipment, workbenches, computers, and instruments; the pallets carry antennae, telescopes, and other equipment and experiments that scientists want to expose to a space environment. Working in Spacelab, astronauts can communicate directly with earthbound scientists in their labs. The first Spacelab mission occurred with the flight of STS-9, *Columbia*, from November 28 to December 8, 1983. During 148 orbits, mission members—including the first Euopean shuttle crewmember (a West German, Ulf Merbold)—worked around the clock in Spacelab, performing over six dozen different experiments contributed by American, European, Japanese, and Canadian scientists.

AEROSPACE TERMS

* Science, language arts

* General

Have students add *space shuttle system, orbiter, solid rocket boosters, external fuel tank, airlock, crew module,* and *payload bay* to their dictionaries of aerospace terms.

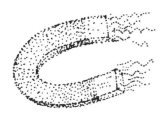

SPACE EXPERIMENTS

* Library research, science, oral communication, language arts

* Intermediate and advanced

First have students do some research to learn what types of experiments have been performed on various shuttle flights. After reporting on them, they plan some experiments on their own. To do this, students will not only need to devise the experiment, explaining clearly the hypothesis being tested, the materials needed, and the procedure to be followed, but also present in written form a cogent argument that would convince NASA officials to accept the experiment. Teachers seriously interested in pursuing space science projects with their students should investigate NASA's Space Science Student Involvement Program (SSIP), which sponsors national conferences and contests for students from middle through senior high school level. SSIP science experiments have been performed on shuttle missions (e.g., STS-26, *Discovery,* September 29-October 3, 1988). For complete information and a teacher resource book, write to Dr. Helenmarie Hofman, Director, SSIP, National Science Teachers Association, 5110 Roanoke Place, Suite 101, College Park, MD 20740; (301) 474-0487.

The Aft Fuselage

The rear of the orbiter is about 18 feet long by 22 feet wide by 20 feet high. It holds the cluster of three main liquid rocket engines, which provide the thrust required to launch the shuttle; when you look at the rear of the orbiter (figure 6.1), you can see the black nozzles of the engines extending outward. These liquid hydrogen/liquid oxygen engines provide the orbiter with its main propulsion. Extending horizontally underneath the nozzles is the *body flap* that helps protect the engines from the high heat encountered at reentry. Above the engines, a fin extends vertically. This is the *vertical stabilizer,* consisting of a rudder/speed brake; that is, while the orbiter is flying through the atmosphere preparing to land, it acts as a rudder surface control, enabling the commander to steer the orbiter to the left or right. When the orbiter is touching down, it functions as a speed brake, splitting in half to decrease the shuttle's speed as it travels along the runway.

SHUTTLE MODEL

* Art, science

* General

Estes Industries (1925 H Street, Penrose, CO 81240. Telephone: 719-372-6565) sells a good model of the shuttle that a patient intermediate or advanced student could make for the class. Have younger students draw the shuttle and label the main parts using figure 6.1 as a guide.

REVIEW OF SURFACE CONTROLS

- Science (physics)

- General

Using models of each, review with your class the similarities in aerodynamic design shared by the shuttle and an airplane (chapter 3), noting the functions of the controls.

How the Shuttle Takes Off

Because the shuttle requires extremely strong thrust to get into space, it uses a combination of power sources: the orbiter's cluster of three main engines, which is fueled by the big orange external liquid-fuel tank and two solid rocket boosters attached to either side of the external fuel tank. (You may wish to review the solid-fuel rocket described at the beginning of chapter 5.) Each solid rocket booster (SRB) is 149.16 feet high and 12.38 feet wide. Propelled mainly by a fuel of aluminum powder and an oxidizer, the SRBs work with the orbiter's main engines during the initial two minutes of the mission not only to help the orbiter escape earth's gravitational pull, but also to help guide its ascent. After the orbiter's main engines are fired, each SRB is fired, providing 2,650,000 pounds of thrust apiece; 0.3 seconds later, the shuttle is released from its eight hold-down posts and it lifts off.

Exhausted of their fuel two minutes later, the SRBs have assisted the shuttle to reach an altitude of about 28 miles. They then separate from the external fuel tank, continue upward for a little over a minute longer to an altitude of 41 miles, and then fall to earth in a ballistic trajectory during which three parachutes on each SRB open to slow its fall. A *ballistic trajectory* is the path followed by an object that is acted upon only by the pull of gravity and the resistance of the medium through which it passes. Hitting the Atlantic Ocean at about 60 miles per hour, the SRBs are rescued by two specially designed and equipped tug boats, which haul them back to the Kennedy Space Center, where they are refurbished for use on another shuttle mission.

The orange external fuel tank, 154 feet high and just under 29 feet wide, curves to a point at the top to overcome drag. The very top of the tank also functions as a lightning rod, reminding us that Benjamin Franklin's eighteenth-century kite experiment, discussed in chapter 3, contributed to the world's most sophisticated spacecraft. Holding over 1,585,000 pounds of propellants (a combination of liquid oxygen in an inner tank at the front serving as the oxidizer and liquid hydrogen in an inner tank at the rear providing the fuel), the tank feeds at liftoff the orbiter's three main liquid rocket engines, each of which has a thrust of 470,000 pounds. Slowly emptying itself of fuel, the external tank is exhausted by the time the orbiter, to which it is attached piggyback style, approximates orbital velocity (70 miles above earth): this is eight minutes and fifty seconds into the flight and between ten and fifteen seconds after the orbiter's main engines have shut down. With the main or launch engines shut down, the fuel tank separates from the orbiter and hurtles in a preplanned path to earth, disintegrating as it reaches the atmosphere. Less than an hour later, the tank's debris falls into the Indian Ocean, which you may remember was the *Skylab*'s final resting place. This tank is the only part of the shuttle system that is not reusable.

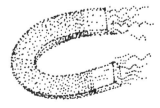

INDIAN OCEAN

- Social studies

- General

Locate the Indian Ocean on the class's world map.

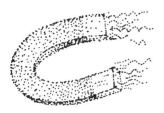

TRAJECTORY

* Science (physics)

* Advanced

The physics teacher can go over trajectories with the class, using the parachute recovery system for the SRBs and the fall of the external fuel tank as examples.

With the SRBs and the external fuel tank gone and the three main engines off, the shuttle's orbital maneuvering system (OMS), two smaller rocket engines located externally on either side of the rear of the fuselage, take over to provide the thrust for getting the shuttle into orbit, changing its orbits, rendezvousing, and getting it out of orbit. Each of the OMS's two engines has 6,000 pounds of thrust. Within ten minutes of liftoff, the orbiter is in space, 172 miles high, and the crewmembers are in a weightless environment, speeding around earth at 17,500 miles per hour and doing a complete orbit every ninety minutes.

FROM THRUST TO HORSEPOWER

* Mathematics and science

* Intermediate

The preceding discussion of the SRBs, main engines, and OMS mentioned the thrust provided by the different rocket engines. Thrust is usually described in pounds. If 1 pound of thrust equals twenty-two horsepower, have students calculate the horsepower of each engine. (*Horsepower* is a unit of measurement of an engine's power output; it is the power required to raise 550 pounds 1 foot in 1 second.) Review from chapters 3 and 5 the Wrights' homemade twelve-horsepower engine and how the development of the rocket engines enabled scientists and engineers to develop modern engines like the shuttle's that provide the immense thrust needed to launch a vehicle into space.

Life on the Shuttle

While in space the crewmembers of a shuttle flight experience weightlessness. To help compensate for this condition, the crew module has footholds, handrails, and handholds; in addition, astronauts can wear shoes with suction cups at the bottom, but most of the astronauts float around the crew module. Food for space travel has come a long way from the Mercury, Gemini, and Apollo astronauts' bland nourishment sucked from tubes. The shuttle carries enough food for the astronauts to have three meals per day plus snacks at an average energy intake of 3,000 calories per person. The menus are designed to compensate for the body's loss of potassium, calcium, and other minerals while at zero g and they are designed to be as tasty as possible.

The shuttle has a galley in the mid-deck with a convection oven, hot-and-cold water dispenser, and water heater. Most of the food is dehydrated or freeze-dried; others are *thermostabilized* (canned) or irradiated, including some meats, which have been precooked and reprocessed. Even some "natural form" foods are on the menu including graham crackers and shortbread cookies, nuts, peanut butter, and soft, seedless rye bread (hard rye crumbles and the crumbs would float around in the shuttle). About twenty different beverages, plus various condiments (barbecue sauce, mustard, ketchup, and liquid salt and pepper) are available. There is enough variety in the foods to insure that no menu is repeated more than once a week.

The crewmember in charge of a meal prepares the food trays for each astronaut in the galley. For example, a dinner might begin with rehydratable shrimp cocktail, then proceed to an entree of irradiated beef steak, rehydratable rice and broccoli au gratin, all packaged in special pouches; thermostabilized fruit cocktail; and a dessert of thermostabilized chocolate pudding, all accompanied by a beverage. The "chef" injects a stated amount of water into the plastic bowls of foods needing rehydration, places the foods that need to be heated into the convection oven, and puts straws into the beverage containers. Cold items and silverware are placed on each astronaut's aluminum meal tray, which is about the size of a small pizza box. Some of these items are held to the tray by tape or magnets. Food in heavy sauces or gravies sticks to the food tray, thus avoiding the problem of flying beef steak and broccoli. The silverware may be slightly smaller than normal because at zero g food sticks all over the utensil, not just the top. The filled food tray attaches with a strap to the astronaut's leg and is compartmentalized for the different foods and courses of the meal. The astronaut can sit down to eat, using restraints. After each meal, the food trays and eating utensils are cleaned with sanitized wipes and stowed for the next meal.

SPACE DIETITIAN AND CAREERS

- Library research, mathematics, science (nutrition), physical education

- General

Students are to plan the meals for four astronauts on a six-day mission aboard a space shuttle. Each astronaut needs to consume 3,000 calories daily over a well-balanced breakfast, lunch, and dinner, as well as compensate for the minerals (potassium, calcium) that the body loses in space and have sufficient roughage. Find the caloric and nutritional values of various foods and design and calculate the daily menus. Remember to provide a different menu for each day of the mission; and remember that the shuttle lacks a refrigerator and has only a convection oven for heating foods.

This would be a practical time to invite either your school nurse or a professional dietitian to the class, perhaps from the school district, a local hospital, or a commercial airline company. Ask the nurse or dietitian to discuss good nutrition, including the food groups, with the students. The dietitian can also talk about the job, the education needed, and its career possibilities. Remind students that NASA has a staff of medical personnel and dietitians working on astronaut health and food for space flights. Have the students write thank-you notes to the visitor(s). McDonald's and Young Astronauts offer a collaborative packet, "Careers in Space," including a poster and curriculum guide with worksheets for beginning students; write to Young Astronauts at the address in the appendix.

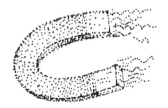

EAT LIKE A SHUTTLE ASTRONAUT

- Science and cooking

- Beginning

If funds are available, the teacher can buy freeze-dried and dehydrated foods at a camping supplies store and some thermostabilized (canned) foods at the supermarket. With the cooperation of the school cook or in the classroom, see if you and the class can prepare some of these foods so everyone can taste them.

LIVING IN SPACE

- Science

- Beginning and intermediate

NASA's *Living in Space* series provides two levels (grades 1, 2, 3 and 4, 5, 6) of activities books for teachers to use with students when dealing with almost any aspect of the space shuttle. See the bibliography entry for Sheila Briskin Andrews and the appendix of addresses for information on ordering this series.

Leaving the Orbiter

As noted in the discussion of space suits, shuttle astronauts wear pressurized suits, called extravehicular mobility units (EMU), with built-in life support systems, called portable life support systems (PLSS) when they enter the payload bay or leave the orbiter. Reasons for leaving the spacecraft include inspecting the orbiter, operating exterior equipment, and retrieving or repairing satellites, which astronaut Dale Gardner did on STS 51-A. In addition to wearing the space suit and PLSS, the exiting astronaut may need to use the *manned maneuvering unit* (MMU) to facilitate movement in space. Latched to the back of the PLSS, the MMU is a one-person propulsive backpack, propelled by nitrogen and run on rechargable batteries. It can run for six hours before the nitrogen and battery need to be recharged. The astronaut directs the movements with hand controllers, which send commands through a microprocessor to two dozen nitrogen thruster jets. It weighs 225 pounds on earth, but is negligible in the weightlessness of space. The space suit, PLSS, MMU, controls module, and other equipment for EVA are together called the extravehicular mobility unit or EMU.

ACRONYMS

- Language arts, library research

- Beginning, intermediate

If your students are unfamiliar with acronyms, this would be a good time to introduce them to the concept. As you have probably noticed, space science has a lot of acronyms: NASA (National Aeronautics and Space Administration); SRB (solid rocket booster); EVA (extravehicular activity or spacewalking); EMU (extravehicular mobility unit); MMU (manned maneuvering unit); PLSS (portable life support system), etc. Discuss why acronyms are so widely used in space science. Can students find other acronyms in use today? Ask the library media specialist to help students discover some acronyms.

Meet an Astronaut: Captain Dale Gardner

Captain Dale Gardner, an engineer by training (bachelor of science in engineering physics, University of Illinois, 1970), was a naval flight officer, involved with the testing of such fighters as the F-14A *Tomcat*, before being selected as an astronaut candidate by NASA in January 1978. After a yearlong training and evaluation period, he became eligible to be a mission specialist astronaut on space shuttle flights. He is a veteran of two shuttle missions, STS-8 (*Challenger*), August 30-September 5, 1983, which was the shuttle program's first night launch and landing; and STS-51A (*Discovery*), November 8-16, 1984, during which he and Dr. Joseph Allen rescued from space two ailing satellites, the *Palapa B-2* and *Westar VI*. Having logged 337 hours in space, Captain Gardner was selected to serve as a mission specialist on the first shuttle flight from the new launch facility at Vandenberg Air Force Base in California.[6]

Following is an interview one of the authors conducted with Captain Gardner:

Author: Captain Gardner, how did you first become interested in space travel?

Captain Gardner: As a child I followed the initial unmanned satellite launches very closely after the Soviets launched *Sputnik*. I remember being shocked that they had reached space before the United States and was stunned when Yuri Gagarin completed the first orbital flight in the early '60s [April 12, 1961]. After school the day of Gagarin's flight, I must have read the headline story in the newspaper ten times in disbelief. As the Mercury, Gemini, and Apollo flights unfolded, I followed every one closely, getting up in the middle of the night to watch launches, key events, and splashdowns. As I watched, I knew this was something I wanted to do, but I was also somewhat of a realist and knew that my chances of actually going into space were exceedingly small.

Author: I know from your biographical data supplied by NASA that you have a degree in engineering physics and that you were a naval flight officer before being selected for the astronaut corps. What kind of additional special training did you need to be an astronaut?

Captain Gardner: Many of the NASA astronauts come from military aviation backgrounds. All of the original astronauts [i.e., for Project Mercury] were military test pilots, for example. NASA obviously felt that they had the prerequisite skills and experience for the job. These days, the pilot astronauts are still primarily from that mold, but the mission specialist astronauts come from diverse educational and professional areas. In selecting astronauts, NASA wants people who have excelled in some scientific or engineering field. After selection, astronaut candidates are put through about a year of specialized training designed by NASA to better prepare the individuals for their eventual space shuttle flight crew duties. Then, once selected for a particular flight, they take intense training for the best part of a year—more for complicated flights such as Spacelab—prior to launch.

Author: You are a mission specialist astronaut; what exactly is a mission specialist?

Captain Gardner: As I mentioned, there are both pilot and mission specialist astronauts in the shuttle program. The pilots fill two positions on a flight crew, the commander and the pilot. These two are responsible for actually flying the vehicle and operating its complicated systems. The mission specialists' prime responsibilities, as their title implies, are focused on executing the particular mission of that shuttle flight once in orbit. One or two mission specialists on a flight also have dual responsibility with the commander and pilot during launch and landing phases, providing assistance, reading checklists, monitoring displays and switches, etc. But their [the mission specialists'] prime functions are centered on deploying satellites, performing experiments, operating the remote manipulator system robot arm, performing space walks, etc. Sometimes, mission specialists are selected for a shuttle mission before a commander and pilot are assigned. This is so they can begin early training on the complex parts of their new payloads and missions.

Author: People seem to be fascinated with the phenomenon of experiencing zero gravity in space. For the weightlessness of spaceflight, what day-to-day things do you need to do differently from doing them on earth?

Captain Gardner: Weightlessness is fun, but if you are not organized and prepared, [it] can also be frustrating. You must learn and accept the fact that you are in a new environment with different rules—if you don't follow the rules, the game does not go well. Specifically, both your body and every item you attempt to work or interact with will try to float away, twist the wrong way, bump into something, or get in your way unless you follow the rules. For example, on the shuttle, footloops are placed in many areas of the floor to give the astronauts a way of anchoring their feet when performing some task. Similarly, loose equipment is provided with Velcro, which can be stuck to small Velcro patches glued all over the shuttle's interior surfaces; cord tethers; foam cutouts inside drawers; or other means of control. For miscellaneous objects, rolls of duct tape are plentiful, allowing the crew simply to tape an item to a wall or panel to hold it in place.

You also learn little helpful things from your experience [in space] or that of others. I remember that while in training for my first flight, Richard Truly, our crew commander and now the administrator of NASA, gave me a hint that seemed trivial at first, but proved to be valuable. We were in the simulator at [the Johnson Space Center in] Houston eating a "space" meal, most of which is packaged in vacuum-packed plastic bags or containers. I was using scissors to cut open the bags, putting the plastic remnants on the table, and then eating the food item. Dick mentioned that this would be bad practice in space—he had already flown once before [STS-2, *Columbia*, November 12-14, 1981]. He told me to only cut the plastic part way off; that way, I wouldn't have extra pieces of plastic to contend with in zero g. I followed his advice, and it worked like a champ in space!

Author: What was the most difficult thing you had to master as an astronaut?

Captain Gardner: That one is easy—the waiting! Most people think that all astronauts do is train and fly in space. Wrong! Most of what they do involves *waiting* to train and fly in space. I was at NASA for eight-and-a-half years and flew two space shuttle flights—one six days and one eight days long. That means I was in space for only 2 weeks out of 442 [weeks], for a percentage of 0.45 percent! I enjoyed every minute of the other 99.55 percent, because NASA always keeps the astronauts busy doing interesting and fun things. But impatience is certainly *not* a virtue if you want to go into the astronaut business!

Author: What was the most exciting moment in spaceflight for you?

Captain Gardner: That one is not so easy. The most exciting moment is probably a tie between the launch on my first flight and the space walks I did on my second flight. My launch on STS-8 was not only my first, but also the first night launch of the Space Shuttle program. As we passed through some cloud layers shortly after liftoff, the light from our five rocket engines [the three main engines and two SRBs] reflected off the surrounding moisture and made it look to us in the shuttle cockpit as if we were inside a ball of fire! The two space walks on STS-51-A were a dream come true. All astronauts want to don a space suit and go outside their spaceship. I had the chance to do that and more. While on the space walks, I also was able to fly free from the shuttle using the manned maneuvering unit (MMU) backpack, becoming my own satellite for a short period of time. It is a moment I will never forget.

Author: What was the most surprising moment you experienced in spaceflight?

Captain Gardner: The most surprising aspect of my spaceflight experience may surprise *you*, for it had more to do with the earth than it did with space. I am referring, of course, to looking at the earth from the vantage [point] of space. Our planet is a beautiful, although fragile, place. I never tired of looking out the shuttle windows whenever there was a free moment, watching continents, islands, clouds, oceans, storms—whatever was in view at the moment.

Author: What would you stress to middle school and/or high school students concerning space travel?

Captain Gardner: There are two things I think students at both levels can understand and appreciate. The first has to do with the inherent dangers and risks of spaceflight. This was, of course, most recently demonstrated by the *Challenger* accident. We must never fool ourselves into believing that anything in life is completely safe or guaranteed. Even at home or at school, you must each day face the possibility—hopefully, an extremely small one—that you could be injured or killed. When performing such activities such as flying, scuba diving, building skyscrapers, law enforcement, etc.—including space travel—those possibilities are increased. Does that mean we should stop doing them because of the risk? Of course, not! We must *control* the risk and danger, not avoid all activities that involve them. Life would be pretty dull, and the human race would quickly stagnate, then wither, if we put protective cocoons around our lives and existence.

This leads to the second point I want to make concerning space travel. It is not unnatural for human beings; it's *natural*! You may find this surprising since the human race evolved here on earth. But if you think of the human race not as a collection of bodies, but rather as a collective force and spirit, it begins to make sense. Our desire to expand, to learn, to explore, and to improve, combined with an intelligence that permits us to invent the ways to do these, means that we cannot forever be confined to this planet. We would cease to be what human beings are all about if we just accepted the status quo and spent the following millennia locked in this home we call earth. We have been given the desire and the intelligence to move out. It is our responsibility to ourselves and to our children to do that. Space is not a forbidding place; it is just a *different* place. As I mentioned earlier, it has different rules than here on earth, but that is what we are good at: figuring out the rules and then playing the game—and winning! We must keep the drama alive and turn it into reality. That responsibility is not just mine—it is *yours*![7]

THE NATURALNESS OF SPACE TRAVEL

- Science, language arts, oral communication, critical thinking

- General

In his interview, NASA astronaut Captain Dale Gardner says that space travel is "natural," and that the human desire to improve and expand will not permit humanity to be confined to earth. Discuss Captain Gardner's comments in class and then ask the students to write essays responding to his points—their response may be an agreement, an elaboration, a refutation, etc.

Reentry to the Atmosphere and Landing the Orbiter

Although a shuttle mission can conceivably last between seven and thirty days, most have lasted around a week.[8] About seven hours before landing, the astronauts start stowing away extraneous items and setting up the specialist seats that were used at launch and then dismantled and stored. They put on their Snoopy caps and their antigravity suits. About two hours before landing, the astronauts don their helmets and strap themselves into their seats, where they sit upright for reentry, and review a checklist of reentry tasks.

With sixty minutes to touchdown and the payload bay doors—which were opened to release heat when the craft entered orbit—now closed and locked, the orbiter begins its *de-orbit burn*: engines will be fired to slow the shuttle down and take it out of orbit and into earth's atmosphere. Using the reaction control system (RCS), which consists of three sets of engines (one set near the orbiter's nose and the other two sets in the rear on the pods), the pilot turns the shuttle around so it is flying backward at a slower speed. The RCS engines enable the orbiter to do the maneuvers of an airplane: pitch, roll, and yaw (see chapter 3). At this point, the two small orbital maneuvering system (OMS) engines, also called *space engines*, fire for about two or three minutes, taking the shuttle out of orbit so that it starts to descend and slows down by about 200 miles per hour. The pilot uses the RCS to turn the orbiter around yet again so that it is now flying with its nose forward and pointing upward.

With thirty minutes until landing, the orbiter has descended to an altitude of 76 miles and is flying 17,100 miles per hour. Computers have set a flight path for the shuttle to the runway (15,000 feet long by 300 feet wide), which is about double the length and width of a runway found at a commercial airport. Recall that the shuttle has special heat tiles to protect the vehicle and its occupants from the searing heat of reentry. At twenty-five minutes before landing, the shuttle, now traveling 16,700 miles per hour, is at an altitude of 50 miles. This is when a thirteen minute communication blackout starts: this blackout is caused by ionizing particles around the shuttle as the protective tiles reflect the extreme heat (2,500-3,000 degrees Fahrenheit).[9] Maximum heat is encountered twenty minutes before touchdown while the orbiter is traveling 15,045 miles per hour at 43.5 miles altitude.

As the orbiter returns to earth's atmosphere, its roll and pitch can be controlled by the elevons on the wings. With sixteen minutes until landing, the orbiter goes through a series of maneuvers, including an S-turn, to reduce its lift and decrease its speed. Four minutes later, and twelve minutes before touchdown, the communication blackout ceases, and the orbiter is flying 8,275 miles per hour at 34 miles altitude. The orbiter makes a series of maneuvers, including two additional S-turns, to reduce lift and speed further and to be in a good position to approach the landing at the right altitude and speed. At 9.5 miles in altitude and a speed of Mach 1, the pilot can steer the orbiter to the right or left by using the tail's rudder: in other words, the orbiter's control surfaces that were nonfunctional in space's vacuum now come into use as the orbiter descends into the increasingly dense air of earth's atmosphere. Going 424 miles per hour at 13,365 feet altitude, the shuttle, now 7.5 miles from the runway's threshold, is guided automatically to a safe landing position by a special microwave scanning beam landing system (MSBLS). Such precision is absolutely vital because the orbiter, unlike an ordinary airplane, lands without its engines running. Rather, the orbiter is now like a high-speed glider and must land correctly during its first and only attempt at touchdown.

The final eighty-six seconds of the flight are largely automatic, with the crew monitoring and supporting the MSBLS. However, with less than thirty seconds to touchdown, the commander maneuvers the gliding shuttle and pulls up its nose so that the steep descent angle will be leveled to a final glide slope of 1.5 degrees. The pilot deploys the landing wheels with twenty-two seconds to go at an altitude of 300 feet. Traveling at a touchdown speed of 215 miles per hour, the orbiter is slowed down further as the commander or pilot uses the speed (tail) and wheel brakes. The orbiter's target is 2,760 feet past the runway's threshold. The rear wheels gently touch down first, and then the nose wheel meets the runway with a thump.

After the orbiter rolls to a stop, the crew remains on board for about thirty minutes to turn off the orbiter's systems, get used to earth's gravity, which after space's zero g makes their bodies feel heavy and a little wobbly, and be checked over by a physician. Meanwhile, a ground crew cools off the orbiter. The mission crew exits, and the ground crew take the orbiter back to its hangar to prepare it for its next flight. The shuttle will be America's workhorse for space travel for the foreseeable future.

SHUTTLE MISSIONS AND FIRSTS

- Library research, science, language arts, art, oral communication

- General

The final *Challenger* flight on January 28, 1986, would have been the twenty-fifth mission in the Space Transportation System or Shuttle program. Up to this writing, thirteen successful missions have followed the *Challenger* tragedy. Ask students to research some of the accomplishments of the various shuttle missions, such as launching and retrieving satellites; the "toys in space" mission (astronauts took certain motion toys into space to test their operation under weightless conditions; see Sumners in bibliography); the first American female astronaut (see June Behrens' *Sally Ride, Astronaut: An American First* and Sally Ride with Susan Okie, *To Space and Back*); the first black American astronaut (Mission Specialist Guion "Guy" Bluford); see James Haskins's and Kathleen Benson's *Space Challenger: The Story of Guion Bluford*); the first American female astronaut to space walk or do EVA (Kathryn Sullivan; see Mary Virginia Fox's *Women Astronauts: Aboard the Shuttle*). Have students present short oral reports and write lengthier reports about specific missions; younger students might also wish to illustrate a particular mission. The teacher can find summaries of the missions through *Challenger* in R. Lynn Bondurant, Jr.'s *On the Wings of a Dream: The Space Shuttle* (p. 27), and Neil McAleer's *Omni Space Almanac*, (pp. 92-96; see bibliography). Teachers also can request mission-by-mission updates and detailed brochures from NASA using the addresses given in the appendix.

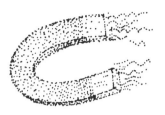

THE SOVIET SHUTTLE *BURAN*

- Library research, social studies, science, language arts

- General

Do your students know about the Soviet Shuttle program? Their shuttle *Buran* (meaning "snowstorm") made its first flight, unmanned, on November 15, 1988. It is scheduled for its first manned launch in 1992, with Cosmonaut Igor Volk as pilot. Have your students investigate the Russian shuttle. How does it compare and/or contrast with ours? Why is it making so few flights? etc. Teachers can find a quick summary and photo of the *Buran* in the 1991 *Information Please Almanac*, p. 325 (see bibliography).

PLAN A SHUTTLE "FLIGHT" AND "LAUNCH" IT!

- All curriculum areas

- Beginning and intermediate with help from advanced

NASA publishes a book called *Launching a Dream: A Teachers* [sic] *Guide to a Simulated Space Shuttle Mission*, which gives a detailed description of how elementary schools, with help from high schools, simulated space shuttle missions in revamped school buses. Over the school year, students plan all aspects of their "mission": they make and wear uniforms, determine schedules, routes, menus, etc. An ambitious project like this requires the collaboration of teachers, principals, school districts, parents, community groups, and local industries, but the results in all areas, from academic skills to school attendance, are reportedly fabulous. You can request information about the book by writing to the NASA resource center for your region listed in the appendix.

READY-MADE SHUTTLE LESSONS

- General curriculum areas

- Beginning and intermediate

The Civil Air Patrol (CAP) has a space shuttle packet complete with posters, a sample certificate for students, and an activities booklet designed for primary students. Teachers can order one complimentary space shuttle teaching packet by writing on school letterhead to the Center for Aerospace Education Development, HQ CAP/EDF, Maxwell Air Force Base, AL 36112-5572. Specify that you want the space shuttle packet. For beginning and intermediate students NASA offers John Hartsfield's and Shirley Norlem's *Space Shuttle: Activities for Primary and Intermediate Students*; you can request it from the NASA resource center for your region (see address in appendix).

Contributions of Space Travel

In these days of economic crunches, some people may wonder about the value of space travel. The aerospace industry has contributed numerous innovative technologies and products that help our everyday lives.[10] Chapter 5 noted how artificial satellites assist us in telecommunications, weather forecasting, and mapmaking. The aerospace industry has also contributed many less obvious advances related to everyday life. Examples include flame-resistant materials used in buses, airplanes, and ships; an abrasion-resistant coating to protect plastics that have been used to make sunglass lenses scratch resistant; lightweight yet exceptionally strong aerospace materials used in the construction of collapsible wheelchairs; and a highly elastic wire material known as Nitinol, which when used for dental braces requires fewer adjustments by the orthodontist and can reduce the total time the patient needs to wear braces. More aerospace contributions are invisible dental braces made of a translucent material called TPA, on the market since 1987; insulin pumps for patients with diabetes using fluid-control technology from the Viking probe to Mars; the "unistik" modeled after the control mechanism on the Apollo moon buggies, which can be attached to a regular car to enable persons with severe physical mobility limitations to drive; apparatus for the blind, including reading machines (the OPTACONs) that translate print into a tactile perceptible form, and a small paper currency identifier that emits signals telling the blind person each bill's denomination; the magnetic resonance imaging (MRI) process, developed from satellite technology, that enables physicians to view internal organs and the insides of bones, where X rays cannot penetrate.

Teachers and/or librarians can obtain NASA's annual illustrated publication called *Spinoff*, which summarizes the aerospace program's technological advances and their practical benefits in fields from art to medicine, from communications to recreation. To order *Spinoff*, write to the Superintendent of Documents, U.S. Government Printing Office, Washington, D.C. 20402.

TECHNOLOGY TRANSFER

- Library research, science, social studies, language arts, art

- General

The library media specialist and teacher should be able to secure copies of *Spinoff* and other materials explaining the technology transfers from the space program. Students can research these, each student reporting on one. Students may illustrate their reports about technological transfers. Do any of your students wear braces made of Nitinol or TPA? If any local orthodontists are using those materials, could one visit the class and talk about them and show them? Are any of your students' parents firefighters? If so, their breathing backpacks use technology from spaceflight. Perhaps a firefighter would visit the class and show the breathing apparatus, which at about 20 pounds replaced the cumbersome equipment used previously. Are any parents oceanographers? Their underwater pens are based on space technology. If any persons from these or other areas visit the class to explain technological transfers, be sure to have the students ask open-ended questions and write thank-you notes to the visitors.

What's in the Future? An Advanced Space Station

In his State of the Union address of January 25, 1984, President Reagan directed NASA "to develop a permanently manned space station, and to do it within a decade."[11] At this writing, the space station *Freedom* is in developmental stages. Artists' conceptions and engineers' mock-ups show an angular complex composed of four cylindrical, pressurized modules—three to serve as laboratories for the United States, the European Space Agency (ESA), and Japan, and the fourth to serve as the living or habitation module for the entire crew—with extended panels and docking facilities to which the shuttle could ferry crew and materials. All of the modules will, of course, be built of several layers of material, including thermal protection.

The U.S. lab module and the habitation module, known respectively as the *lab* and *hab* modules, will each be 44 feet long and 14 feet in diameter. Contractors from Connecticut to California are building components.[12] Current plans propose that between 1993 and 1995, astronauts would build the modular station in space, traveling between the station and earth in the shuttle; by 1994, the station could be inhabited.[13] A versatile structure, it could conceivably house from six to (eventually) eighteen crewmembers working on varied experiments in separate pressurized laboratory modules, one of which would be a "space factory" devoted to processing materials, such as medicine and crystals. Certain pharmaceutical items, for example, require expensive vacuums and refrigeration on earth, but such conditions would be comparatively easy to supply in the vacuum of space. Likewise, microgravity can reduce the defects in crystals produced for computers and data processors.[14]

In addition to being a space laboratory, the station would be a way station or launch station for missions to Mars and to the Moon. The station would travel about 17,500 miles per hour in a low earth orbit (the same speed that the shuttle orbits) above the equator at an angle or inclination to the equator of 28.5 degrees. It would not, however, be a geosynchronous orbit (see discussion of orbits in chapter 5). An orbit will take ninety minutes, just as the shuttle's does.

The module containing the living quarters would be pressurized and include amenities similar to, but in some ways superior to, those found on the space shuttle. For example, each crewmember would have small but private sleeping quarters; the station would also have a freezer, shower, and dishwasher. Both the living and working conditions within the pressurized modules would be a "shirtsleeve" environment. The habitation module would include exercise equipment to help the crewmembers compensate for the physically debilitating effects of a prolonged stay in space. The tour-of-duty for the crew would be ninety days.[15]

Just as the Spacelab that is sometimes carried on board the shuttle is a multinational venture, so too is the planned space station, with ESA, Canada, and Japan collaborating on the project.[16] In particular, Canada is planning to supply an "arm," as it did for the space shuttle's payload bay. The space station should have a life expectancy of at least thirty years.

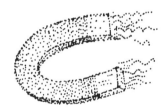

DESIGN A SPACE STATION

- Library research, science, art, language arts

- General

By now students know some of the requirements of a space station from their study of the crew module, payload bay, and Spacelab of the space shuttle, as well as the features of other stations such as *Skylab, Salyut*, and *Mir*, discussed in chapter 5. Ask them to design a space station for NASA. For advanced students, designs should include not only a to-scale artistic rendering of the station, but also a prose commentary about the station's features for living, working, and transportation. Include habitation quarters, considering the need for privacy, the facilities required, and even the color schemes. Teachers of beginning students can adapt this activity to study the constituents of a community. What are some of the services we have in our community, and which of these would we need in a space colony or space station?

Because the space station will function as a potential way station or launch point for missions to the Moon or to Mars, teachers may want to incorporate an earlier Aerospace Magnet from chapter 5, asking students to plan a colony on Mars or the Moon, and include a space factory in those plans. The library media specialist can help teachers and advanced students find the 1987 report to (then) NASA Administrator James Fletcher by a committee (National Commission on Space) headed by Dr. Sally Ride (America's first female astronaut and a physicist), which includes recommendations for colonies on the Moon and Mars. Have students do some research to see which materials would benefit from space manufacturing.

LIVING IN A NICHE

- Science, social studies, oral communication, problem solving

- General

As observed in the discussion of the planned space station, six to eight crewmembers would initially serve a ninety-day tour-of-duty at the station. Each crewmember would have a privacy niche in the living module, a little more than nine feet wide and just under seven feet high. First, measure out this space with chalk and a ruler along the floor and wall or board. Then discuss how people might cope with the confines of life on the station.

The National Aero-Space Plane

Working together in 1984 and 1985, NASA and the Department of Defense began formal planning of the next Space Transportation System, the National Aero-Space Plane (NASP or the X-30), a hydrogen-powered, delta-winged aircraft able to takeoff and land horizontally on a runway, like an airplane, but fly at orbital altitudes at hypersonic speeds (from Mach 5 up to Mach 25) (see figure 6.2).[17] The decision on whether or not to build this plane, propelled by supersonic ramjet engines called *scramjets*, will be made in 1993. Although somewhat similar to the ramjet, the scramjet does not have moving parts to overheat. Theoretically, the NASP would have advantages over the current shuttle because it would not require the extensive and expensive facilities and liftoff procedures used in vertical launches.

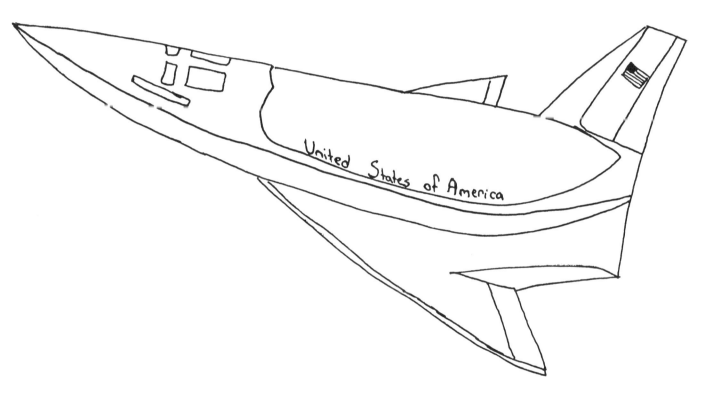

Fig. 6.2. National Aero-Space Plane.

As a space plane, the NASP would fly into orbit from regular runways and reach speeds of 17,500 miles per hour; as a commercial plane, it would fly about 2,000 to 3,500 miles per hour. Such a plane would make the flight between Washington, D.C. and Tokyo in under two hours instead of eighteen hours. Today, supercomputers are generating data about the X-30's potential performance and work is being done on new materials for the construction of the plane that will need to be heat- and pressure-resistant at hypersonic speeds.

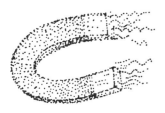

SHRINKING THE GLOBE

- Mathematics, social studies, problem solving

- General

Chapters 4 and 5 noted how advances in commercial air travel, especially with the jumbo jets and the Concorde, have seemed to make the world smaller. This is especially true of hypersonic flight, which will enable people to fly to distant locations in two or three hours instead of a day or longer. First, have students locate some routes for which commercial hypersonic travel would be desirable (New York City to Sidney, Australia; Boston to Tokyo, etc.). Discuss the implications of this phenomenon in terms of world economies, politics, etc. Then, have students do some calculating: If at 40,000 feet altitude, the speed of sound (Mach 1) is 660 miles per hour, how long would it take a plane flying at Mach 5 to reach point A from point B? etc.

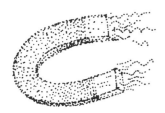

WORKSHOPS, PROGRAMS, AND NASA *SPACE LINK*

- All curriculum areas

- Teachers

The final Aerospace Magnet is devoted to teacher education. Teachers who are interested in getting some hands-on experience in teaching aerospace science may wish to apply for some of the numerous workshops and programs available. For example, the United States Space Foundation and U.S. Air Force Academy cosponsor a summer graduate program, "Getting Comfortable Teaching with Space," at the U.S. Air Force Academy in Colorado Springs, Colorado. As of this writing, graduate credit is available through the University of Colorado at Colorado Springs. The Space Foundation also offers other programs and has many resources for teachers. (See the appendix for the Space Foundation's address; write to them for information. Scholarships are available for the summer USAF Academy program.)

The National Science Teachers Association (NSTA) and NASA collaboratively offer summer programs for teachers geared to teaching level (NEWEST for grades 1-6; MEWMAST for grades 7-12) at key sites, including (as of this writing) the Johnson Space Center, Texas; Langley Research Center, Virginia; Lewis Research Center, Ohio; Stennis Space Center, Mississippi; and the Jet Propulsion Laboratory, California. Teachers attend the workshop for their geographical area. These are highly selective programs and cover teachers' expenses, including airfare and per diem (see appendix for NSTA's address to request detailed information and an application).

The Challenger Center offers workshops, publications, and conferences for teachers, some of which are broadcast via satellite downlink and cablevision (see appendix for address and phone number).

NASA also offers educational satellite videoconferences for teachers, K-12, in all subject areas. For information, write to NASA's Educational Technology Branch (see appendix for address).

The Civil Air Patrol also offers workshops for teachers (see appendix).

An ambitious and expensive but enjoyable workshop is held at the U.S. Space Camp in Huntsville, Alabama (see the appendix for their address and the addresses of other space camps).

Teachers in the Washington, D.C. area have access to the many programs offered by the Smithsonian's National Air and Space Museum.

Teachers interested in astronomy may wish to attend the National Workshop on Astronomy for the Teacher sponsored by the Astronomical Society of the Pacific (see address in appendix).

Workshops for teachers and students are sponsored by the Kansas Cosmosphere and Space Center (see appendix for address).

Teachers may want to start a chapter of the Young Astronauts Program at their school or for their class. Young Astronauts provides all types of teaching resources on all aspects of space travel (see address in appendix).

In addition, innumerable teaching aids for teaching aerospace science, ranging from activities books to videos and movies to computer software, are available (see appendix for summary).

Teachers with access to a computer and modem and who are anxious for up-to-date information from NASA on the latest space events may be interested in NASA *Spacelink*, an electronic information system for educators. The program includes current NASA news, classroom materials, space program spin-offs, even contact with educational specialists. It can be accessed by telephone. The computer access number is (205) 895-0028, and the data format is eight bits, no parity, and one stop bit. For more information, dial direct via modem (205) 895-0028; or write to Spacelink Administrator, Marshall Space Flight Center, Mail Code CA-20; Huntsville, AL 35807, or phone (205) 544-6527.

Notes

[1]NASA, *Space Shuttle News Reference* (Houston, Johnson Space Center: NASA. n.d.), 1.6. This is a detailed manual providing comprehensive technical data about the shuttle. See also R. Lynn Bondurant Jr., *On the Wings of a Dream: The Space Shuttle* (Washington, D.C.: National Air and Space Museum, n.d.), 2. Bondurant's booklet, among the many available from the museum and from NASA, gives an overview of the Shuttle program written for the common reader. For information on gliders, see chapter 3.

[2]Neil McAleer, *The OMNI Space Almanac* (New York: OMNI, World Almanac Books, 1987), 73.

[3]NASA, *Space Shuttle News Reference*, 8.17; Bondurant, *Wings of a Dream*, 3.

[4]All information about the crew module is from NASA, *Space Shuttle News Reference*, 3.5-3.12; about job responsibilities, 7.4; about the shuttle's main engines, solid rocket boosters, and liquid fuel tank, 2.1-2.43 passim; about the orbiter's structure, 3.1-3.26 passim; about food, clothing, and equipment, 5.5-5.45 passim.

[5]Sally Ride with Susan Okie, *To Space and Back* (New York: Lothrop, Lee and Shepard Books, 1986), 13, 80, 93.

[6]Information about Captain Gardner comes from NASA's "Biographical Data Sheet" (Houston, Johnson Space Center: NASA, May 1986).

[7]Captain Dale A. Gardner, interview with author, Colorado Springs, Colo., 8 January 1991.

[8]NASA, *Space Shuttle News Reference*, 1.9; Bondurant, *Wings of a Dream*, 27.

[9]Bondurant, *Wings of a Dream*, 24. Also, NASA's *Space Shuttle News Reference* gives a comprehensive account of the landing procedures, 6.34-6.37, from which the information in this text is taken.

[10]All the information on technology transfers from the aerospace industry to our lives comes from NASA's annual publication, *Spinoff*, which focuses precisely on this subject. See James J. Haggerty, *Spinoff* (Washington, D.C.: U.S. Government Printing Office, 1982, 1984, 1986, 1987, 1988, 1989), passim.

[11]"Transcript of Message by President on State of the Union," *New York Times*, 26 January 1984, p. B8, col. 3; David A. Anderton, *Space Station* (Washington, D.C.: U.S. Government Printing Office, n.d.), ii. This booklet is sponsored by NASA and sold by the U.S. Government Printing Office, Washington, D.C. 20402.

[12]*Space Station Freedom Media Handbook* (Washington, D.C.: NASA, Office of Space Station, 1989), 27, 103, et passim. Designed for the media, this book has everything you need to know about the space station *Freedom*. All information about the space station, except data indicated by other notes, comes from this book. See bibliography for information on ordering a copy.

[13]Lynn P. Hagan, Elizabeth Elsen, and Kathleen Beauford, *A Teacher's Companion to the Space Station: A Multi-disciplinary Resource*, a project of Martin Marietta and the Louisiana Nature and Science Center (New Orleans: Martin Marietta, n.d.), 59.

[14]Leonard David, *Space Station Freedom: A Foothold on the Future* (n.p.: NASA, [1988]), 15.

[15]Hagan, et al., *Teacher's Companion*, 59.

[16]*Space Station Freedom Media Handbook*, 4-5.

[17]Information about the X-30 National Aero-Space Plane comes from the following: Walter Froehlich, *National Aero-Space Plane* (n.p.: NASA, n.d.); *One Step to Space: The X-30 National Aero-Space Plane* (Washington, D.C.: NASA, n.d.); *National Aero-Space Plane: Pioneering New Frontiers* (n.p.: n.d.); James J. Haggerty, *Spinoff 1989* (Washington, D.C.: U.S. Government Printing Office, 1989), 26.

Bibliography

Andrews, Sheila Briskin, and Audrey Kirschenbaum. *Living in Space*. Washington, D.C.: U.S. Government Printing Office, 1987.
Two series of manuals at the elementary level—one for grades 1, 2, 3, another for 4, 5, 6—giving lots of activities related to all aspects of a shuttle mission. One caveat: procedures for activities are sketchy, if given at all, so if you use this series study it well and try some procedures on your own before bringing this into the classroom; also do not be confused by their mixing up flight suits with shuttle "shirtsleeve" crew module wear!

Baker, David. *I Want to Fly the Shuttle*. Vero Beach, Fla.: Tourke Enterprises, 1988.
Illustrated book for beginning and intermediate students on astronaut qualifications and training, life on a mission, etc.

Behrens, June. *Sally Ride, Astronaut: An American First*. Chicago: Childrens Press, 1984.

"Biographical Data" sheet on astronaut Dale Gardner. Houston, Johnson Space Center: NASA, May 1986.
NASA has data sheets on all the astronauts.

Bondurant, R. Lynn, Jr. *On the Wings of a Dream: The Space Shuttle*. Washington, D.C.: National Air and Space Museum, n.d.
Readable for intermediate students through teachers; good photos; follows a typical shuttle mission from launch to landing.

Bryan, C. D. B. *The National Air and Space Museum.* 2d ed. New York: Harry N. Abrams, 1988.
    Great photos of exhibits from the museum; great reading; the school library should own this.

DeOld, Alan R., Joseph W. Judge, and Teri-Lynn Judge. *Space Travel: A Technological Frontier.* Worcester,
    Mass.: Davis Publications, 1989.
    A text covering the shuttle, NASP, space station; includes lots of diagrams. Designed for teachers of
advanced students, for whom activities and brainstorming exercises are included; emphasizes the technology but
clear and readable enough for nonspecialists.

Dewaard, E. John, and Nancy Dewaard. *History of NASA: America's Voyage to the Stars.* New York: Exeter
    Books, 1984.
    Interesting text and great photos.

Educational Technology: NASA Educational Satellite Videoconferences. NASA Fact Sheet. Washington, D.C.:
    NASA, 1989.

Fox, Mary Virginia. *Women Astronauts: Aboard the Shuttle.* New York: Julian Messner/Simon and Schuster,
    1985.

Froehlich, Walter, *National Aero-Space Plane.* n.p.: NASA, n.d.

Furniss, Tim. *Our Future in Space.* New York: Bookwright Press, 1985.
    For beginning students, this looks ahead to space stations, satellites, etc. Easy text and good photos.

Gardner, Captain Dale. Interview with author, Colorado Springs, Colo., 8 January 1991.

Hagan, Lynn, Elizabeth Elsen, and Kathleen E. Beauford. *A Teacher's Companion to the Space Station: A
    Multi-disciplinary Resource.* Project of Martin Marietta and the Louisiana Nature and Science Center. New
    Orleans: Martin Marietta, n.d.
    Contains guides for lesson plans, drawings. Write to Michoud Aerospace, Public Relations Department,
P.O. Box 29304, New Orleans, LA 70189, to request a copy.

Haggerty, James J. *Spinoff.* NASA: U.S. Government Printing Office, 1982, 1984, 1986, 1987, 1988, 1989.
    Spinoff is published annually and includes illustrated pieces about aerospace science's contributions to all
walks of life. Write to the U.S. Government Printing Office about ordering copies; see appendix for address.

Hartsfield, John, and Shirley Norlem. *Space Shuttle: Activities for Primary and Intermediate Students.* Wash-
    ington, D.C.: U.S. Government Printing Office, 1987.

Haskins, James, and Kathleen Benson. *Space Challenger: The Story of Guion Bluford.* Minneapolis: Carol-
    rhoda Books, 1984.

Information Please Almanac, Atlas, and Yearbook. Boston: Houghton Mifflin, 1991.

Launching a Dream: A Teachers [sic] Guide to a Simulated Space Shuttle Mission. Lewis Research Center,
    Cleveland, Ohio: NASA, 1988.

Martin, Franklin D., and Terence T. Finn. *Space Station: Leadership for the Future.* Washington, D.C.: U.S.
    Government Printing Office, [1987].
    A NASA publication.

Matricardi, Paolo. *The Concise History of Aviation*. New York: Crescent Books, 1984.

McAleer, Neil. *The OMNI Space Almanac*. New York: OMNI, World Almanac Books, 1987.
Lots of details and photos; younger students will like the photos, but the reading level is for advanced students and teachers.

Miller, Jay. *The X-Planes: X-1 to X-31*. rev. ed. New York: Orion/Aerofax Books, 1988.
Loads of pictures and data; for advanced students and teachers, although younger students will love the pictures.

Moore, Patrick. *Man's Future in Space*. London: Wayland Publishers, 1978.
For beginners; looks at lunar bases, shuttle, planetary travel; easy reading with good photos.

National Aeronautics and Space Administration. *Seeing in a New Light: Astro-1 Teacher's Guide with Activities*. Huntsville, Ala.: Essex Corporation, 1990.
Designed to complement the *Astro-1* shuttle observatory mission, devoted to astronomy in orbit; excellent; request from NASA resource center for your region; see address in appendix.

National Aeronautics and Space Administration. *NASA Spacelink*. n.p.: NASA. [1988].
A pamphlet from NASA describing the Spacelink electronic information system for teachers.

National Aeronautics and Space Administration. *NASA Space Plans and Scenarios to 2000 and Beyond*. Park Ridge, N.J.: Noyes Publications, 1986.

National Aeronautics and Space Administration. *Space Shuttle News Reference*. Houston, Johnson Space Center: NASA, n.d.
This manual, designed for news reporters, tells just about everything anyone would want to know about the shuttle, but it is extremely hard to get. One of the authors obtained one as a participant in an NSTA program for teachers at the Johnson Space Center; see appendix for information on such programs.

National Aero-Space Plane: Pioneering New Frontiers, n.p.: n.d.
Charts and illustrations about the NASP; hard to get.

National Air and Space Museum. *Discovery*. Washington, D.C.: National Air and Space Museum, n.d.
Activities for beginning students; contact the museum at address in appendix.

One Step to Space: The X-30 National Aero-Space Plane. Washington, D.C.: NASA, n.d.
A pamphlet giving data and drawings of the X-30.

Reichhardt, Tony. *Proving the Space Transportation System: The Orbital Flight Test Program*. Washington, D.C.: U.S. Government Printing Office, n.d.
Part of the NASAFacts Series; available from NASA resource centers; see addresses in appendix.

Ride, Sally, with Susan Okie. *To Space and Back*. New York: Lothrop, Lee, and Shepard Books, 1986.
Generally easy reading and lots of great photos; the first American female astronaut's own story about a shuttle mission.

Shayler, David. *Shuttle Challenger*. New York: Prentice Hall, 1987.
Traces the shuttle from its maiden voyage through its final tragic flight; lots of photos.

Smolders, Peter. *Living in Space: A Manual for Space Travellers*. Translated by Sidney Woods. Blue Ridge Summit, Pa.: TAB (Aero Books), 1986.
Lots of pictures and information about daily life on the shuttle, space stations, etc.

Space Program Benefits. n.p.: NASA Scientific and Technical Information Facility, n.d.
A concise, illustrated summary of aerospace technological transfers; could be used as a wall chart in the classroom or library.

Space Science Student Involvement Program (SSIP). *Teacher Student Resource Book*. College Park, Md.: NASA and the National Science Teachers Association, 1989.
Middle school and junior and senior high school teachers may wish to contact the NSTA for information on the SSIP, which has sponsored student experiments on the shuttle; see appendix for address.

Space Station: A Research Laboratory in Space. Washington, D.C.: NASA, Office of Space Station, n.d.

Space Station Freedom Media Handbook. Washington, D.C.: NASA, Office of Space Station, 1989.
Everything you want or need to know about the space station *Freedom* through April 1989. Write to Mark Hess, Public Affairs Officer, Office of Space Station, NASA Headquarters, Washington, D.C. 20546-0001.

Space Station Power System. Washington, D.C.: NASA, Office of Space Station, n.d.
Explains and illustrates station's configuration and its power options, including solar power.

Spangenburg, Ray, and Diane Moser. *Living and Working in Space*. New York: Facts on File, 1989.
Lots of data; great photos.

Stofan, Andrew J. *Space Station: A Step into the Future*. Washington, D.C.: NASA, Office of Space Station, [1987].
An illustrated pamphlet emphasizing station's benefits by NASA's associate administrator for the space station.

Sumners, Carolyn, Gary Young, and Chris Meister. *Toys in Space: Results of the Space Shuttle Mission STS-51D*. Washington, D.C.: U.S. Government Printing Office, 1987.
Sumners developed the program for the 1985 shuttle mission STS-51D. The illustrated booklet explains the various toy experiments and includes a series of predictions on how the toys would behave at zero g. NASA also has a *Toys in Space* video. Teachers may contact their nearest NASA Teacher Resource Center to obtain the video (addresses listed in the appendix).

Torres, George. *Space Shuttle: The Quest Continues*. Presidio Power Series, Airpower #1006. Novato, Calif.: Presidio Press, 1989.

Trefil, James S. *Living in Space*. New York: Charles Scribner's Sons, 1981.
Interesting thoughts about future space colonies by a physics professor; good reading for teachers and advanced students.

Wilson, Andrew. *The Eagle Has Wings: The Story of American Space Exploration, 1945-1975*. London: British Interplanetary Society, 1982.
Filled with information and beautiful photographs of America's early space program.

Appendix of Useful Addresses

General suggestions: Allow plenty of time when writing for materials; request catalogs first so you know what is available (see "Bibliography of Bibliographies" for suggested catalogs and note specific publications listed in chapter notes and bibliographies); write on school letterhead.

Aviation Information and Materials

Estes Industries, 1925 H Street, Penrose, CO 81240 (719) 372-6565. Sells model rockets and kites, computer software, and also has teaching guides. Produces *Estes Educator News*, edited by Robert Cannon, filled with ideas for activities, reports on what other teachers are doing, photos, and information about Estes products. Estes rockets can be launched relatively easily with apparatus sold by Estes. Rockets range from simple to complex. Schools normally get a discount on their orders. See also The Civil Air Patrol Depot's catalog under CAP.

The *FAA* has numerous free materials—pamphlets, posters, teaching guides, activities booklets, pictures, software, videos and films—for the teacher. Many of these are listed in the chapter notes and bibliographies. The agency makes its materials available by mail through its various offices. The FAA has a main office and nine regional offices. Contact the regional office serving your location.

Main Office:
FAA Headquarters
  Aviation Education Office
  800 Independence Avenue, SW
  Washington, D.C. 20591   (202) 267-3476

Regional Offices:
AK
  FAA-Regional Education Officer
  701 C. Street
  Box 14
  Anchorage, AK 99513-7587   (907) 271-5169

IA, KS, MO, NE
  FAA-Regional Education Officer
  601 East 12th St.
  Federal Building, RM 1501
  Kansas City, MO 64106   (816) 374-5811

DE, District of Columbia, MD, NJ, NY, PA, VA, WV
  FAA-Regional Education Officer
  John F. Kennedy International Airport
  Fitzgerald Federal Building
  Jamaica, New York 11430   (718) 917-1056

IL, IN, MI, MN, ND, WI
  FAA-Regional Education Officer
  O'Hara Lake Office Center
  2300 East Devon Avenue
  Des Plaines, IL 60018   (312) 694-7727

CT, MA, ME, NH, RI, VT
  FAA-Regional Education Officer, Box 510
  12 New England Executive Park
  Burlington, MA 01803   (617) 273-7391

CO, ID, MT, OR, UT, WA, WY
  FAA-Regional Education Officer
  17900 Pacific Highway South
  C-68966
  Seattle, WA 98168   (206) 431-2017

AL, FL, GA, KY, MS, NC, SC, TN, PR, VI
  FAA-Regional Education Office
  P.O. Box 20636
  Atlanta, GA 30320   (404) 763-7201
  or
  3400 Norman Berry Drive
  East Point, GA 30344

ΛR, LA, NM, OK, TX
    FAA-Regional Education Office
    4400 Blue Mound Road
    Fort Worth, TX 76193-0005   (817) 877-2087

AZ, CA, NV, HI, Pacific/Asia
    FAA-Regional Education Office
    P.O. Box 92007
    Worldway Postal Center
    Los Angeles, CA 90009   (213) 536-6431

Beech Aircraft Company offers a manual for sale, *Aviation for the Elementary Level*, filled with activities dealing with airplanes, weather, airports, and related topics. It includes suggested lessons and student activities. Write to Beech Aircraft Corporation, Aviation Education Department, Wichita, KS 67201.

Boeing Airplane Company offers posters and an information packet. Write to Boeing Aircraft Company, MS 65-47, P.O. Box 3707, Seattle, WA 98124.

Cessna Aircraft Company offers publications, posters, and demonstration aids for sale. Write for a catalog of available materials on school letterhead: Cessna Aircraft Company, Air Age Education Department, P.O. Box 1521, Wichita, KS 67201.

Federal Express offers free polystyrene jets that students can put together; item code DC-10. Write to Federal Express Corporation, Box 727, Memphis, TN 38194, (800) 238-5355.

McDonnell Douglas offers materials including airplane posters; write to McDonnell Douglas, P.O. Box 516, St. Louis, MO 63166-0516.

Sikorsky Aircraft offers free materials on helicopters and on Igor Sikorsky; write to Sikorsky Aircraft, Public Relations, North Main Street, Stratford, CT 06601.

General Aerospace Materials

For grades 4-6, the *Civil Air Patrol* (CAP) sells a kit called "The Falcon Force." Write to Civil Air Patrol, Aerospace Education, HQ-CAP-USAF/EDF, Maxwell AFB, AL 36112; (205) 893-5371. Some separate activities booklets, including several listed in chapter 3, are available free in single copies; write to the CAP on school letterhead, requesting a specific activities booklet such as on August Martin, the space shuttle, Amelia Earhart, Charles Lindbergh, Eddie Rickenbacker, or James "Jimmy" Doolittle.

The Civil Air Patrol Supply Depot *1991 Catalog of Aerospace Education Classroom Support Materials* offers items for sale ranging from kites and balloons to space ice cream, models, posters, pins, and hats. It also provides ordering information for Estes Industries. Write to CAP Supply Depot, 14400 Airport Blvd., Amarillo, TX 79111-1207. Telephone 1-800-858-4370.

The *Smithsonian Institution, National Air and Space Museum's Education Resource Center* (ERC) offers materials and information related to aviation, space, and the museum's collection for teachers of all levels and subjects. Included are curriculum packages (K-12), lesson plans, software, videodiscs, videos, slide sets, NASA audiovisuals, science kits, posters, and brochures. They also do a quarterly newsletter, *Skylines*. Limited services by mail; use school letterhead. Write to Office of Education, P-700, National Air and Space Museum, Washington, D.C. 20560. The Educational Resource Center phone is (202) 786-2109. As of this writing, the Educational Resource Center is open Monday-Friday, 10 a.m.-5 p.m.; Saturday, 10 a.m.-4 p.m.; closed federal holidays and on Saturday from Memorial Day through Labor Day; other closures possible, so if you are planning to visit Washington, D.C., call ahead.

Space Information and Materials

The *Challenger Centers for Space Science Education* in Houston, TX, and Washington, D.C. (with more sites being considered) offer workshops, including televised conferences, various teaching tools, simulated work stations and mission controls, etc. Write to Challenger Center, 1101 King Street, Suite 190, Alexandria, VA 22314, (703) 683-9740.

The *National Aeronautics and Space Administration* (NASA) has nine NASA Teacher Resource Centers. These centers have NASA publications, videos (bring a blank tape and tape your own), posters, slides, etc. If you are planning to visit in person, call or write ahead to get on the list of visitors because some of the centers have limited space and get heavy teacher traffic, especially during the summer. You will get the most access to the most material at the center serving your region. Contact the office appropriate to your state by mail or phone.

AK, AZ, CA, HI, ID, MT, NV, OR, UT, WA, WY
NASA Ames Research Center
Teacher Resource Center
Mail Stop 204-7
Moffett Field, CA 94035   (415) 694-6077

NASA Jet Propulsion Laboratory
Teacher Resource Center
JPL Educational Outreach
Mail Stop CS-530
Pasadena, CA 91109   (818) 354-6916

CT, DE, District of Columbia, MA, ME, MD, NH, NJ, NY, PA, RI, VT
NASA Goddard Space Flight Center
Teacher Resource Laboratory
Mail Stop 130-3
Greenbelt, MD 20771   (301) 344-8981

CO, KS, NE, ND, NM, OK, SD, TX
NASA Lyndon B. Johnson Space Center
Teacher Resource Room
Mail Stop AP-4
Houston, TX 77058   (713) 483-8696

FL, GA, PR, VI
NASA John F. Kennedy Space Center
Educator Resource Laboratory
Mail Stop: ERL
Kennedy Space Center, FL 32899   (305) 867-4090

KY, NC, SC, VA, WV
NASA Langley Research Center
Langley Teacher Resource Center
Mail Stop 146
Hampton, VA 23665-5225   (804) 865-4468

IL, IN, MI, MN, OH, WI
NASA Lewis Research Center
Teacher Resource Center
Mail Stop 8-1
Cleveland, OH 44135   (216) 267-1187

AL, AR, IA, LA, MO, TN
Alabama Space and Rocket Center
Teacher Resource Room
Tranquility Base
Huntsville, AL 35807   (205) 544-5812

MS
NASA National Space Technology Laboratories-Stennis Space Center
Teacher Resource Center
Building 1200
NSTL (Stennis Space Center), MS 39529
(601) 688-3338

NASA CORE: Central Operation of Resources for Educators: CORE is designed to enhance distribution of NASA aerospace educational videotapes, filmstrips, slides, and slide/audio cassette programs (no publications) nationally and internationally. CORE will process teachers' requests by mail for a small fee. Write on school letterhead for their catalog (*NASA CORE's Guide to Resources*) and a CORE order form: NASA CORE, Lorain County Joint Vocational School, 15181 Route 58 South, Oberlin, OH 44074; (216) 774-1051 ext. 293 or 294.

NASA also sponsors many *NASA Regional Teacher Resource Centers*, which have materials in more limited quantities but which may be more convenient. These include:

Bossier Parish Community College
NASA Regional Teacher Resource Center
2719 Airline Drive
Bossier City, LA 71111   (318) 746-7754 or 0226

Central Michigan University
NASA Regional Teacher Resource Center
Ronan Hall, Rm 101
Mount Pleasant, MI 48859   (517) 774-4387

Chicago Museum of Science and Industry
NASA Regional Teacher Resource Center
57th Street and Lakeshore Drive
Chicago, IL 60637-2093   (313) 684-1414, ext. 429

The Children's Museum
NASA Regional Teacher Resource Center
P.O. Box 3000
Indianapolis, IN 46206   (317) 921-4001

The City College
NASA Regional Teacher Resource Center
NAC Building, Room 5224
Convent Avenue at 138th Street
New York, NY 10031   (212) 690-6993

Delaware Teacher Center
Central Middle School
Delaware Avenue
Dover, DE 19901   (302) 736-5569

Discovery World Museum
NASA Regional Teacher Resource Center
818 West Wisconsin Avenue
Milwaukee, WI 53233   (414) 765-9966

Education Service Center
NASA Regional Teacher Resource Center
Region XVI
1601 South Cleveland Street
Amarillo, TX 79102   (806) 376-5521

Kansas Cosmosphere and Space Center
NASA Regional Teacher Resource Center
1100 North Plum
Hutchinson, KS 67501   (316) 662-2305

Mankato State University
NASA Regional Teacher Resource Center
Department of Curriculum and Instruction
MSU Box 52
P.O. Box 8400
Mankato, MN 56001-8400   (507) 389-5710 or 16

Murray State University
NASA Regional Teacher Resource Center
Waterfield Library
Murray, KY 42017   (502) 762-4420

National Air and Space Museum
Smithsonian Institution
Educational Resource Center, P-700
Washington, D.C. 20560   (202) 786-2109

NASA Industrial Application Center
Christa McAuliffe Teacher Resource Institute
823 William Pitt Union
University of Pittsburgh
Pittsburgh, PA 15260   (412) 648-7008

Northern Michigan University
NASA Regional Teacher Resource Center
Olson Library Media Center
Marquette, MI 49855   (906) 227-2270

Oakland University
NASA Regional Teacher Resource Center
O'Dowd Hall, Room 216
Rochester, MI 48309-4401   (313) 370-2485

Oklahoma State University
NASA Regional Teacher Resource Center
300 North Cordell
Stillwater, OK 74078-0422   (405) 774-7015

Parks College of St. Louis University
NASA Regional Teacher Resource Center
Route 157 and Falling Springs Road
Cahokia, IL 62206   (618) 337-7500

St. Cloud State University
Center for Information Media
NASA Regional Teacher Resource Center
St. Cloud, MN 56301   (612) 255-2062

Southern University
NASA Regional Teacher Resource Center
Downtown Metro Center
610 Texas Street
Shreveport, LA 71101   (318) 674-3444

University of Evansville
NASA Regional Teacher Resource Center
School of Education
1800 Lincoln Avenue
Evansville, IN 47714   (812) 479-2393

University of North Carolina-Charlotte
NASA Regional Teacher Resource Center
Atkins Library
Charlotte, NC 28223   (704) 547-2559

University of Wisconsin-La Crosse
NASA Regional Teacher Resource Center
Morris Hall, Room 200
La Crosse, WI 54601   (608) 785-8148

United States Space Foundation
NASA Regional Teacher Resource Center
1525 Vapor Trail
Colorado Springs, CO 80916   (719) 550-1000

NASA's Educational Technology Branch sponsors videoconferences for teachers in all subject areas, K-12; perhaps your school district would like to participate. For information, write to NASA Educational Technology Branch, Educational Affairs Division, Office of External Relations, Washington, D.C. 20546, (202) 453-8388. NASA's Educational Technology Branch is developing aerospace educational software for Apple II computers, plus clip art for Macintosh computers. The first software program deals with the Hubble space telescope; future packages will have satellite pictures of and from space and reference databases on manned space missions and planetary probes. They also have interactive videodisc lesson plans on space. The plans are for all NASA Teacher Resource Centers (TRC) to have laser videodisc systems. Contact the NASA TRC for your region or write: NASA Educational Technology Branch, Mail Code XE, NASA Headquarters, Washington, D.C. 20546, (202) 453-8388.

NASA and the 4-H Club have jointly developed a television (video or 16mm film) series and accompanying materials series for a program called "Blue Skies Below My Feet — Adventures in Space Technology," which can be purchased. 4-H also sells space posters, T-shirts, model rockets, etc., for its program. Contact your local 4-H or write for a supply catalog to the National 4-H Council, National 4-H Supply Service, 7100 Connecticut Avenue, Chevy Chase, MD 20815, (301) 961-2934 (Monday-Friday, 8:30 a.m.-5 p.m., Eastern time).

The *National Science Teachers Association* (NSTA) offers programs for teachers in collaboration with NASA, including NASA/NEWEST (grades 1-6) and NASA/NEWMAST (grades 7-12, teachers of math, science, technology); and programs for students, the Space Science Student Involvement Program (SSIP). As noted in the book's final Aerospace Magnet, some of the teacher programs involve workshops at NASA research centers. For information on the many programs that NSTA offers, contact Dr. Helenmarie Hofman, Director, or Shelagh R. Lane, Associate Director, 5110 Roanoke Place, Suite 101, College Park, MD 20740, (301) 474-0487. Another address for NSTA is 1742 Connecticut Avenue NW, Washington, D.C. 20009, (202) 328-5800.

The *U.S. Government Printing Office*, Superintendent of Documents, Washington, D.C. 20402, sells many NASA publications. Write for their catalog of free materials: Free Catalog, P.O. Box 37000, Washington, D.C. 20013-7000.

The *United States Space Foundation*, one of the many NASA Regional Teacher Resource Centers, also offers other materials related to space science, sponsors the annual National Space Symposium, and collaborates with the U.S. Air Force Academy, also in Colorado Springs, Colorado, on a summer workshop called "Getting Comfortable Teaching with Space." Especially useful from the foundation is their voluminous file of lesson plans, covering grades K-12 and all subject areas, supplied by teachers from around the country who have taken the "Getting Comfortable Teaching with Space" workshop; plans are to compile all the lesson plans into a manual and sell it. With a major grant from the National Science Foundation, the U.S. Space Foundation is also working on a three-year middle school science textbook series to be published by D. C. Heath and Company, called *Project First Step*. A number of agencies such as NASA, the FAA, and the CAP are providing support for this huge project. Write to U.S. Space Foundation, Education Center, 1525 Vapor Trail, Colorado Springs, CO

80916, (719) 550-1000. The contact person for Project First Step only is Dr. Norris Harms. For all other educational resources at the foundation, write to the same address, attention Dr. Victoria Duca.

Space Voyage offers an educational simulation that invites students to imagine they are astronauts directing shuttle flights and safely building space station *Freedom*. Space voyage stimulates excitement about learning and makes reading, science, and math meaningful and relevant to students. Space Voyage offers students in-depth, hands-on activities, exposes them to career possibilities, allows them to focus on positive concepts, and facilitates team building, problem solving, and communication skills. Space Voyages are available for K-12 from Space Voyage Simulations, 1504 South Johnson Court, Lakewood, CO 80232; or call Dr. Mark "Doc" Palmere, (303) 985-3143.

The *Young Astronauts Program* is a national and international network of teachers and students at the primary and middle-school levels; as of this writing, the annual dues are $40. Mailings and activities include membership cards and certificates, Chapter Leader's Handbook, curriculum documents, and student activities packets, posters, etc. Write to the Young Astronaut Council, 1211 Connecticut Avenue, NW, Suite 800, Washington, D.C. 20036, (202) 682-1985.

Space camps can be expensive, but they offer simulated experiences of space travel. Most are for children, but the Huntsville Space Camp offers programs for adults, too. This list does not imply endorsement.

Aerospace Camp
Cradle of Aviation Museum
Museum Lane
Mitchell Field
Garden City, Long Island, NY 11530   (516) 222-1190

Shuttle Camp
Space Center
Alamogordo, NM 88311   1-800-545-4021

Space Camp
Tranquility Base
Huntsville, AL 35807   1-800-63SPACE
You can also request information about their Titusville, Florida Space Camp.

Michigan Space Camp
2111 Emmons Road
Jackson, MI 49201   (517) 787-4425

Future Astronaut Training Program
Kansas Cosmosphere and Space Center
1100 North Plum Street
Hutchinson, KS 67501   (316) 662-2305

Pacific Rim Spaceflight Academy
Oregon Museum of Science and Industry
4015 SW Canyon Road
Portland, OR 97221   (503) 222-2828

Martin Marietta has several publications dealing with aerospace, including one on the space station (cited in chapter 6) and one on careers in the aerospace field at Martin Marietta. Write to Martin Marietta, Michoud Aerospace, Public Relations Department, P.O. Box 29304, New Orleans, LA 70189. If Martin Marietta has a division near you, you might contact it.

Dover Publications has some very reasonably priced books about model gliders and shuttles, as well as coloring books about flight and space travel. Write for their catalog: Dover Publications, Inc., 31 East 2d Street, Mineola, NY 11501.

Bibliography of Bibliographies

Each chapter in this book includes a bibliography listing resources relevant to the chapter's topics. This concluding bibliography lists some of the teaching tools available from the various agencies whose addresses are given in the appendix.

Federal Aviation Administration (FAA)

FAA, *List of FAA Aviation Education Materials*. Washington, D.C., FAA, 1987.
Pamphlet listing publications for K-12 and university-level teaching; single copies of titles listed in the pamphlet are free. Write to the FAA regional office listed in the appendix.

FAA, Office of Public Affairs. *Teacher's Guide to Aviation Education Resources*, Publication no. APA-5-149-85. Washington, D.C.: FAA, 1985.
This is a very comprehensive list of aviation teaching resources covering teaching guides, career information, audiovisuals, periodicals, and publications, available from various sources. It includes addresses and phone numbers of the suppliers; costs, if any; etc. For teachers from K-12. Write to the FAA regional office listed in the appendix.

National Aeronautics and Space Administration (NASA)

Aerospace Education Services Department, Oklahoma State University. *Software for Aerospace Education: A Bibliography*. draft ed. Washington, D.C.: NASA, 1987.
Lists all available software, system requirements, costs, grade levels. Contact the NASA Teacher Resource Center for a copy; see appendix for center serving your state.

NASA Educational Affairs Division Programs and Services. Washington, D.C.: NASA, 1989.
Summarizes NASA's multifaceted educational endeavors. Contact the NASA Teacher Resource Center serving your location; see address in appendix.

NASA Educational Publications. Washington, D.C.: U.S. Government Printing Office, 1987.
Lists NASA's periodicals, posters, wall sheets, resource books, activities books, etc., and their costs. The catalog and most materials can be ordered from the Superintendent of Documents, U.S. Government Printing Office 20402-9325. Or request the catalog from the NASA Teacher Resource Center serving your state (see appendix).

NASA Lyndon B. Johnson Teacher Resource Center. *Teacher Resource Center Catalog*. Houston, Johnson Space Center (JSC): NASA, 1989.
Lists all the videocassettes and audiocassettes available from JSC. Also shows if lesson packets accompany tape. Check with your local NASA Teacher Resource Center for a similar catalog.

U.S. Government Printing Office

U.S. Government Printing Office Subject Bibliography: NASA Educational Publications. Washington, D.C.: U.S. Government Printing Office, 1988.
Lists all publications available from this office with their prices and ordering information (see address in appendix).

United States Space Foundation

United States Space Foundation. *Video Tapes Available for Free Duplication*. Colorado Springs, Colo.: U.S. Space Foundation, n.d.

Write to the United States Space Foundation at the address in the appendix; teachers send new blank video-cassette(s) with return postage, along with their request(s), and the foundation will duplicate the tape(s) and return.

United States Space Foundation. *Material Request Form*. Colorado Springs, Colo.: United States Space Foundation, n.d.

Lists all the publications and teaching aids available; includes grade level use. Write to the United States Space Foundation (see address in appendix) and request this pamphlet/order form.

Index